POPULATION AND DEVELOPMENT
OF THE ARAB GULF STATES

T0293349

Population and Development of the Arab Gulf States

The Case of Bahrain, Oman and Kuwait

NADEYA SAYED ALI MOHAMMED

Routledge
Taylor & Francis Group

LONDON AND NEW YORK

First published 2003 by Ashgate Publishing

2 Park Square, Milton Park, Abingdon, Oxon OX14 4RN
711 Third Avenue, New York, NY 10017, USA

Routledge is an imprint of the Taylor & Francis Group, an informa business

First issued in paperback 2016

British Library Cataloguing in Publication Data
Mohammed, Nadeya Sayed Ali
  Population and development of the Arab Gulf states : the
  case of Bahrain, Oman and Kuwait
  1.Bahrain - Population - Economic aspects 2.Kuwait -
  Population - Economic aspects 3.Oman - Population -
  Economic aspects 4.Bahrain - Economic conditions 5.Kuwait -
  Economic conditions - 1991- 6.Oman - Economic conditions
  I.Title
  304.6'09536

Library of Congress Control Number: 2003102976

ISBN 978-0-7546-3220-7 (hbk)
ISBN 978-1-138-25848-8 (pbk)

Transferred to Digital Printing in 2014

Contents

List of Figures

List of Tables

Introduction

The Arab Gulf States are associated with average total population growth rates of four percent (1981-91),[1] stemming from rapid declines in mortality, relatively modest fertility declines (from an average TFR of 6.75 in 1975-80 to an average of 5.63 in 1985-90),[2] and the influx of large numbers of migrant workers. These growth rates are exceptionally high, even relative to the other developing countries that are commonly associated with rapid growth (2.9 percent in Sub Saharan Africa, 2.7 percent in North Africa, 1.8 percent in Asia during the same period), and imply that the current young age structure of the Gulf States,[3] will continue at least for some time in the near future.

This demographic reality needs to be set within the context of dependence on one non-renewable and 'unreliable' source of income: sale of oil reserves. 'Unreliable' because these revenues are subject to fluctuations in oil prices in the world markets. However, the relatively high oil prices during the 1970s and 1980s ensured that the revenues of the Gulf States were sufficient to stimulate a 'growth' in the economy averaging two percent per annum. This, when distributed amongst a numerically small population, led to the registration of high GDPs per capita (averaging $10423.29 (1989-90)).[4]

Given such a favourable economic context, the high population growth rates have not been considered a problem. Indeed, it has been assumed that Gulf population growth was a matter of little consequence, having neither negative nor positive effects. After all, it could be argued that there was no obvious poverty, overcrowding, or deteriorating infrastructure.

Yet since the 1990s, the governments across the Gulf States have become increasingly concerned with employment of their young nationals. In addition, most Gulf States have reduced their generous welfare subsidies, and all have become concerned about the lack of diversification of their economic base. While the rapid population growth of the past cannot be argued to be the sole cause of these strains, this Book, through its focus on assessing, measuring and critically examining the (potentially negative) effects of rapid population growth rates, will

---

[1] United States Bureau of the Census. International Programmes Centre Estimates. On-line Database July 1998. Internet url: http://www.census.gov/ipc/www/idbsprd.html
[2] United Nations. (1989). *World Population Prospects*. Geneva, Switzerland: UN Publications.
[3] On average 48 percent of the population are aged below 15 years. United Nations Economic and Social Commission of Western Asia. (2000). *Demographic and Related Socio-Economic Data Sheets*. Jordan: UNESCWA.
[4] Gulf Cooperation Council Office. (1992). *Economic Bulletin*, Issue No 7.

argue that it is a significant contributing factor to lower levels of overall development.

The Population-Development Debate

Few development issues have aroused as much dissension as the relations between population growth, economic growth and human welfare. The issue of the effect of rapid population growth affecting the development of a country has been debated with regard to developing and poor countries for the past two decades, and as yet no consensus has been reached.[5] At the heart of the issue is the fact that the causal links between population growth and economic growth are reciprocal and simultaneous.

Different periods have been characterized by specific approaches. During the 1950s, concern focused on population increase limiting the amount of capital available for productive investment, leading to slower growth. These neo-Malthusian theories were based on the Harrod Domar models that assumed income growth rates were a function of rates of personal savings.[6] Hence, rapid population growth was considered to affect economic growth and social advancement negatively, through slowing per capita and GDP income growth rates, maintaining income inequalities, depressing savings and productive investment.[7] The 1960s questioned this view, though consensus on action was based on a recognition that family planning led to health and welfare benefits for individuals.[8] The 1970s concentrated on the relationship of population to land, food and poverty.[9] Research focused on understanding reproductive behaviour and how intervention may accelerate fertility decline, though there was little empirical research conducted on the consequences of rapid population growth.

---

[5] Cassen, R. (1994). *Population and Development: Old Debates, New Conclusions.* Washington, DC: Overseas Development Council.

[6] Teitelbaum, M.S. (1974). Population and Development: Is a Consensus Possible? *Foreign Affairs,* July, 749-757. See also Ehrlich, P, and Ehrlich, A.H. (1972). *Population, Resources and Environment: Issues in Human Ecology.* San Francisco: Freeman.

[7] Hoover, E, and Coale, A. (1958). *Population Growth and Economic Development in Low Income Countries: A Case Study of India's Prospects.* Princeton: Princeton University Press.

[8] Kuznets, S. (1974). *Fertility Differentials between Less Developed and Developed Regions: Components and Implications.* Discussion Paper No 217. New Haven, Connecticut: Yale University.

[9] King, T, and Kelley, A. (1985). The New Population Debate: Two Views on Population Growth and Economic Development. *Population Trends and Public Policy Paper No. 7.* Washington, DC.: Population Reference Bureau.

During the 1980s, revisionism prevailed.[10] Now rapid population growth was given secondary importance in economic development, and its deleterious effects were believed to be easily countered by the (free) market reaction. While no quantitative estimate of population's effect on development were produced, qualitative assessments varied between countries over time, and with population growth rates. Micro-level data supported the view that population growth under high fertility had negative effects: mothers exposed to many pregnancies are more likely to die earlier and children with more siblings are more likely to be deprived in some way.[11] And if the girls are deprived of education, then inter-generational transmission of poverty and high fertility is the likely result. However, macro-level evidence was unclear. Statistical analysis across developing countries, examining the effect of population growth on income per head, yielded no firm results. Yet, on an individual country basis, there were near term problems, of provision of employment, adequate schooling and health services. In these cases, the institutional capacity to set the right policies and incentives in place was considered critical to determining whether or not population growth could be accommodated without major negative consequences. Overall, it was granted that rapid population growth aggravated development problems: the National Academy of Sciences accepted a qualitative conclusion that slower population growth would be beneficial for most developing countries.[12] However, population fell low on the list of causes of those problems, and other causes: poor management, distorted incentives etc., were considered as more important.

Marginalization of the Gulf States in the Debate

Thus far, this debate has neglected the Gulf region, and all research conducted has tended to focus on the developing countries of Asia, South America and Sub Saharan Africa. The combination of high fertility rates, obvious economic inequalities and poverty made them easier research candidates. In fact, many of the models were based on the conditions specific to the particular country under

---

[10] Birdsall, Nancy. (1988). Economic Approaches to Population Growth. In H.B. Chenery, T.N. Srinivasan (Eds.), *Handbook of Development Economics.* Vol. 1. (pp. 478-542). Amsterdam: North Holland.
[11] World Bank. (1989). *Malawi: Human Resource Development Study* Report No 7854-MAI, Washington, DC: World Bank. Also, World Bank. (1989). *Rapid Population Growth in Pakistan: Concerns and Consequences,* Report No 7522-PAK. Washington, DC.: World Bank. World Bank. (1989). *Zimbabwe Population Sector Report,* Report No., 7703-ZIM. Washington, DC.: World Bank. Also, Ogawa, N. Gavin W. Jones, and Jeffrey G. Williamson. (1993). *Human Resources in Development Along the Asia-Pasific Rim.* New York: Oxford University Press.
[12] National Research Council. (1986). *Population Growth and Economic Development: Policy Questions.* Washington, DC.: National Academy Press.

investigation: e.g., Coale and Hoover's model being based on India. But there are many reasons for the Gulf States not being considered.

Were the economic system of the Gulf States similar to other countries, such economic models could have been easily applied. However, the economy characteristic of an oil state is based on the distribution of wealth generated from the sale of oil, rather than the production capabilities of its population. This, plus the lack of domestic taxation, means that wealth does not tend to circulate in the economy.[13] Further, the social-cultural basis of these models is not applicable: the Gulf is unique, with a population that has great purchasing power, governed by a tribal cultural ethic, an Islamic moral code and a large 'guest worker' sub-population that remits most of its wages regularly. Therefore, the fundamental basis on which the above economic-population models rest may not be applicable.

Yet even if the models could have been adapted or modified, the lack of detailed reliable demographic and economic data, would have rendered macro and micro-level economic analysis almost impossible. Historical data is sketchy due to:

i. A then largely illiterate population: Schooling in the Quranic 'kutabs' meant merely the recitation of the Quran. Only a handful of merchants and traders[14] had some knowledge of basic rudimentary arithmetic to enable them to deal with merchants in Bombay. The first modern school for Sunni boys in Bahrain (and in the Gulf) was set up in 1921, and that for Sunni girls was established in 1928. Kuwait had two schools by 1936 and there were three schools in Oman by 1969. Certainly a project of estimating inhabitants in the region would have seemed not only difficult, but unnecessary.

ii. The lack of administrative 'state' structures: On the Arabian mainland, small wadies were separated by large expanses of uninhabited desert, roamed by wandering tribes whose survival depended on trading the produce of their herds, and their livestock with the coastal towns, as well as on frequently raiding neighbouring villages and tribes. Coastal towns with their settled populations were led by tribal sheikhs:[15] the closest that the region came to having a 'government' structure. Bahrain was the only place where a rudimentary administrative system existed, managed by a literate minority. The lack of central medical facilities ensured that there were no records of births and deaths: births were delivered by midwives at home, and deaths involved religious burials without any registration.

---

[13] This is a 'rentier' economy since it is based on rent. Beblawi, H. and Giacomo Luciani (Eds.), 1987. *The Rentier State*. Kent: Croom Helm Ltd.
[14] For pearls in Bahrain, spices in Oman, other goods in UAE, and the educated Hijazis of Saudi Arabia.
[15] For example, the port of Kuwait under the Al Sabahs, the town of Doha under the Al Thanis, that of Abu Dhabi under the Qawasims.

iii.   The frequent and unmonitored population movements: Demographic estimates made by British Political Residents refer to settled populations and the tribes 'associated with' a particular port or town: an association which would have, of necessity, been flexible, depending on the current sheikh and tribal relations. Also, people continually migrated to and from Southern Persia, and large communities of Persians, existed in every coastal town on the Arabian side of the Gulf. The Hajj pilgrimage brought many Muslims to Mecca and Medina, some of whom may have stayed on in Mecca, or elsewhere in the region. Finally, the slave trade introduced people of African origin into the region. This was, in addition to the frequent seasonal migrations of the local inhabitants to other coastal ports in search of employment, especially during the pearling seasons.

iv.   The social and cultural norms of the region: The conservative population would not have comprehended the need for the collection of such private information, even if enough literate people were found to physically conduct the surveys. And, Islam, unlike other religions, does not require baptismal or confirmation services, therefore eliminating the possibility of seeking alternative information sources.

The existing historical population estimates, made by the British Political Residents, do not lend themselves to demographic analysis: the population is not divided by age or sex (the male Political Residents could not have been in contact with local females), and the basic underlying assumption was that there were five people in every house counted, a number which even they admitted was too low. Further, the estimates refer to towns, villages and tribes, all of which are not necessarily incorporated into the same modern State found today.[16]

However, some of the Gulf States began laying the foundations for statistical data collection in the 1940s. It was the need to redistribute oil revenues, after the first oil shock of 1973, that made collection of data on vital events, and census taking, necessary. Yet, even such recently published sources of data are not free from problems and errors, whether deliberate or accidental. The first Censuses were not conducted at the same time in every Gulf State: Bahrain's first Census was in 1941, Kuwait's in 1957, Oman's in 1991, and the content and depth of detail that these Censuses go into vary. Further, the tribal correlation of numbers and size with power and authority, may translate into an attempt at inflating their population numbers to gain prestige amongst themselves. This need to exaggerate numbers is reinforced by their acute awareness of the presence, in the region, of two strong, larger and more populous States, Iran and Iraq. This may explain why the governments of the smaller Gulf States are wary of publishing any data which may disadvantage them vis a vis these two countries, especially given the historic claims

---

[16] Lorimer, J.G. (1908). *Gazetteer of the Persian Gulf, Oman and Central Arabia* Vol II. India: Calcutta Superintendent Government Printing Press.

that each of them have had (or continue to have) on neighbouring Arab States: Iraq on Kuwait, Iran on Bahrain.

In addition, their reliance on the large numbers of foreign workers (at all skill levels), has intensified their need to conceal any data which may show their acute dependence on the external world, on the pretext of it being provisional, inaccurate or confidential. While Censuses and sample surveys do provide some data on the proportion of non-nationals, they rarely identify the reason for their residence, nor their ethnic origins. However, since the pioneering work by Birks and Sinclair,[17] and especially since the 1990 Gulf War, which highlighted the plight of migrants in the Gulf, the quality of data on non nationals in the Gulf has improved.

Therefore, existing demographic data on the Gulf States is, in addition to being relatively recent, either incomplete, irregular or full of gaps, and can rarely be checked for accuracy.

Thus, at the time when population economists across the world were struggling to investigate the relation between population growth and development, and to develop appropriate frameworks for its analysis, Bahrain and Kuwait were just beginning to record basic demographic information. By the time the debate on population growth and development abated in the 1970s, the oil boom boosted the Gulf region's economy, and laid the necessary infrastructure for the relatively sophisticated Censuses to be conducted. By the time the revisionist approach was being upheld in the 1980s, Oman was conducting its first Census. Given such a context, of a lack of data and obvious economic strain, of inapplicable models and theories and of a political system not open to dissemination of data, it is not surprising that the debate totally disregarded the Gulf and its demographic peculiarities.

Yet by the late 1980s, it was becoming increasingly evident that the Middle East region was experiencing amongst the highest population growth rates in the world, though understanding the exact magnitude of the problem was difficult to gauge.

Methodology

This Book adopts a revisionist approach: that population growth is one important variable (amongst others) that hinders long term development – and avoids a purely quantitative or statistical analysis, because of the data inadequacies explained above. In addition, we focus on those aspects of the economy that affect human capital development, because within a context of good economic resources, high per capita GDPs (averaging $10423.29 (1989-90))[18] and relatively good economic

---

[17] Birks, J.S., and Clive A. Sinclair. (1980). *International Migration and Development in the Arab Region*. Geneva: International Labour Office.
[18] Gulf Cooperation Council. (1992). *Economic Bulletin*, Issue No 7.

growth rates (averaging 9.6 percent in 1975-80),[19] human capital and its development becomes the critical measure of future progress, rather than growth in savings, consumption and so on. In addition, human development (in the form of people being better educated, more healthy, gainfully employed etc.) is both a means and an end: constituting a better quality of life whilst contributing to individual productivity and thereby to material prosperity. Therefore, any variable that may influence the provision of the services, that result in the creation of human capital, would negatively affect human development, and hence a country's progress towards material prosperity in the long term.

The argument in this Book is based on an examination of the ability of the Gulf governments to continue providing quality education, health and employment under conditions of rapid population growth: specifically, on three alternative population growth scenarios. This Scenario approach has been selected because it would:

i.   trace the different paths along which Gulf Demographic Transition could proceed toward an assumed low mortality-low fertility equilibrium by 2025.

ii.   illustrate the implications for population growth of fertility and mortality trends, which could be modified by public policy.

iii. demonstrate the likely alternatives of future population growth in the context of unrealistic/unlikely projections based on implausibly rapid/slow assumed trends of fertility decline.

iv.   highlight the importance of integrating population matters in Gulf development planning through outlining the implications of the variant scenarios on the provision of various public services, and hence human capital development in the long run.

As judgment needs to be exercised in the choice of scenarios and their relative likelihood, the demographic characteristics, the health, education and labour status of Gulf populations are first examined. Based on the analyses, assumptions are made for each of the demographic components, as well as for various indicators of health, education and employment. Three Alternative Projection Scenarios are then generated using the International Labour Organization's projection software,[20] which is based on the cohort component method.

The alternative scenarios differ from projections made by the United Nations and other international organizations: in the specification, justification and combination of assumptions. UN projections do not segregate Gulf populations

---

[19] International Monetary Fund. (1974-1997). *World Economic Outlook.* World Economic and Financial Surveys Series.
[20] Green, G. (1986). *Planning for Population, Labour Force and Service Demand: A Microcomputer based Training Module. Background Papers for Training In Population, Human Resources and Development Planning.* Geneva: International Labour Organisation.

into national and non-national parts, nor do they assume separate and different demographic characteristics for each segment, an oversight which may lead to certain misconceptions. Non-national populations have different demographic characteristics: age structures, fertility and mortality levels, which must be taken into account. Most importantly, the UN projections try to forecast future demographic trends as accurately as possible, at any given moment in time. Instead, the alternative scenario projections merely illustrate certain likely future demographic developments to demonstrate a particular outcome. Hence, rather than generating one most probable variant based on a complex set of assumptions, the scenario projections are based on some simple alternative fertility level assumptions. The results of the scenarios are then compared, and their impact, in terms of stimulating demand for public services, health, education and employment, are assessed.

Sources of Data

The argument focuses on three of the Gulf States: Bahrain, Oman and Kuwait. Not only do they have the most extensive records of demographic and other data,[21] but they also represent the range of demographic, economic and social characteristics found in the Gulf (Table 1, below), thereby avoiding the danger of classifying all Gulf Arab States into one category.

Table I.1 Socio-Economic Indicators 1990-1994

Indicators	Bahrain	Kuwait	Oman
TFR	4	5	7
Percent females literate	59	75	42
GDP $mn (1989)	4094	25988	6621
Oil Reserves mb	100	96500	4480
Cultivated hectares	1000	2000	58000

Sources: Population Reference Bureau, Census/Statistical Abstracts, UNDP: Human Development Report 1995

Among these three States, greater emphasis is placed on data from Bahrain. This is due to the following reasons:

i.   the author was permitted to conduct independent research (discussed below).
ii. availability of detailed and relatively good demographic census information (dating from 1971).

---

[21] Though other Gulf States are referred to when appropriate, and when data is available.

iii. society being open to debate given relatively educated status.
iv.   personal experience of the society, culture and people, given author's
      Bahraini nationality.

The author conducted individual fieldwork in Bahrain. The first fieldwork, conducted during the summer of 1993, was a quantitative Knowledge Attitudes and Practice of Contraception Survey (KAP), with 250 currently married Bahraini women aged 15-49. The sample was designed to be representative of the Bahraini population and as random as possible. The interviews were conducted amongst women who attended the public health Clinics in Bahrain during the period June-July 1993.

In addition, two qualitative focus group sessions were held in September 1996. One session was with two groups of female Bahraini Doctors, averaging 30 years of age, employed by the Ministry of Health with an average of four years of work experience in the Public Health Clinics. The second session was with two groups of primary level female teachers employed by the Ministry of Education with an average of 13 years of teaching experience in various public primary schools in Bahrain.

Census results were also analyzed. For Bahrain, this included Census findings from 1957 to 1991, with emphasis on the results of the more recent Censuses, given their better quality. Kuwait's relatively good Census taking history was disrupted by the Gulf War in 1991, during which time the definition of the Kuwaiti nationality was re-evaluated. Since 1991, it has been reported that the non-national population has increased to numbers similar, if not more, than those found in the pre-War days.[22] Hence, the analysis uses the historical data up to 1988, when the last labour survey was conducted. The data on Oman, on the other hand, relies on the only Census that has been conducted, in 1993.

Other primary data sources included demographic estimates from the different organizations within the United Nations, the World Bank, World Health Organisation, CIA Factbook, the International Programmes Division of the United States Bureau of the Census, as well as the Population Reference Bureau.

Various secondary literature sources were also studied: local Arabic newspapers and magazines, Gulf State's Development Plans and other Government documents. Most significant of the secondary sources, are the two Gulf Family Health Surveys, published in 1990 and 2000 (with the fieldwork having been conducted in 1989 and 1996 respectively), under the auspices of various United Nations agencies (UNFPA, UNICEF, UNDP) and in collaboration with and under supervision of the local Ministries of Health.

---

[22] Economic Intelligence Unit. (1994). *Kuwait Country Report.*

The Findings

Currently, Gulf fertility rates are declining gradually. However, the Scenario approach highlights the gains that Gulf governments could enjoy if they were to speed this process. At the macro level, the high population growth rates of the Gulf States would increase demand for public services, and hence would require increased public expenditure within a short span of time. Further, such growth rates, under the current socio-economic context, could lead to growing unemployment. Under such circumstances, it would be expected that lower levels of human capital formation would result and this would slow the progress towards development in the future.

Gulf States cannot afford to wait for fertility decline to occur naturally: the current population growth rates of the Gulf States are higher than those found in today's developed countries when at comparable stages of development (due to the speedy reduction in mortality and the spread of modern medication, in the absence of contraception), and current population growth rates are higher than in many other countries with similar per capita income levels. Such population growth rates will heighten the current economic and social difficulties of the Gulf States. The limited government revenues (especially given the declining price of oil) will have to be divided amongst ever increasing numbers of people who will continue to expect the same luxuries (e.g., food subsidies, no taxation, free health and education services, etc.) rather than being invested in the development of the human and economic resources. This will occur at the expense of the future human development of the region. Hence the urgency and the need for the formulation and implementation of an active and broad ranging population policy.

Structure

The first part of the Book, Chapters 1 to 4, explain the current demographic situation of the Gulf States, considering each of the three components of population growth in turn: migration (Chapter 1), mortality (Chapter 2) and finally fertility (Chapters 3 and 4).

Part 2 of the Book, comprising Chapters 5 to 6, is concerned with assessing the public services that underpin the main components of human capital: education and health (Chapter 5) and employment (Chapter 6).

The final, third part of the Book, links the demographic and development components through the scenario approach. Chapter 7 focuses on the assumptions underlying the three alternative population projections for the national populations in each of the three Gulf States, and the one projection for the non-national population. Chapters 8 and 9 demonstrate the effect of the population growth rates, resulting from these projections, for the provision of public services and employment. Attention is particularly paid to the gains that could be made if the population growth rate were to be moderated.

The Conclusion examines the official 'laissez-faire' position of the Gulf States vis a vis their population growth rates. Continuing to ignore, or minimizing the importance of population growth rates would result in a dramatic increase in the population, within a short span of time. Gulf governments, which have so far not formulated rigorous Development Plans, will be ill-equipped to meet the demands, which would consequently be made on them. As part of their development planning process, firm, yet culturally sensitive population policies need to be devised, that would aim to reduce fertility at a more rapid pace.

PART I
DEMOGRAPHIC COMPONENTS OF GULF POPULATIONS

Chapter 1

Non-Nationals in the Gulf: Transient Migrants or Adopted Siblings?

General theories of migration tend to concentrate on the decision to migrate at the individual level, which is assumed to be based on a rational comparison of relative costs and benefits of migrating or remaining. Therefore, the causes for migration are sought in terms of 'push' and 'pull' factors. The existence of undesirable factors in the area of origin (for example, overcrowding, low incomes and living standards) compels people to leave, while the merits of the destination (for example, better economic opportunities, political freedom, higher living standards), beckons them to it. Such a framework is instrumental to the analysis of migration, but it does not encompass all the factors at work in the migratory process. It either totally disregards the role of the State and its policies, or treats it as an aberration, which, because it disrupts the functioning of the rational market, should be removed. Further, the push-pull model cannot explain why certain groups of migrants go to one country rather than another.

No single cause is ever sufficient to explain why people decide to leave their country and settle in another. Migration is a collective phenomenon and should be examined as a part of the global economic and political system. Migratory movements are the result of global interdependence: of interacting macro and micro structures: large scale institutional factors (the political economy of the world market, interstate relationships, laws, structures and practices established by the states) and informal networks (psychological adaptations, personal relationships, family and household patterns, friendship and community ties), practices and beliefs developed by the migrants themselves to cope with migration and settlement. To understand migratory movements, it is essential to consider all aspects of the process.

Within such a framework, this Chapter shall trace and explain the main characteristics of the migratory flows into and out of the Gulf States: the increase in the size of this population, the shifts in its ethnic composition, and the tendency towards 'settling' found in some States. It will also reflect on the official policies of the Gulf States with respect to their non-national populations, and tease out the potential future trends.

Tracing the Characteristics of the Non-Nationals

The non-national population in the Gulf has been increasing, in absolute numbers and percentage terms since the 1950s. Qatar's total population increased from 12,000 (1940) to 190,000 (1976), of whom 6,000 were thought to be foreign.[1] In the United Arab Emirates, non-nationals make up more than 70 percent of the 2.5 million inhabitants. Abu Dhabi's population increased from 46,375 (1968) to 235,662 (1975) of whom an estimated 176747 were foreign.[2] In 1993, non-nationals accounted for an average of 26 percent of the total population in Oman[3] and in Saudi Arabia.

As Table 1.1 indicates, between 1957 and 1993, the proportion of non-nationals in Kuwait increased from 45 to 57 percent, and from 12 to 36 percent (1959-1991) in Bahrain. The increase was most rapid between 1970 and 1980 for Kuwait and, between 1960 and 1970 for Bahrain. Since 1990, the rate of increase has been slowing down in Bahrain, while that in Kuwait has been negative because of the Kuwait-Iraq War (1991).[4]

Table 1.1 Change in the Non-National Population's Size

Year		Population in 000s		Average Increase Per	
		Bahrain	Kuwait*	Bahrain	Kuwait*
1950		19	93	n/a	n/a
1960		24	160	2.6	7.2
1970		38	391	5.8	14.4
1980		112	971	1.9	14.8
1990		185	2208	6.5	12.7
1993		199	1428	2.5	-11.8
%	Increase (per	4	32		

* Kuwaiti data refers to the Censuses of 1957, 1970, 1980, 1989, 1993.

Source: National Censuses and Statistical Abstracts, various years

---

[1] Bonine, M.E. (1980). The Urbanisation of the Persian Gulf Nations. In Alvin J. Cottrell, (Ed.). *The Persian Gulf States* (pp. 260, 597-598). Baltimore: John Hopkins University Press.

[2] Bonine, M.E. (1980). The Urbanisation of the Persian Gulf Nations. In Alvin J. Cottrell. (Ed.), *The Persian Gulf States* (pp. 260. 597-598). Baltimore: John Hopkins University Press.

[3] Ministry of Development. (1996). *Statistical Yearbook. Sultanate of Oman, 24th Issue.* Oman: Information and Documentation Center.

[4] All the emigration out of Kuwait was resumed, and it is estimated that the proportion of non-nationals now equals that of the pre war levels, if not higher.

National Origins of the Non-Nationals

The non-national population in the Gulf States has comprised specific nationalities at different times, not by coincidence. Initially, nationals from within the Arabian Peninsula, particularly Omanis, Bahrainis and Iranians constituted the bulk of the 'non-national' population in any State. The construction of the Saudi Arabian pipeline (Tapline) at Ras al Mishab in 1944 employed 450 Americans, two Britons, and 1200 'native labourers' (mainly Bahrainis, and Saudi Arabians).[5] In 1960, there were claims that the United Arab Emirates government, with help from the British, was trying to 'Iranize' the country, by granting too many naturalizations to the Iranians.[6] Between 1959 and 1971, Gulf Arabs and Iranians accounted for an average of 55 percent of the non-national population in Bahrain (see Table 1.2).[7] In Kuwait, this was 23 percent by 1965.[8]

Table 1.2 Nationality Distribution of Non-Nationals in Bahrain

Year	Iranians	Omanis	Saudis
1941	47	n/a	n/a
1950	37	12	n/a
1959	17	30	10

Source: State of Bahrain, Fourth and Fifth Population Census, p. 3 and p. 166

By the early 1960s, the first shift in nationality occurred: the proportion of Arabs from the Fertile Crescent began increasing steadily. In Kuwait, it increased from 65 percent (1965) to 76 percent (1975).[9] Between 1953 and 1963,[10] the proportion of other Arabs working in the Kuwait Oil Company increased from 22 percent to

---

[5] Indian Office Records: *R/15/5/179 Letter No B/PG/20* Office of Staff Officer (Intelligence) Persian Gulf (10/4/1948).

[6] Indian Office Records: *R/15/5/179 Letter No B/PG/20* Office of Staff Officer (Intelligence) Persian Gulf (10/4/1948).

[7] Central Statistics Organisation. (1987). *Fourth Population Census* (p. 3). Bahrain: Central Statistics Organisation. Also, Central Statistics Organisation. (1987). *Fifth Population Census* (p. 14). Bahrain: Central Statistics Organisation.

[8] Ministry of Planning. (1978). *State of Kuwait, Statistical Abstract, 1978. Edition XV* (Table 96. p. 109). Kuwait: Central Statistics Organisation.

[9] Ministry of Planning. (1978). *State of Kuwait, Statistical Abstract, 1978. Edition XV* (Table 96. p. 109). Kuwait: Central Statistics Organisation.

[10] Finne, D.H. (1958). *Desert Enterprise: The Middle East Oil Industry in its Local Environment* (p. 119). Cambridge, Mass.: Harvard University Press.

36 percent, while that of Asian workers declined from 37 to 31 percent.[11]   In Bahrain, the increase was less significant and never large, the total number of non-nationals increased from 15930 to 38389 between 1950 and 1965, and just under 50 percent of these were other Arabs.[12]   Between 1959 and its peak in 1965, the proportion of other Arabs increased by about 0.6 percent per annum to reach 11 percent of the non-national population.[13]   In 1957, Saudi Arabia's ARAMCO's foreign labour force was divided between ten percent Indians and Pakistanis and nine percent other Arabs.[14]

The second shift in nationality occurred by the late 1970s: this time towards Asians, initially Indians and Pakistanis, then including Far East Asians as well.   Since 1977, the proportion of Asians in the non-national workforce in Bahrain has been increasing by three percent per annum, and accounting for 91 percent of non-nationals on the Island. In 1980, Asians accounted for 88 percent of all work permits issued, a proportion which increased to 92 percent by 1984. Indians comprised 51 percent of these Asians. The share of Asians in the Omani non-national workforce increased by two percent per annum between 1980 and 1983: from 88 percent to 93 percent.[15]   In Qatar, Asians represented 60 percent of total employment in the period 1980-1984.

The Non-National Population's Sex and Dependency Structure

Overall, the non-national population across the Gulf States are largely workers, given the relatively high labour force participation rates: 60 percent in Kuwait, 80 percent in Bahrain, 55 percent in Qatar and an average of 47 percent in Saudi Arabia and the United Arab Emirates.[16]   Since the proportion of dependents amongst the non-national population is relatively small, it can be assumed that the non-national females are either migratory workers, or employed spouses, and

---

[11]   *Arab Economic Report.* (1965). (pp. 48-59). Beirut: General Union of Chambers of Commerce, Industry and Agriculture for Arab Countries.

[12]   Bonine, M.E. (1980). The Urbanisation of the Persian Gulf Nations. In Alvin J. Cottrell, (Ed.), *The Persian Gulf States* (p. 262). Baltimore: John Hopkins University Press.

[13]   Central Statistics Organisation. (various years). *State of Bahrain: Statistical Abstracts.*

[14]   Finne, D.H. (1958). *Desert Enterprise: The Middle East Oil Industry in its Local Environment* (pp. 110, 119). Cambridge, Mass.: Harvard University Press.

[15]   Ministry of Development. (1996). *Statistical Yearbook. 1996. Sultanate of Oman, 24th Issue.* Oman: Information and Documentation Center.

[16]   Numbers may be underestimates, given that many non-nationals work illegally.

are in the Gulf States for employment, rather than settlement purposes (Figure 1.1).[17]

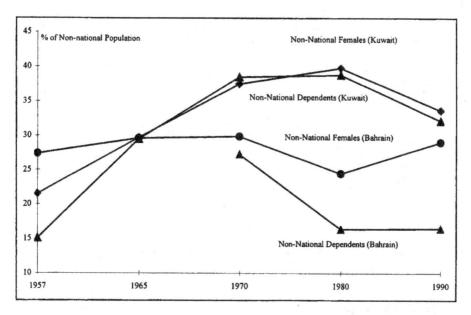

Figure 1.1 Non-National Females and Dependants in Bahrain and Kuwait
Source: UNESCWA, 2001. Demographic and Related Socio-Economic Datasheets, and Statistical Abstracts, various years

Further evidence of this can be found in both Kuwait and Bahrain, where the rate of natural increase (per 1000 of the non-national population) has been declining. In Bahrain, the rate of natural increase declined from 18 in 1980 to 16 by 1991, while in Kuwait, it declined by two percent per annum between 1967 and 1976, and by six percent between 1988 and 1989.

Characteristics of the Non-National Workforce

On average, 62 percent of the workforce in the Gulf States is accounted for by non-nationals, a proportion which has been increasing, in absolute and percentage terms in every State, and has been most rapid in Saudi Arabia and least rapid in the UAE, as illustrated in Figure 1.2.

---

[17] Demographic evolution (whereby the age pyramid of a migrant community, initially unbalanced towards males of working age, transforms into a normal shaped sex/age pyramid) occurs as the families of migrants join the workers.

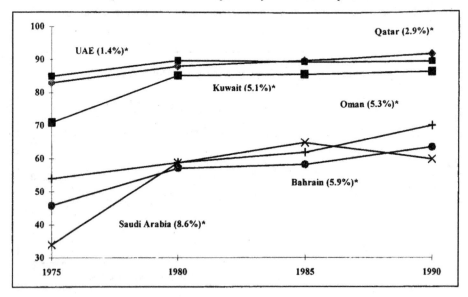

* the average % increase per annum between 1975-1990.

Figure 1.2 Participation of Non-Nationals in the Workforce (1975-1990)
Source: ILO estimates

Sex distribution Across the Gulf States, more non-national males than females are employed. However, while the proportion of non-national male workers has been declining in both Kuwait and Bahrain, that of female workers has been increasing. In Kuwait, between 1957 and 1993, the proportion of female non-national workers increased by 35 percent in two stages: a slow increase of 0.2 percent per annum between 1957 and 1975, followed by a rapid increase of three percent per annum between 1980 and 1993.   In Bahrain, the proportion of working non-national females has been steadily increasing from 12 percent in 1971 to 41 percent by 1993.

Economic segmentation Non-national workers have tended to concentrate in the services[18] and construction sectors. Two changes are noteworthy: banking is employing an increasing share of non-nationals, from a base of 0 in the 1950s to four percent in Kuwait, and to nine percent in Bahrain, by the 1990s. The share of non-nationals in the mining and quarrying sector has declined (by 0.2 percent per annum in Kuwait and 0.6 percent in Bahrain).

---

[18] Defined in the Kuwait Statistical Abstract as including community, social and personal services; in Bahrain this includes educational, medical, social and households with employed people.

In Bahrain, employment of non-nationals in manufacturing, and trading/ hotelling has been increasing (at an average of 0.35 percent per annum), whilst that in 'Gas, Water, Electricity' and 'Transport and Communication' sectors has been declining (by 0.3 percent per annum). In Kuwait, employment of non-nationals in all sectors, except for 'Banking', 'Services', 'Trading and Hotelling' (where there have been modest increases) and 'Transport and Communication' (which has remained constant), has been declining. While time series data is not available for Oman, it is evident that its economy is still in the 'construction' phase, as 37 percent are involved in 'Construction and Manufacturing' (see Table 1.3).

Table 1.3 Average Distribution of Non-National Workers Across Sectors

	Kuwait (1957-1993)	Bahrain (1959-1991)	Oman 1993
Services	44.0	28.0	24.0
Construction	17.9	21.0	24.0
Trading/Hotelling	14.0	12.8	21.2
Manufacturing	8.9	7.3	13.0
Transport and Communication	5.0	7.3	3.0
Electricity, Gas, Water	1.7	10.1	0.8
Others	8.5	13.5	14.0

Source: National Censuses, Statistical Abstracts, various years

In both Kuwait and Bahrain, an average of 83 percent of non-national female workers are employed in the 'services' sector. In Kuwait, this proportion increased by 0.2 percent per annum from 90 percent (1957) to 94 percent (1975), after which it declined to 89 percent in 1985. In absolute numbers, it increased 62 times between 1957 and 1985. In Bahrain, their share declined from 82 percent to 75 percent, though in absolute numbers it increased 13 times. While a detailed breakdown of this 'services' sector is not available, maids accounted for 81 percent of the non-national female workers in the services sector of Bahrain in 1991, and in 1993, Kuwait estimated that 68 percent of female workers were in the 'household sector'.[19] Between 1971 and 1991, the share of female non-national workers in trading and hotelling in Bahrain increased 19 times, from 3 to 7 percent, while in Kuwait, it increased 22 times from 2 (1965) to 3 percent (1985).

Skill composition As Table 1.4 indicates, most non-national workers in the Gulf have tended to be unskilled labourers. Between 1971 and 1993, the average ratio of labourers: service workers: professionals was 3:2:1 in Kuwait, and 5:3:1 in Bahrain. However, the share of labourers has been declining by 0.7 percent per

---

[19] *Al Watan*, Wednesday, 24/8/1994. No 6609.

annum in Kuwait (1970-1988)[20] and by 0.3 percent per annum in Bahrain (1971-1991). On the other hand, the proportion of professional non-nationals has been increasing by 0.5 percent per annum in Kuwait (between 1988 and 1993), and by 0.3 percent per annum in Bahrain (between 1981 and 1991). Per annum increases of three percent and 0.5 percent have been registered for service workers in Kuwait and Bahrain, respectively, during the same period. Workers at other skill levels have maintained their share in the workforce.

Table 1.4 Skill Distribution of the Non-National Workforce

	Kuwait (1971-93)	Bahrain (1971-91)	Oman 1993	Saudi Arabia (1983-1992)	UAE (1992)
Labourers/Production	42.9	47.9	44.8	64.5	44.8
Service	23.5	25.2	20.9	14.3	30.6
Professional/Technical	13.7	10.0	16.0	13.1	12.7
Clerical	8.9	5.2	3.0	4.3	10.6
Others	11.0	11.7	15.6	3.8	1.3

Source: Statistical Abstracts, various years

The 'Need' for Non-Nationals in the Gulf States

While it can be argued that demographic and economic reasons underlie the presence of these non-nationals in the Gulf States, some of the characteristics identified above demand additional analysis.

Demographic Structure

In addition to being numerically too small to be able to implement the ambitious development plans formulated, Gulf nationals are too young. Table 1.5 indicates that in every Gulf State, almost 40 percent of the national population is aged less than 15 years.

In addition, the rapid increase in education (an average annual increase of seven percent for University students) has meant that a large proportion of those who would have normally joined the workforce, are otherwise occupied (Table 1.6).

---

[20] This ignores the post Iraq-Kuwait War period, as Kuwait had to import even more labourers to reconstruct its damaged infrastructure.

Table 1.5 Gulf Nationals (000s) and Proportion of Dependants (1970-1990)

States	1975		1980		1992	
	Nationals	% Dependant	Nationals	% Dependant	Nationals	% Dependant
Bahrain	214	53.5	238	46.2	323	46.2
Kuwait	472	53.2	562	51.6	669	40.5
Oman	550	na	635	na	1481	46.3
Qatar	68	na	na	na	123	47.9
Saudi Arabia	4593	na	5101	na	12196	53.4
UAE	200	na	na	na	493	52.7

Source: UNESCWA, 2001, Demographic and Related Socioeconomic Datasheets

Table 1.6 Total Enrolment Ratios (percent of population aged 20-24)

	Kuwait	Saudi Arabia	UAE
1975			
Males	7.1	6.0	n/a
Females	11.2	1.8	n/a
1980			
Males	8.0	8.8	1.6
Females	15.0	5.0	3.8
1985			
Males	14.0	13.5	5.4
Females	17.7	10.5	14.9
1988			
Males	15.7	13.9	4.5
Females	20.2	10.3	15.4

Source: UNESCO Statistical Yearbook, 1991

Finally, until recently, female nationals have not been joining the workforce,[21] for structural and social reasons, further exacerbating the 'shortage' in national manpower (see Figure 1.3). While the trend in female labour force participation has been increasing, by 1985, only five and eight percent of the national workforce of the United Arab Emirates and Saudi Arabia were females.

---

[21] This issue will be further analyzed in Chapter 6 on labour forces.

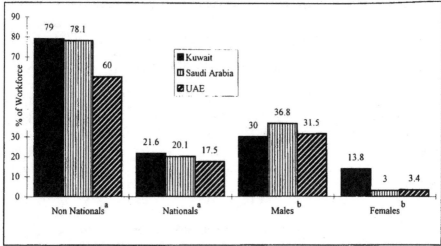

a.   Working population as a proportion of working age population (aged 15-65) by nationality.

b.   percent of national working males as a proportion of total working age national males and similar for females.

Figure 1.3 Labour Force Participation Rates by Nationality and Sex
Source: Latest available Statistical Abstracts

Economic Reasons

Immediately after the discovery of oil, workers were 'pulled' to the oil industry, despite it being a capital-intensive industry. It was a source of employment for a population that was suffering from the effects of the collapse of the pearling industry, so much so, that it stimulated labour migrations from other less fortunate (in terms of oil discoveries) Gulf States. Migrant Omanis, Saudis, Bahrainis and Iranians were attracted to the oil sector not only by higher wages, but also, by the luxury of a regular source of income. The higher wages of the Arabian American Oil Company (ARAMCO) attracted so many Bahrainis that the Bahraini government imposed restrictions on migrations to Saudi Arabia. Migrations resumed once the restrictions were lifted, so that by 1946, 1300 left for the Mainland.[22] Similarly, the poor living conditions in Oman (first oil exports were in 1967), and the effects of the tribal war in Dhofar (1950s), forced an estimated

---

[22] Government of Bahrain. (1957). *Annual Report, 1366 H* (p.35). Bahrain: Central Statistics Organisation. Also Littlefield, R.E. (1958). *Bahrain as a Persian Gulf State*. M.A. Thesis. Beirut: American University of Beirut. pp. 93-110.

100,000 Omanis, by 1970, to seek employment and better living standards in neighbouring countries.[23]

After the oil shock of 1973, the financial surpluses that the oil exporters were beginning to accumulate, and the concurrent financial losses that oil importers shouldered, prompted fears about the long-term effects that this would have on the world economy.[24] Hence, the Gulf States were encouraged, by international financial institutions, and their own populations, to spend money on the rapid 'development' of their countries: the deposition of Sultan Taymour of Oman in 1970, by his son, with the help of the British, was a reminder to other Gulf Emirs of the danger of not spending.[25]

Table 1.7 Government Expenditures (US $ millions) 1973-1980

States	1973	1975	1978	1980	Percent change per annum
Bahrain	87	324	749	818	120
Kuwait	1768	3567	n/a	n/a	
Oman	120	1288	1456	2403	273

Source: National Census and Statistical Abstracts, various years

Economic arguments were also made in defence of this 'Instant Development Drive': inflation erodes away the purchasing power of oil revenues to buy foreign capital equipment, and in the long term, oil prices decline vis a vis the prices of imported manufactured goods[26] (even though increased demand for foreign capital, in itself, exacerbates inflation in domestic and international markets). For these reasons, after 1973, the pressure and temptation, to spend was great (see Table 1.7).

The Gulf States therefore 'bought', within a decade, what had taken the industrial countries a century to achieve. Large industrial (state funded) projects were implemented to transform, simultaneously, all Gulf countries in industrial terms, in the shortest possible time span: at Jebel Ali and Ruwais in the UAE, refineries and other industrial projects at Jubail and Yanbu in Saudi Arabia, Umm Said in Qatar, ALBA and ASRY in Bahrain. They concentrated on producing petrochemicals (ethylene, methanol and nitrogenous fertilizers); salt, chlorine and

---

[23] *Conference on the Population Distribution and Development in the Arab World.* Kuwait: International Labour Organization, Kuwait University and Kuwait Planning Institute, 22-27 November 1981. Translated from Arabic. (pp. 394-396).

[24] Yergin, D. (1993). *The Prize* (pp. 634-636). Washington, D.C.: Princeton Press.

[25] Indian Office Records: *R/15/5/179 Letter No B/PG/20* Office of Staff Officer (Intelligence) Persian Gulf (10/4/1948).

[26] Wilson, R. (1980). The Rising Costs of Industrial Construction. In May Ziwar Daftari (Eds.), *Issues in Development: The Arab Gulf States* (pp. 66-67). London: MD Research and Services Ltd.

sulphur; natural liquid gas (the Saudi Arabian gas gathering project provided methane and ethane (fuel and feedstock) for other industrial plants); oil refining, aluminium, steel mills (mainly import substituting industries) and dry docks. At the same time, large-scale extravagant infrastructural investments were also made to create large highways, large buildings, and luxurious houses. Saudi Arabia spent $3.5 billion on infrastructural projects (roads, airports, schools, universities, hospitals, defence, industries).[27] Bahrain's infrastructural expenditure increased from $36 million to $359 million between 1973 and 1980 (an increase of 129 percent).[28] This development drive, and the employment opportunities it offered, accelerated the pace of migration of non-national workers, and particularly labourers, to the Gulf States.

But the non-nationals' presence was not just a simple matter of the demand for workers being higher than the supply in the Gulf: it was economically rational for Gulf employers to recruit non-nationals. The ease of immediately importing skilled, qualified and experienced labour whenever needed, made the option of the costly and time consuming investment in the development of indigenous manpower unattractive to employers. Non-national workers also helped reduce production costs, as they accepted lower wages and were more productive than the nationals. In 1988, despite non-national workers putting in, on average, 1.3 times more working hours than a Kuwaiti worker, they earned, on average, 2.3 times less. The difference was especially marked for workers in fishing and agriculture, where Kuwaitis worked two times less hours than their non-national colleagues, and yet earned five times more.[29]

Employers in the Gulf States found non-national workers from the Indian subcontinent and the Far East even more attractive than workers from other countries. In addition to being cheaper, they were more organized and transient. With the 'contract labour' method, the responsibility of the Gulf Kafeel (sponsor)[30] was limited to the provision of employment visas. Associated problems of discipline, accommodation, maintenance expenses and so on, were all borne by the contracting firms who established and operated 'work camps' or enclaves in which the non-nationals lived: ASRY in Bahrain, Shuaiba in Kuwait, Umm Said in Qatar,

---

[27] Wilson, R. (1980). The Rising Costs of Industrial Construction. In May Ziwar Daftari (Eds.), *Issues in Development: The Arab Gulf States* (pp. 66-67). London: MD Research and Services Ltd.

[28] Ministry of Finance and National Economy. (1991). *Thirty Years of Economic and Social Development in the State of Bahrain* (p. 100). Bahrain: Directorate of Evaluation and Economic Research, Ministry of Finance and National Economy.

[29] *Kuwait Statistical Abstract, 1993* (p. 113, Table 107 and 108). Kuwait: Central Statistics Organization.

[30] The Kafeel system emerged in the 1930s as a means of ensuring that government regulations were implemented as the bureaucracies did not have the organizational structure to police them themselves. With increasing powers that were granted to Kafeels, their political influence increased.

Jebel Ali and Ruwais in the UAE[31] all had associated work camps. The location of these work camps, close to the work place and away from the main residential areas, minimized the impact of the non-national workers on the local society, as their presence was concealed and therefore posed no threats to the fragile Gulf identity and cultural norms.

Furthermore, it was also economically rational for Gulf nationals to encourage non-national labour recruitment. Initially, the explosion in the non-national numbers in States that had only recently been awarded their independence,[32] where State structures were still in their infancy, and which were undergoing rapid and unpredictable changes, posed serious challenges to the immature national identity. Therefore, Gulf governments designed employment regulations specific to the recruitment of non-nationals that aimed at reducing the impact of the large numbers of non-nationals and at expressing the link between the nationals and their State. The Saudi Labour regulations (1947), the Kuwaiti Labour Law (1957), the Bahraini Labour Law (1958) were conditioned by the labour strikes in the Oil Companies in 1938, 1947 and 1953 (in Bahrain) and 1956 (in Dhahran) and tended to benefit locals at the expense of non-nationals. For example, Kuwaiti Law No 36[33] granted the right of conducting commercial agencies to Kuwaitis only; Law No 43[34] allowed only nationals (and their companies) to import; the Central Tenders Board decreed that only registered Kuwaiti merchants could issue tenders. Non-nationals could only work if they had national Kafeels who theoretically enforced the other regulations:[35] two year contracts, employment in one task, Kafeel's permission required for changing jobs, the right of residence being linked to the work permit, which lapsed upon unemployment or with an unauthorized change in employment, right of arbitrary deportation by a local Minister of the Interior. Furthermore, until 2000, non-nationals were not able to either own property or invest in the Gulf Stock markets.

These regulations ensured that nationals could make a sizable, virtually unearned income from 'sponsoring' a non-national into a Gulf State: in exchange for being a 'nominal' business partner,[36] a Gulf national could extract fees from non-nationals for the sponsorship visas, a proportion of their business profits and rental income for accommodation. This is in addition to the entrepreneurship

---

[31] Sooying Kim. (1982). Contract Migration in the Republic of Korea. *IME Working Paper* (p. 28). Geneva: International Labour Organisation.

[32] With the exception of Saudi Arabia, all the Gulf States were British Protectorates until 1970-1971.

[33] *Kuwait Official Gazette.* No 486, July 19, 1964.

[34] *Kuwait Official Gazette.* No 486, July 19, 1964.

[35] Owen, R. (1985). Migrant Workers in the Gulf. *The Minority Rights Group Report,* 68, 8-10.

[36] Commonly referred to as 'sleeping' partner.

opportunities that the presence of a large subpopulation presented (in terms of specialised goods and services that only nationals could own and manage).

Structural Reasons

Until the 1980s, recruitment of non-nationals was necessary, especially given that employment in the oil industry demanded skills more sophisticated than those which pearl-diving, fishing or kutab-training provided. As Table 1.8 highlights, the population of the Gulf, in addition to being illiterate, did not possess the appropriate skills that were required in this and the other modern sector industries that were rapidly being created.[37]

Table 1.8 Literacy Levels of the National Labour Force (1970-1980)[38]

State	1971/5			1981		
	Population	Labour	% literate	Population	Labour	% literate
Bahrain	178193	47	47	238420	54	69
Kuwait	347396	46	55	386695	48	73
Oman	550000	n/a	20	n/a	n/a	n/a

Source: National Census, Statistical Abstracts, various years

However, the scale of recruitment of non-nationals was only made necessary due to the unexpected repercussions of the policies that were adopted by the Gulf governments to redistribute oil revenues to their nationals. These un-elected governments found, in the redistribution of oil wealth, an easy means by which they could maintain, or buy, if not outright political support, then acquiescence from their populations, without having to resort (from their point of view) to the drawbacks of democracy, mainly, people's right to participation in and the formulation of policies.

The main means of redistribution of wealth took the form of welfare state provisions: the most generous of which was found in Kuwait, to which other Gulf States either aspired, or tried to outperform, depending on the size of their oil revenues and populations. These provisions ensured that Gulf nationals led comfortable lives at minimum cost to themselves, subsidized charges for electricity,

---

[37] The American oil men (in Bahrain) had been told by British friends that not much should be expected of Arab labour, and that for all but the lowest unskilled grades, it would be necessary to import Indians or others for training. The local labour, consisting of peasants, villagers, tribesmen, fishermen, pearl divers and town fringe indigents, was 'indeed unskilled illiterate, impoverished, undernourished and diseased.' From Thornburg, M.W. (1964). *People and Policy in the Middle East* (p. 64). New York: W.W. Norton and Co.
[38] National labour force is the population aged 15-60.

water, fuel and food. Other social benefits accrued from being a Gulf citizen:[39] right to property ownership, establishing a business, social security assistance (for marriage ceremony expenses, dowries, and for each child born), easy access to cheap credit, loans, mortgages and grants of land. Qatar and the UAE were especially generous to their people: more people than in Kuwait and Saudi Arabia qualified for free housing, and both States sent their sick nationals, along with an accompanying family member, overseas, at the government's expense, for medical treatment.[40] Scholarships to study abroad were also more generous and numerous. In 1991, Emirati women married to non-nationals, spinsters and married students were all entitled to allowances. Finally, until recently, nationals in most Gulf States were guaranteed employment in the large public bureaucracies, where productivity tended to be low, demanded minimal effort, required few skills, provided little training and offered large salaries. This nurtured a social acceptance and expectation of administrative and managerial positions, and converted Gulf nationals into white-collared salaried middle classes, who frowned upon manual blue-collar work.[41]

Such benefits, in addition to rendering the large investments made in the new educational and medical facilities in the States themselves ineffectual, have had detrimental consequences for human resource development in the Gulf. It has curbed the nationals' motivation to join the labour force: why work when one can receive a virtually unearned income? The employment of non-nationals in the Gulf States was thereby rendered a necessity, rather than an option.

Political Reasons

Yet the demographic, structural and economic factors outlined thus far, do not provide a full explanation for the shifts in nationality of the non-national workforce. Why did the switch from Iranian to other nationalities occur in the 1950s, that from Arabs to Asians in the late 1970s? Why are non-national workers still being recruited in 2001, despite a more educated and skilled national workforce, and amid high and increasing national unemployment (estimated at 15 percent in Bahrain in 2001)?

The proximity of Iran has ensured a long tradition of migration between the two sides of the Gulf, as attested to by the contemporary presence of the 'stateless' groups in the Gulf States: 'Ajams' in Bahrain, 'Bidoons' in Kuwait and

---

[39] Kuwaiti Laws Nos. 36 (1964), 43 (Nov 29, 1964) and the Central Tenders Board regulations which confine the ability to conduct any business to Kuwaiti nationals. *Kuwait Official Gazette.* No 486, July 19, 1964.

[40] Field, M. (1984). *The Merchants: The Big Business Families of Arabia* (pp. 58-59). London: John Murray Publishers Ltd.

[41] Chatelus, M and Y. Schmeil. (1984). Towards a New Political Economy of State Industrialization in the Arab Middle East. *International Journal of Middle Eastern Studies,* 2, 225-226.

elsewhere. Yet, the proportion of Iranians in the workforces of Bahrain and Kuwait began declining in the 1950s: the proportion of Iranian workers in the total population in Bahrain declined from eight percent in 1941 to three percent by 1959. The proportion of Iranians in the non-national workforce in Kuwait declined from 20 percent in 1965 to 14 percent by 1975.[42]

Both Bahrain and Kuwait include large ethnically Iranian and Shi'a communities that (it is assumed by the authorities) owe allegiance to Iran, rather than to the Sunni Gulf Sheikhs. Bahrain's concern has been compounded by the historic claims Iran has made on the Island (dating back to 1605). Hence, in the 1950s, the main employer on the Island, the Bahrain Oil Company, began reducing its Iranian workforce, because it did not want to be seen as supporting these claims.[43] After the collapse of the Pahlavi dynasty and the rise to power of Khomeni in 1980, Iranian labour was further eschewed, to avoid exacerbating the effect that the Ayatuallah's calls for revolution were already having on the Gulf States.

A political reason also underlies the increase in the 'other' Arab populations in the Gulf. Initially, the local and British authorities, believed it would be easier for these conservative Gulf societies to incorporate other Arabs, given the similarities in culture and language. But, the increase in their proportion also coincided with the creation of Israel in 1948,[44] and the Lebanese political crisis. Offering employment to the Arabs of the Levant, particularly the Palestinians, was easier working towards achieving a solution to the political crises. Even Oman, with its meagre revenues, under the money-cautious Sultan Taymour,[45] reserved ten teaching positions especially for Palestinians, which the British authorities subsequently helped to fill.[46]

However, this preference for the 'appropriate' Arabs was undermined by the political orientations of the governments of the Fertile Crescent in the 1970s. Nasser's brand of Pan Arabism, his appeal for a Pan Arab Republic, and Sadat's Camp David Accords with Israel (1978) were frowned upon by the Gulf States. The fear of the potentially destabilizing effect that the introduction of such Arab

[42] *Kuwait Statistical Abstract,1978.* (1993). Kuwait: Ministry of Planning. Central Statistics Organization.

[43] Indian Office Records: *R/15/5/179 Letter No B/PG/20* Office of Staff Officer (Intelligence) Persian Gulf (10/4/1948).

[44] Hourani. A. (1991). *A History of the Arab Peoples* (p. 360). London: Faber and Faber.

[45] Oman's revenues increased between 1930 and 1966 from 50000 pounds to one million pounds. *Conference on the Population Distribution and Development in the Arab World Kuwait:* International Labour Organization, Kuwait University and Kuwait Planning Institute. 22-27 November 1981. Translated from Arabic p. 394.

[46] Indian Office Records: *R/15/6/380:* series of letters and telegrams from The British Consulate in Muscat to the Minister for Foreign Affairs. B. Woods-Ballard: dated 18 September 1949 (537/28-C), 8 December 1949 (962/28-C), 29 December 1949 (64/II/32/49).

nationalism would have, on the undemocratic Gulf societies led to the reversal of the policy, and the switch towards Asian nationalities. This shift was given a boost in 1990, during the Kuwait-Iraq Gulf Crisis: the governments of Yemen, Jordan and Palestine had chosen not taken a stance against Iraq during the War, a choice with grave repercussions for their workers in the Gulf. By the end of 1990, about 800,000 Yemenis, 54000 Palestinians and 300,000 Jordanians 'returned' to their countries from the Gulf States (mainly from Saudi Arabia).[47] Meanwhile, Mubarak's prominent anti-Iraq stance secured Egyptian workers a larger share in the employment opportunities that arose in the wake of the reconstruction of Kuwait.

Furthermore, the Iranian Revolution demonstrated the potential threat that the presence of a disgruntled (ethnic or other) community poses, to even the seemingly most powerful government. Hence, recognizing the political and economic security that fragmentation provides, Gulf governments sought to balance the potentially politically demanding national population, with the socio-economically and legally incarcerated non-national masses. Furthermore, they ensured that the non-national segment was itself fragmented into diverse nationalities,[48] not merely to avert the emergence, in strength, of any one community, but also to limit the economic impact that strained relations with any given labour exporting country could have.

Finally, labour-exporting governments have had a role in encouraging larger numbers of their nationals to seek employment in the Gulf States. While workers from other Arab countries have tended to rely primarily on kinship ties and other informal means of gaining employment in the Gulf States, the recruitment of workers from Asia has been, on the whole, more organized and systematic. In fact, an Indian Recruiting Office was opened in Bombay as far back as July 1936, to recruit workers for the oil companies of Bahrain and Kuwait, under proper contract, and subject to the supervision of the Government of India Office for the Protector of Emigrants.[49] Other Asian labour exporting countries, like the Philippines, Thailand and Pakistan, have made the export of manpower a main feature in their economic plans. Still others have encouraged migration indirectly through 'de-regulation', embassies playing a minimal role in protecting the legitimate rights of their workers, lack of studies on the social and economic status of their migrant workers, limited involvement in trying to improve their migrants' wages, their

---

[47] Van Hear, N. (1992). Migrant Workers in the Gulf. *Minority Rights Group International Update*. London: MRG.

[48] Ibrahim, S.E. (1982). *The New Arab Social Order; A Study of the Social Impact of Oil Wealth* (p. 12). London: Croom Helm.

[49] Indian Office Records: *R/15/5/179 Letter No B/PG/20* Office of Staff Officer (Intelligence) Persian Gulf (10/4/1948).

disregard for the many illegal or private recruitment agencies in their countries:[50] in the hope that Gulf employers would find their workers more 'economical' and thus attractive, to recruit.

Not only does migration translate into remittances,[51] but also employment for their unemployed masses. Estimated remittances sent back have been as high as 80 percent of earnings for Koreans in labour camps where housing and food is provided, and 20 to 30 percent for those with dependents (see Table 1.9).

Table 1.9 Workers' Remittances (debits in US $ millions)

States	1975	1980	1985	1990	1992
Bahrain	187	219	115	253	218
Kuwait	n/a	n/a	1044	770	870
Oman	171	278	947	856	1157

* All transfers are negative

Source: IMF, *Balance of Payments Statistical Yearbooks, 1993.* Part 1. Vol. 44. pp. 419, 443, 449. *Balance of Payments Statistical Yearbooks, 1985.* Vol. 36. Part 1. pp. 42, 352, 470

Monthly remittances are believed to vary from $200 to $450 for Yemenis to $170 for Asians and $319 to $444 for Thai and Indonesians workers.[52] The wage and salary differentials between labour importing and labour exporting states have been high enough to ensure a long waiting list of prospective workers to fill the vacancies in the Gulf, despite the working and living conditions.

Non-Nationals in the Gulf: Social Status

The social (class) position of non-nationals is a function of their ethnic origins and economic status. The social relationships between the different nationalities within each Gulf State follow a set of rules that are unofficial, yet publicly acknowledged and strictly observed.

---

[50] Gunatilleke, G. (1991). *Migration to the Arab World: Experience of Returning Migrants* (pp. 55, 103). Japan, United Nations University Press.
[51] In 1983, Bangladesh earned 12.2 billion Taka from Middle Eastern remittances, which were used mainly to finance imports under the Bangladesh Wage Earners Scheme. Gunatilleke, G. (1991). *Migration to the Arab World: Experience of Returning Migrants* (p. 281). Japan, United Nations University Press.
[52] Sooying Kim. (1982). Contract Migration in the Republic of Korea. *IME Working Paper* (pp. 28, 38-40). Geneva: International Labour Organisation.

Generally, Westerners tend to occupy the highest strata in this non-national hierarchy. They are a group that are grudgingly respected by the nationals: for their physical appearance, education, their 'developed' country origins, and their modern liberal outlook to life (relative to the conservative Muslims). In addition, they tend to be recruited for the well-paid executive positions, which may additionally offer full expatriate packages (accommodation, club membership, vacation allowances and so on). From the Gulf sponsor's point of view, recruiting a Western expatriate is socially prestigious - not only does it reflect the financial strength of the business (to have been able to retain such an 'expensive' employee), but it is more 'classy' to be represented by a Western national. However, despite their high-ranking position, social intermingling between locals and Westerners tends to be confined to work relationships with Gulf males.

The other Arabs, predominantly from the Levant and North Africa, occupy the second level in this non-national social hierarchy. They are socially accepted mainly because of their Arabic lineage, and the shared cultural and religious beliefs. However, the extent to which they network socially with Gulf nationals is a function of their economic status, greater with wealthier business families and almost non-existent with the lower wage earners.

Finally, at the lowest rung of this social ladder are the Asians: Indians, Pakistanis, Koreans, Filipinos and so on. They are generally the poorly paid (bachelor) workers who perform the hard manual labour, often in adverse working conditions (for example, building roads in the heat of the Gulf summers). They are geographically isolated in work camps, or in cheap council housing,[53] and make minimal social and economic demands. Socially, they are ridiculed and stripped of any rights, given their low incomes and their uneducated status. Therefore, they tend to be outcasts in a society that depends on them for its basic functioning, and whose infrastructure their efforts built.

Yet, regardless of the position that non-nationals may occupy in this social stratification system, a similar pattern of lifestyle is adopted: mingling in their own respective social circle, returning to their home country every year, usually during the summer vacation, marrying with members of their own social circle or from their home country, and remitting their salary back abroad. Those non-nationals with families register their children in private schools, usually offering the same curriculum as that given in their home country: for example, the New Indian School, the Oxford School, the American School and so on. The ease with which they can be deported has made non-nationals wary of even exposing themselves to the risk of encountering the police: many would prefer to avoid any interaction with the nationals for fear of disagreement and its potential repercussions.[54] Institutionalising this social hierarchy are the many social and economic regulations

---

[53] A one bedroom flat could be shared by up to 10 bachelor workers.

[54] Because they know that overall, the police/justice system would favour the national over the non-national.

that discourage intermarriage with non-nationals: for example, Kuwaiti and Emirati women who may choose to marry non-nationals forfeit their right to subsidies and allowances, and their children are not granted Gulf citizenship.[55]

Future Expectations for Non-Nationals in the Gulf

Table 1.10 outlines the official position of Gulf governments with respect to their non-national populations. The authorities have repeatedly asserted that their demand for non-national workers is a temporary expedient, that once their nationals are qualified (educated and trained to the required standard), they will be replaced. However, given that the need for the non-nationals is not merely economic, it is doubtful that this process of replacement will materialize.

The governments have made several attempts at reducing the number of non-nationals in their countries. Since the oil shock of 1986, stricter procedures have been adopted for issuing work permits, for ensuring that new workers come for a stated job for a stated period of time, after which they return, and regulations have been tightened on accompanying dependants and for deporting illegal migrants. Saudi Arabia allows only teachers, lawyers, engineers, defence experts, and executives with companies of more than 100 employees or capital of about $272500 to bring their families.[56]

The United Arab Emirates accepts applications for work permits only if the employer is a national, authorized to engage in commercial, industrial or service activities, and shows evidence that the vacancy could not be filled by nationals or resident non-nationals, and requires that a minimum of one year be spent with the same employer before an alternative position is sought.[57] Kuwait's April 1985 Employment Bill proposed that contractors employ a minimum share of Kuwaitis on government contracts (15 percent at technical or managerial level, 30 percent at other levels).

---

[55] Marrying a non-national makes one ineligible for marriage grants, and the Gulf nationality is not easily extended to the wife. If Gulf women were to marry non-nationals, neither their husbands nor children are granted Gulf nationality.

[56] *An-Nahar Arab Report and Memo.* 8 September 1980.

[57] Owen, R. (1985). Migrant Workers in the Gulf. *The Minority Rights Group Report.* 68, 9.

Table 1.10 Gulf Government's Official Policies on Non-National Populations

State	Official stance on the non-national proportion	Regulations concerning residence and work permits
Bahrain	Proportion is too high. Since 1978, have been seeking to reduce it.	Only temporary residence permits are issued. New job seekers need to apply for work permits. Strict control is enforced over labour imports.
Kuwait	Proportion is too high. Have tried to maintain rates.	Amendments have been made to the period of residence and the inflow of dependents has been regulated. Two-year work permits are issued. Regulations have been issued pertaining to working conditions, organization, contract termination, and compensation is now offered for occupational injuries. Stricter control is enforced over illegal migrants.
Oman	Proportion is satisfactory overall. Since 1986 have been trying to reduce rates.	
Saudi Arabia	Proportion is considered significant, yet satisfactory. Have tried to maintain rates.	Arab non-nationals are prioritised, though there is a preference for 'contract labour'. Since 1978, registration of non-nationals has been compulsory.
UAE	Proportion is considered too high. Have tried to maintain rates.	Since 1980, non-national workers need national sponsor. Visa and other controls and strict penalties have been imposed.

Sources: Adapted from UN, Kuwait Statistical Yearbook, Kohli[58]

Gulf governments have also tried to reduce the proportion of illegal migrants, a significant proportion of whom either travel to Saudi Arabia for the Hajj pilgrimage, or to other Gulf States as visitors of resident non-nationals, and then remain after the expiration of their visas. Such has been the magnitude of the problem that the governments of Bahrain, the United Arab Emirates and Saudi Arabia have at various times staged crackdowns and granted amnesty periods

---

[58] *Kuwait 1964 Act.* (1979). State of Kuwait, Ministry of Social Affairs and Labour. United Nations. (1982). *International Migration Policies and Programs: A World Survey*, ST/ESA/Series A/80. Sales No E.82.XIII.4. Kohli, K.L. (1989). Population Policy in Kuwait. In E. Mahadevan (Ed.), *Fertility Policies of Asian Countries* (pp.223-227). New Delhi, Newbur Park, London: Sage Publications.

during which time such illegal non-nationals could voluntarily leave without penalty.[59] The numbers were estimated to be half a million in the UAE, and about 800000 in Saudi Arabia.

Concluding Remarks

The discovery of oil in the 1950s prompted a large influx of workers from around the world, seeking employment and the higher salaries that Gulf employers paid. Over time, a network has been forged which benefits all parties involved, the non-national, nationals and the authorities, socially, financially, economically and politically, and is a powerful force frustrating the governments' half-hearted attempt to change the status quo.

Gulf nationals have not tried to build or to acquire skills or experience relevant to productive modern sector employment. Their 'rentier'[60] ethic militates against the acceptance of employment positions, at the same working and remuneration conditions as those offered to non-nationals. Their polarization in the public sector, and preference for white-collar positions, and the cultural discouragement of female employment, despite public investment in their education, all contribute towards creating a 'shortage' in the pool of available labour, and hence a demand for non-national workers. At the same time, Gulf nationals have become personally dependent on the services offered by non-nationals, doctors, teachers, mechanics, chauffeurs and maids, and on the financial rewards they reap from the markets that their presence creates, for accommodation, business ventures and so on.

For their part, Gulf governments need non-nationals to build and continue maintaining their fragile economies, to ensure continued political support from the important Gulf merchant families who benefit the most from the continued presence of these non-nationals, and to neutralize any potential political and/or economic threat that disgruntled national subgroups may pose. And labour-exporting governments encourage the out-flow of their workers to the Gulf States, not only to reduce the scale of unemployment that they face in their countries, but more significantly, to secure a source of foreign exchange for their economies.

Bahrain provides clear evidence of the complexity of the situation. Despite a national unemployment rate, estimated at 15 percent in 2001, a relatively well-educated population that accepts blue-collar work, and dwindling oil revenues, there continue to be increases in the proportion of non-national workers. Bahrain knows, as do the other Gulf States that any attempts at eliminating non-nationals from the equation would have serious repercussions for the domestic and world political economy, a risk that few governments would be willing to consider.

---

[59] *Khaleej Times, Gulf News, Al Ayam*, October 1996.

[60] Beblawi, H. (1987). The Rentier State in the Arab World. In H. Beblawi, Giacomo Luciani (Eds.), *The Rentier State* (pp. 49-52). Kent: Croom Helm Ltd.

Therefore, while the in-flow of non-nationals cannot be expected to cease totally, a reduction in the pace of the increase, as Gulf economies and the national population mature further, is feasible. The non-nationals will remain a significant sub-population within the geographic boundaries of the Gulf States, yet external to their socio-economic and demographic systems.[61]

---

[61] Forecasting the pattern of growth of any migrant population is extremely hazardous, mainly because their presence is vulnerable to shifts in the political agendas. Further, given that the non-nationals in the Gulf tend to be a segregated sub-population, and tend to attend fee-paying private schools, and pay for their own medical requirements, their impact on demand for these services is likely to be limited.

Chapter 2

The Gulf Epidemiological Transition

In 1960, Omanis could expect to live for 38 years, while Saudi Arabians could look forward to enjoying 44 years of life. Today, a Gulf national can expect to live to an average of 74 years. Increased material well being (individual wealth effects), improved medical knowledge and technology, better nutrition, improved transportation, the effect of international agencies and foreign aid[1] have all contributed towards improving the health of Gulf populations. Since the 1960s, average life expectancies have increased by 1.2 percent per annum in Bahrain and the United Arab Emirates, 0.8 percent per annum in Kuwait and two percent per annum in Oman and Saudi Arabia.[2]

The four-stage Epidemiological Transition[3] theory tries to explain such mortality decline in a structured manner. It focuses on the demographic, socioeconomic and biological determinants underlying changes in health and disease patterns, and their implication at the population level. The four stages of the transition include pestilence and famine, receding pandemic, degenerative and man-made diseases (aging, chronic diseases, emerging new scourges), and resurges of older diseases. With changes in disease patterns, the average age at death increases, with corresponding increases in life expectancy. Young people, women, and the 'privileged' tend to benefit from mortality declines first. With the widening in the gap between birth and death rates, population growth becomes dependent on the fertility level.

Several models of the Epidemiological Transition have been formulated, each specific to particular societies, given that the pattern, pace and peculiarities of the transitional changes vary in different historical, socioeconomic and cultural settings:[4]

---

[1] WHOSIS, Internet url. http://www.worldbank.org.

[2] World Bank. *World Bank Socioeconomic Datasheets 1960-1986.* Internet url: http://www.who.int/whosis/hfa/index.htm#Evaluation.

[3] Omran, A.R. (1971). The Epidemiological Transition: A Theory of Population Change *Milbank Memorial Fund Quarterly,* 49(4), 509-538. Also, Omran, A.R. (1983). The Epidemiological Transition Theory: A Preliminary Update. *Journal of Tropical Paediatrics,* 29, 305-316.

[4] Omran, A.R and F. Roudi. (1993). The Middle East Population Puzzle. *Population Bulletin,* 48(1), 8.

i   Classical Model (Europe and USA): mortality decline occurred over a long period of time (mid eighteenth to early twentieth centuries)

ii   Accelerated Variant of the Classical Model (Japan): mortality decline progressed rapidly after a late start (late nineteenth century)

iii. Delayed Model (most developing countries): mortality decline started very late (mid twentieth century) and progressed at varying rates:

- Rapid Transitional Variant (Taiwan, South Korea, and newly industrialized countries): steady declines in mortality and fertility since 1945
- Intermediate Transitional Variant (Egypt, Mexico): mortality decline (in mid twentieth century) accompanied with gradual fertility declines
- Slower Transitional Variant (Yemen, Bolivia): mortality declines not matched by fertility declines.

Within the framework of the epidemiological transition model, this Chapter will first chart and then explain the mortality trends of the Gulf States. Given the inadequacy of Gulf vital statistics data, particularly those related to mortality statistics, the analysis will rely on various observed rates (simpler rates computed from actual data), and some adjusted rates (hypothetical representations of the mortality level), drawn primarily from Bahraini and Kuwaiti data.

Tracking the Mortality Declines

Since 1965, mortality rates for the Gulf States have been reduced by an average of 30 to 40 percent. Crude Death Rates in the Gulf States are significantly lower than those found in the developed and developing countries: averaging 4.6 against 9.7 and 9.5 per 1000 population, respectively. However, while this rate is a general indicator of the level of mortality, it merely reflects the underlying age structure of the population: low rates being registered for young populations (as in the Gulf States) and higher rates for older populations (as in the developed countries).

A more accurate indicator of the health and living conditions of a community is the age-specific, Infant Mortality Rate (IMR).[5] The IMRs of the Gulf States have been declining over time, indicating a rapid rate of improvement in the living conditions (Figure 2.1). Average IMRs for Bahrain, Kuwait, Oman and the United Arab Emirates declined by three per 1,000 live births per annum between

---

[5] Approximates the probability of death among infants in a given year, and is widely used as an indicator of the health conditions of a community and its level of living, and tends to be tracked over time to reflect progress in a society.

1975 and 1988.[6] Oman, the UAE and Bahrain reduced their IMRs by an average of 66 percent (from very high IMRs in 1975), whilst Kuwait experienced the least change (36 percent) mainly because its 1975 IMR was already, on average, 55 percent lower than the others.

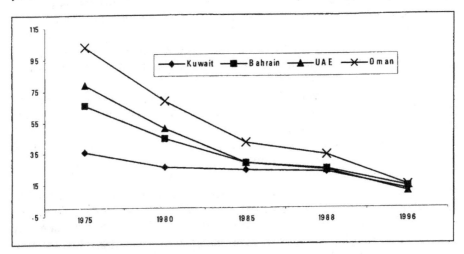

Figure 2.1 Infant Mortality Rates of the Gulf States Since 1975
Source: Family Health Surveys, 1989, 2000

The trend in neonatal[7] and post neonatal[8] mortality rates further reflect the mortality achievements made. Since 1981, Bahraini post-neonatal mortality (weeks five to 52) has been declining by two percent per annum, while the neonatal mortality (weeks one to four) has been declining by 0.8 percent per annum.

However, a more careful analysis of the mortality statistics reveals certain anomalies. Figure 2.2 graphs the close and expected relation between age and the risk of death in Bahrain and Kuwait. High mortality is experienced at the youngest ages declining steeply to ages 34, then rising again, gradually at first, then sharply

---

[6] Rashood, R., Alnesef, Y., and Farid, S. (2000). *Kuwait Family Health Survey*. Council of Health Ministers of GCC States. Naseeb, T., and S. Farid. (2000). *Bahrain Family Health Survey*. Council of Health Ministers of GCC States. Suleiman, A.J.M., Al Riyami, A., and S. Farid. (2000). *Oman Family Health Survey*. Council of Health Ministers of GCC States. Fikri, M., and S. Farid. (2000). *United Arab Emirates Family Health Survey*. Council of Health Ministers of GCC States. Khoja, T.A., and S. Farid. (2000). *Saudi Arabia Family Health Survey*. Council of Health Ministers of GCC States. Jaber, K.A., and S. Farid. (2000). *Qatar Family Health Survey*. Council of Health Ministers of GCC States.

[7] The number of deaths of infants under 4 weeks of age during a year, per 1000 live births during the year.

[8] The number of infant deaths at 4 to 51 weeks of age during a year per 1000 live births during the year.

after the age of 50. However, while this pattern has been maintained over time, the 1991 and 1988 Age Specific Mortality Rates (ASMR) are higher than the corresponding rates for 1981 and 1975 for Bahrain and Kuwait, respectively.

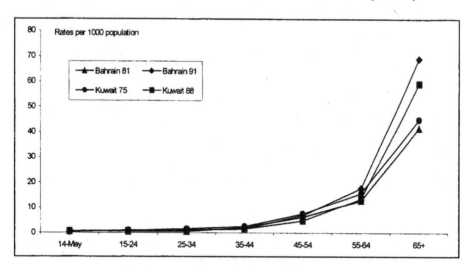

Figure 2.2 Age Specific Mortality Rates (ASMRs) in Bahrain and Kuwait
Source: Statistical Abstracts and Census, various years

The direct standardization technique, which eliminates the effect of different age structures,[9] indicates that the 1991 Bahraini death rate (standardized on the 1981 Age Specific Mortality Rates) should have been four per 1,000, as compared with the actual observed five per 1000. Hence, if the 1991 population had experienced the 1981 ASMRs, the mortality rates would have been lower. This suggests that the 1991 death rates were 1.3 times as bad as those in 1981.

Another peculiarity of Gulf mortality decline is identified when estimates are generated for other Gulf States, using the indirect standardization method.[10] Table 2.1 uses Bahrain's 1991 ASMR as the standard and applies it to the 1992 United Nation's Economic and Social Commission for Western Asia's (UNESWA) national population estimates. Bahrain has been chosen because its mortality data is the most complete for that year, and it is considered to have the most accurate

---

[9] Direct standardization method uses the following formula: $m_1=((\Sigma m_a\ P_a)/P)\times1000$ or $m_1=(\Sigma m_a(P_a/P))\times1000$ where $m_a= d_a/p_a$ is the age specific death rate in a given area, P_a is the standard population at each age, and P or ΣP_a is the total standard population. (capitals refer to standard population, lower case letters refer to other populations).

[10] The indirect method was chosen since age specific data is not available for the many of the Gulf States. The formula is $m2=M(d/\Sigma Mapa)$, where for the standard population Ma=ASDR, M=CDR, d=total number of deaths, pa=population at each age.

registration system, relative to the other States.[11] The results determine the difference between the rates, assuming there were no differences in the age structure.

Table 2.1 Indirect Standardization of the Death Rate for Kuwait, Oman and the UAE

	Kuwait	Oman	UAE
Observed Deaths*	1831.0	1676.0	6907.0
Expected Deaths	3924.0	524.0	6303.0
Ratio Observed/Expected	0.5	3.2	1.1
Adjusted Rate	2.0	13.8	4.7
Percent difference from Bahrain	-53.3	219.8	9.6

*these are likely to be lower than the actual figure, given under-registration of actual deaths

Source: UNESCWA 1992, Demographic and Related Datasheets

The calculation indicates that Oman's mortality rates can be expected to be the highest from amongst the four States, and Kuwait's would be the lowest.

Finally, when compared to other countries with similar income levels across the world, the average life expectancy of Gulf nationals remains lower and Gulf IMRs remain almost four times higher (see Table 2.2).[12]

Table 2.2 General Health Indicators for 2000

	Life Expectancies	IMR	CDR
Bahrain	78	12	3.9
Kuwait	77	12	2.4
Oman	71	21	4.4
Saudi Arabia	72	25	4.0
Qatar	75	22	4.3
UAE	75	14	4.0
Average Gulf States	74	18	3.8
High Income	77	7	9.0

Source: World Bank, World Tables, 1995, UNESCWA Datasheets 2001

---

[11] United States Bureau of the Census. (1998). International Programme. Internet url: http://www.census.gov/ipc/www/idbsprd.html

[12] World Bank. (1989). *World Bank Data Sheets*, International Economics Department. Internet url: http://www.who.int/whosis/hfa/index.htm#Evaluation.

Therefore, while overall, the Gulf States have made dramatic strides in reducing their mortality rates since the 1960s, these achievements are not uniform across the six States, and it is possible that the reductions may be moderating. On the one hand, the death registration system may have improved and hence more accurately reflects the level of mortality experienced in Gulf populations. Alternatively, this could be a reflection of the failings of a public health system that may be under strain or may not be equipped to adequately meet the demands of the public.[13] A final explanation may be that the Gulf States are progressing through the different stages of the epidemiological transition. It is to this analysis that the remainder of this Chapter is devoted.

Explaining Gulf Epidemiological Achievements

Theoretically, the dynamics that cause death and birth rates to drop during the Epidemiological Transition reflect changes in patterns of health and disease.

Urbanization Mortality declines would be first felt in the urban areas, given public services tend to concentrate there. Mortality tends to be lower when parents reside in capital cities, even if their conditions are unfavourable (for example, if the mother is semi-literate or illerate).[14] The relatively small physical size of the Gulf States (except for Saudi Arabia and Oman), and the proximity of the urban centers to each other and of the population to urban areas would have facilitated the dissemination of and access to medical and other facilities (see Table 2.3).

Table 2.3 Urbanization of the Gulf States

	Urban population	Paved Roads (% of total)
Bahrain	88	77
Kuwait	100	81
Qatar	91	90
UAE	86	100
Saudi Arabia	86	30
Oman	72	30
High Income	79	91

Source: UNICEF, 2000, World Bank Data Indicators, 2000

---

[13] This issue will be considered in detail in Chapter 5 on Public Services.

[14] Cramer, J.C. (1987). Social Factors and Infant Mortality: Identifying High Risk Groups and Proximate Causes. *Demography*, 24 (3), August, 299-322.

Housing Quality   In addition to urbanization's effect on reducing mortality levels, the quality of housing has an impact on child mortality and nutritional status (especially for those aged below three years).[15] Housing quality depends on the family's economic standing and on other contextual factors, amongst others, the development level, housing construction and water distribution policies.

Table 2.4 Gulf States Housing Characteristics (1998)

Characteristics	Bahrain	Kuwait	Qatar	Saudi Arabia	UAE	Oman
Household size	6.4	7.0	6.9	7.0	7.8	8.4
No of bedrooms	2.8	4.3	4.1	2.5	3.4	2.4
People per room	1.4	0.9	1	1.3	1.4	1.9
Dry drainage	97.0	99.0	98.5	95.0	95.8	99.2
Gas/Electricity for cooking	100.0	100.0	99.6	97.0	99.6	96.1
% with flush	97.9	99.6	98.0	78.4	92.4	77.8

* On average 69 percent of the population in all developing countries have access to safe water, 48 percent in Least Developing countries, and 43 percent in Sub Saharan Africa[16]

Source: Gulf Family Health Survey, 2000

The distribution of oil revenues, the provision of subsidized housing, land and low interest or interest free mortgages has secured a relatively high standard of housing for most Gulf nationals. Table 2.4 indicates the relatively smaller gains made by Oman and Saudi Arabia, given their larger geographic areas and rural populations.

Public Health Care While this issue will be dealt with in detail in Chapter 5, it is important to highlight the relatively well-supported public health system found in the Gulf States. Between 1970 and 1980, the proportions of medical personnel, ratio of facilities and medical personnel to population have all increased. In absolute terms, the number of beds and medical personnel are continuing to increase across the Gulf States.

---

[15] Tekce, B., and F.C. Shorter. (1988). Determinants of Child Mortality: A Study of Squatter Settlements in Jordan. In W.H. Henry and L. Chen (Eds.), Child Survival: Strategies for Research. *Population and Development Review, Supplement,* 10, 257-280.

[16] Tekce, B., and F.C. Shorter. (1988). Determinants of Child Mortality: A Study of Squatter Settlements in Jordan. In W.H. Henry and L. Chen (Eds.), Child Survival: Strategies for Research. *Population and Development Review, Supplement,* 10, 257-280.

Food and Nutrition Oil revenues have enabled Gulf governments to increase the range and quantity of food imports, and to offer these at subsidized prices to their populations, consequently improving their population's nutritional status. Total food imports for Bahrain increased by six percent per annum between 1985 and 1992, whilst those for Kuwait increased by nine percent per annum between 1992 and 1994.[17]

Moderating The Gulf Epidemiological Transition

Therefore, high urbanization levels, good housing and living standards, good medical facilities and a diverse range of affordable imported food products have secured the initial dramatic declines in Gulf mortality indicators, and have increased life expectancies within a short span of time.

Degenerative Diseases   The first explanatory factor is the increase in the incidence of degenerative diseases and those related to man-made hazards, for example, accidental, occupational and environmental. Between 1965 and 1987, Kuwaiti deaths attributable to accidents increased by 0.8 percent, those to heart disease by three percent, those to stroke by two percent and those to cancers by 12 percent per annum. In Bahrain, circulatory diseases were one of the main causes of death in 1991 (Table 2.5). Between 1995 and 1999, the number of cancer cases in Bahrain increased by 34 percent, positioning it as the second leading cause of death (accounting for 12 percent of all deaths in 1999). Those aged 40 to 49 experienced the highest (and increasing) incidence of cancers: increasing from 18 percent in 1996 to 20 percent by 1998.

---

[17] Statistical Abstracts, various years.

Table 2.5 1991 Bahraini Cause Specific Death Indices

Disease	Rates ('000)	Ratios ('000)
Circulatory/Blood[18]	17.00	0.302
Neoplasm[19]	0.55	0.101
Unknown	0.47	0.086
Accidents	0.46	0.084
Digestive/Urinary	0.43	0.789
Respiratory	0.38	0.071
Endocrine/Nutrition	0.38	0.069
Skin/Sensory	0.11	0.021

Source: Bahrain Statistical Abstract, 1992. p. 98

Furthermore, the incidence of diabetes across the Gulf States is relatively high: 11 percent of the population in the UAE, 12 percent in Kuwait, ten percent in Oman, nine percent in Bahrain, 16 percent in the Western provinces of Saudi Arabia, 13 percent in the Northern provinces, ten percent in the Eastern provinces and three percent in the southern provinces. In 2001, the Gulf States harboured 1.5 million diabetics and it is expected that 25 percent of the total Gulf population are or would be at risk of developing diabetes by 2010.

This increase in degenerative diseases is a byproduct of the exposure to different cultures and an affluent lifestyle, especially the adoption of a modern (Western) lifestyle (including habits like smoking, a higher-fat diet, sedentarization), urbanization and increased stress. 55 percent of Saudi women, and 35 percent of Saudi men, 33 percent of married Emirati women and 40 percent of married Emirati men were estimated to have been overweight in 2000. 38 percent of married Emirati women, and 16 percent of married Emirati men were considered obese in the same year.

Furthermore, a larger proportion of Gulf populations are surviving to older age groups, therefore increasing their probability of suffering from degenerative diseases. In addition, the newly established health facilities may not be prepared to deal with such diseases (which may partially explain why many are sent overseas for treatment) whether due to inexperience in the early diagnosis of such diseases, or not being able to offer the most effective medication. Finally, these diseases respond to a preventative approach, taken by an educated populace that understands the root causes of these ailments. Many older Gulf people are semi/illiterate and hence may not fully appreciate their role in reducing their risks.

---

[18] This is a combination of the International Disease Category 280-289 and 390-459.

[19] This refers to tumors (carcinogenic/not).

Rural-Urban Differentials The benefits of improved living conditions have not yet percolated to all regions within the Gulf.

Table 2.6 Rural-Urban Differentials (1998)

Indicators	Bahrain	Oman*	Kuwait	Saudi	Qatar	UAE
		Infant Mortality Rate				
Urban	8.4	18.4	28	18.3	8.0	11.3
Rural	16.2	23.6	13	27.9	14.9	14.5
		Child Mortality Rate				
Urban	3.3	5.5	35	7.8	2.3	1.9
Rural	3.1	7.3	17	7.5	10.0	4.7

* Omani data is drawn from the 1989 Family Health Survey

Source: Gulf Family Health Survey, 2000

Table 2.6 confirms that infant and child mortality is higher amongst rural populations.[20]   Such rural areas are more likely to suffer limited health and education services, and poorer housing conditions.

Furthermore, with the exception of Bahrain, children in rural areas, and those born to semi-/illiterate mothers were less likely to have been immunized. In 1991, the proportion of immunized children was highest in Muscat (23 percent) and lowest in Al Wusta (Central) region (0.6 percent) for TB, Tetanus and Polio, and Measles vaccinations. In Bahrain, in 1984, the proportion of rural deliveries attended by doctors was 39 percent as against 55 percent in urban areas, and the proportion of rural deliveries attended by nurses was 52 percent verses 42 percent for those in urban areas. Rural women were least likely to have had a postnatal checkup, and overall, only 46 percent had a postnatal checkup at any time. Similarly, residence in the Kuwaiti capital denotes the highest likelihood of a pregnancy check and speedier access to a hospital.

High Fertility and Maternal Care 'Poorly-managed' fertility is associated with high rates of fetal death, still births, prenatal and child mortality and morbidity. High fertility rates, limited child spacing (with birth intervals of less than two years), early (before the mother is 18) and late (after the mother is 35) births all contribute

---

[20]   Guzman, J.H. (1984). Trends in Socioeconomic Differentials in Infant Mortality in Selected Latin American Countries. *Seminar on Social and Biological Correlates of Mortality in Tokyo.* Washington: International Union for the Scientific Study of Populations.

towards higher maternal,[21] child and infant mortality rates.[22] In 1998, in the Gulf, all the various child mortality rates were highest for those births in the order 7+ (Table 2.7).[23]

Table 2.7 Mortality Rates and Birth Order

Mortality Indicator	Infant		Under Five		Child		Post Neo-Natal	
Birth Order	7+	1-6	7+	1-6	7+	1-6	7+	1-6
Qatar	11.1	10.5	19.3	15.9	8.3	4.4	7.7	4.4
Saudi Arabia	31.4	18.1	42.0	24.7	11.0	6.7	13.0	8.4
UAE	15.4	11.3	19.1	13.9	3.8	2.6	6.0	4.0
Kuwait	28.9	8.0	36.2	14.0	7.6	6.0	14.4	4.5
Bahrain	19.1	13.2	26.4	15.2	7.3	2.1	6.3	2.4
Oman	20.1	22.3	24.9	28.6	4.9	6.4	8.3	9.5

Source: Gulf Family Health Survey, 2000

Parental Education[24] This affects child survival directly through knowledge of appropriate child health care, and is related to the greater role of an educated parent in family decision-making about resource allocation, food distribution among its members, personal hygiene and use of modern medical services.[25] Not only is parental education inversely related to child mortality, but its importance is greater for those aged less than four.[26] Whilst a one percent rise in national income is associated with a 0.05 year gain in life expectancy, a one percent increase in primary schooling (amongst the adults) would result in an estimated gain of four to

---

[21] Maternal Mortality Rates were indirectly estimated for the Bahraini Family Health Survey and was found to be 188 deaths per 100,000 live births for 1977. The lifetime risk of maternal death was found to be 0.0105, or 1 in 95.

[22] Cramer, J.C. (1987). Social Factors and Infant Mortality: Identifying High Risk Groups and Proximate Causes. *Demography,* 24(3), August, 299-322.

[23] This is also associated with the fact that these older women had access to poorer health service facilities prior to their development.

[24] D'Souza, S. and A. Bhuiya. (1982). Socioeconomic Mortality Differentials in a Rural Area of Bangladesh. *Population and Development Review,* 8(4), December, 753-769.

[25] Tekce, B. and F.C. Shorter. (1988). Determinants of Child Mortality: A Study of Squatter Settlements in Jordan. In W.H. Henry and L. Chen (Eds.), Child Survival: Strategies for Research. *Population and Development Review, Supplement,* 10, 257-280.

[26] Hobcraft, J.N., MacDonald, J.W., and S.O. Rutstein. (1984). Socioeconomic Factors in Infant and Child Mortality: a Cross-National Comparison. *Population Studies,* 38(2), July, 193-223.

eight years in life expectancy (with a time lag).[27] Finally, parental educational levels indicate the socioeconomic condition of the parental household, illustrating a generational effect of social class on child survival.[28] In fact, maternal education is considered to be the more decisive factor for a child's survival: for each additional year of maternal education, there is a three percent reduction in child mortality, once effects of all controllable independent variables are eliminated.[29]

Illiterate Gulf women are more likely to use traditional medication and less likely to understand the importance of immunization and other modern means of infectious disease prevention (Table 2.8).

Table 2.8   Relation Between Maternal Education and Diarrhea Treatment and Child Immunization

	Diarrhea				Immunization		
	Kuwait	Oman	UAE	Oman	UAE	Bahrain	Kuwait
Illiterate	24	11	35	96.9	73	97.4	90
Incomplete Primary	4	12	36	99.3	83	97.8	90
Primary	11	}	}	98.2	}	97.2	93
Intermediate	32	12	34	98.4	90	99.0	93
Secondary	13	}	}	99.3	95	98.1	94

Source: Pan Gulf Maternal Child Health Survey, 1989

Government Policies   Government policies and investment decisions, external economic forces and other national level changes can exert an important effect on mortality trends. The balance governments choose between development strategies favouring capital accumulation and concentrated investments (to maximize economic growth) and those oriented towards meeting basic needs, reducing wealth and income inequalities is vital. Gulf governments spend disproportionately more on military purposes than on the health and education of their population.

---

[27] Preston, S. (1978). Mortality, Morbidity and Development. *Population Bulletin of the United Nations Economic Commission for Western Asia*, 15, December, 63-75.

[28] Farah, A., and S.H. Preston. (1993). Child Mortality Differentials in Sudan. *Population and Development Review*, 8(2), June, 365-383.

[29] United Nations. (1985). *Socioeconomic Differentials in Child Mortality in Developing Countries*. Sales No E85, XIII.6. pp. 31-53.

Table 2.9 Government Expenditures and Mortality Rates (1990)

	IMR	Social Security[a]	Health[b]	Education[c]	Military[b]
Qatar	26	-	3	3	13
Bahrain	12	0.1	6	-	5
UAE	23	-	9	2	5
Kuwait	15	-	-	5	7
Oman	30	-	2	4	16
Saudi Arabia	31	1.0	3	6	14
Similar Income[30]	7	11.0	8	7	2

[a] percent of Gross Domestic Product for the years 1985-1990
[b] percent of Gross Domestic Product for the years 1985-1990
[c] percent of Gross National Product for the years 1985-1990

Source: UNDP, Human Development Report, 1994

Table 2.9 indicates that Oman, with the highest military expenditures, has the highest Infant Mortality Rates too. Gulf States military expenditures are also higher and their health and education expenditures lower than those countries with a similar GNP per capita.

Concluding Remarks

Although not as critical as fertility in determining population growth rates, future mortality trends are important in determining the size and distribution of a population, especially for prospects for future infant, child and 'old-age' mortality since these account for the bulk of total deaths. Modernization in the Gulf States has been accompanied by a range of mortality responses. For infants and children below 15 years of age, mortality has been declining progressively with a dramatic reduction in infectious diseases through environmental sanitation and good nutrition.[31] Among adults, there have been mixed effects: declines in death rates caused by infections (especially TB) have been balanced with the concurrent rise in mortality caused by the 'diseases of affluence', coronary heart disease, cancer, motor vehicle accidents and so on.[32] However, there is scope for improvement, particularly in the

---

[30] Similar Income countries include: Canada, USA, Japan, Netherlands, Finland, Iceland, Norway, France, Spain, Sweden, Australia, Belgium, Switzerland, Austria, Germany, Denmark, New Zealand, UK, Ireland, Italy, Israel, Greece, Luxembourg, Malta and Portugal.

[31] United Nations. (1984). *International Conference on Population. Mortality and Health Policy: Proceedings of the Expert Group on Mortality and Health Policy.* Rome, 30 May to 3 June 1983. ST/ESA/SER.A/91. New York.

[32] Bourgeois-Pichat, J. (1984). Mortality Trends in the Industrialized Countries. In United Nations, *International Conference on Population, Mortality and Health Policy:*

rural areas of the larger Gulf States of Oman and Saudi Arabia. In addition, a critical component in lowering mortality among women of childbearing age would be the availability of integrated family planning and effective maternal and child health care (MCH) services throughout all health facilities.

Prospects for a continuation in the declines in morality rates are relatively good, especially given that the importance of health care is clearly stated in the health programs of the Gulf States, and given their attention to infant and child mortality. Their commitment to the World Health Organization's program of 'Health for All by the Year 2000' was specifically designed to reduce infant and child mortality and morbidity. Saudi Arabia's Royal Decree linked the issuing of birth certificates with the completion of the vaccination schedule to increase the vaccination coverage. It focused on extending health care programs to rural and Bedu populations, and on preventive services, health education, maternal and child health programs. The United Arab Emirates set itself an ambitious target of immunizing 95 percent of all children under the age of one by 1990.[33]

Regionally coordinated efforts have also been devised: one such program has been to combat health hazards posed by smoking, another has been the Child Health Surveys (funded by AGFUND and various UN organizations) to collect and analyze data on which to base future child health programs, and finally the regional health education and awareness programs covering a diverse range of issues. While the impact of these interventions on mortality cannot yet be fully examined, evidence from other countries implies that declines in mortality levels are likely.

Proceedings of the Expert Group on Mortality and Health Policy. Rome, 30 May to 3 June 1983. ST/ESA/SER.A/91. New York.

[33] United Nations. (1985). *World Population Trends and Population Policies, 1983 Monitoring Report.* Vol. II. ST/ESA/SER.A/93/Add.1. Population Studies. No 93. UN: New York.

Chapter 3

Explaining Fertility, Theoretically

Chapter 1 highlighted the closed nature of the Gulf States: despite their heavy dependence on foreign manpower, and the non-nationals' economic contribution, this 'sub-population' remains socially and demographically distinct and external to them. Chapter 2 showed that better nutrition and the provision of good medical care has dramatically reduced Gulf nationals' mortality rates and increased their life expectancies and thereby curbed mortality's effect as a check on population growth. Therefore, while mortality and migration do contribute to the size and structure of Gulf populations, fertility must be the main and most important component underlying Gulf population changes.

The Demographic Transition Theory

Despite the lack of uniformity and of a clear relationship between socioeconomic indicators and demographic rates, the framework of the Demographic Transition (from a pre-modern regime of high mortality and fertility to a present day regime of low mortality and fertility),[1] is applied to the analysis of demographic trends in the contemporary developing world.

The Demographic Transition is divided into four stages. Prior to its onset (and except for periodic fluctuations), population growth is very slow,[2] as high mortality rates (due to environmental factors: poor hygiene, sanitation, nutrition and disease outbreaks, etc.) offset the high fertility rates (equilibrium period). Then, sustained mortality declines (improved socioeconomic and living conditions: better nutrition, decline in disease etc.), lead to a period when births exceed deaths, and the population growth rate increases (disequilibrium period). After this time lag, fertility declines, and a new equilibrium is achieved with a subsequent decline in population growth rates, thereby completing the 'transition' from one form of stable population to another.

---

[1] Ohlin, G. (1976). Economic Theory Confronts Population Growth. In A.J. Coale (Ed.), *Economic Factors in Population Growth* (pp. 3-16). London: Macmillan Press.

[2] World Bank. (1994). *Development in Practice: Population and Development: Implications for the World Bank*. Washington, D.C.: World Bank.

The precise mechanism by which fertility reduction is initiated and proceeds to stable low levels is unclear. The number and scope of the theories and models that have been devised highlight the difficulty of encompassing, within one framework, all the factors that would explain how individual couples determine their family size and the non random (sometimes unsystematic and unpredictable) fertility variation within and between societies.[3] Theoretically, these explanations can be classified into the biological (affect reproduction, determine fecundity) and behavioural (conscious or inadvertent modifications determining the extent to which the biological maximum is realized) factors, though an empirical distinction between them is difficult (unless the factor is clearly exogenous, that is, not subject to individual or social choice, e.g., age).[4]

Modern demographic theory highlights the relations between fertility, nuptiality, mortality, age and sex distribution and population growth rates. It has also been argued (though not proved) that socioeconomic changes (arising from 'modernization') need to occur before fertility declines.[5] These include urbanization, industrialization, social mobility, changes in women's status (education, age at marriage, roles in society, income earning opportunities outside the home), in values and aspirations (religious, cultural), family functions and structure, a shift in dependence from local self contained institutions and communities to larger specialized socioeconomic and political units,[6] institutionalization of old age support and insurance schemes, reduced mortality (infant, child, maternal) and better living standards, the financial 'cost' and 'returns' from childbearing and rearing (declining production value, increased rearing costs, returns to child labour and demand for educated labour), due to compulsory education and child labour laws.

The causal relationship between development and fertility is complex, indirect and the indicators emphasized tend to reflect only one dimension of the explanation.[7] Evidence is also mixed on whether the relationship is continuous (fertility varies directly and evenly over a range of development indicators) or has threshold levels (fertility is unchanged until a threshold level after which fertility changes with alterations in development indicator).

---

[3] Simmons, G.B. (1985). Theories of Fertility. In G.M. Farooq and G.B. Simmons (Eds.), *Fertility in Developing Countries: An Economic Perspective on Research and Policy Issues.* London: Macmillan Press.

[4] Schultz, P. (1976). Determinants of Fertility: A Microeconomic Model of Choice. In A.J. Coale (Ed.), *Economic Factors in Population Growth* (p. 89). London: Macmillan Press.

[5] United Nations. (1961). *The Mysore Population Studies,* ST/SOA/Ser.A/34, New York.

[6] Freedman, R. (1979). Theories of Fertility Decline: A Reappraisal. In P.M. Hauser (Ed.), *World Population and Development: Challenges and Prospects* (p. 63). New York: UNFPA.

[7] Hauser, P.M. (1979). Introduction and Overview. In P.M. Hauser (Ed.), *World Population and Development: Challenges and Prospects* (p. 15). New York: UNFPA.

Modern Demographic Theory

Blake and Davis highlighted eleven intermediate variables[8] linking the socioeconomic and cultural factors with the physiological processes[9] of fertility. Seven were considered as important in determining fertility: the proportion married, contraceptive use, prevalence of abortion, postpartum infecundability, fecundability, spontaneous intrauterine mortality and permanent sterility (these last four are also components of natural fertility).[10] Bongaarts transformed this theoretical approach into an operational framework.[11] After rating the seven variables according to sensitivity of fertility to variations in them, and the extent of variability among populations or over time, he included only the first four variables[12] in his measure of the Total Fertility Rate (TFR):

$$TFR=TF.(C_m.C_c.C_a.C_i)^{13}$$

TFR=   Total Fertility Rate (legitimate births only) is the actual observed fertility level in the presence of the four fertility inhibiting variables

TF=   Total Fecundity Rate is the number of children a woman would have in the absence of any fertility inhibiting factors (ranges from 13 to 17 births), with an average of 15.3.

C_m=   Index of Marriage is a proxy measure for exposure to sexual intercourse[14] (this would equal one if all women aged 15-44/49 are currently married; and 0 if none are married).

---

[8] Davis, K., and J. Blake. (1956). Social Structure and Fertility: An Analytical Framework. *Economic Development and Cultural Change*, 4(3).

[9] Freedman, R. (1986). Fertility Determinants. In J. Cleland and J.C. Scott (Eds.), *World Fertility Survey: An Assessment of its Contribution* (p. 773). London: Oxford University Press.

[10] Fertility in the absence of deliberate fertility control (includes social practices influencing post partum infecundability, for example prolonged breastfeeding or abstinence from intercourse after childbirth, not consciously practiced at the individual level to reduce fertility).

[11] Bongaarts, J. (1978). A Framework for Analyzing the Proximate Determinants of Fertility. *Population and Development Review*, 4(1), 105-132. Also Bongaarts, J. (1982). The Fertility Inhibiting Effects of the Intermediate Fertility Variables. *Studies in Family Planning*, 13(6/7), June-July, 179-189.

[12] Fecundity, spontaneous intrauterine morality, permanent sterility show less variation, are not powerful explanatory factors and are difficult to measure.

[13] Bongaarts, J. and R.G. Potter. (1983). *Fertility, Biology, and Behaviour: An Analysis of the Proximate Determinants* (pp. 78-101). New York: Academic Press Inc.

[14] Brunborg, H. (1983). *An Economic Model of Fertility, Sex and Contraception.* Unpublished Ph.D. thesis in Economics, University of Michigan.

$C_c=$ index of contraception measures the prevalence of deliberate marital fertility control (this would equal one if no contraception is used, and 0 if all couples use a totally effective technique).

$C_a=$ index of induced abortion (this would equal one if abortion never occurs, and 0 if all pregnancies are aborted).

$C_i=$ index of post partum infecundability (this would equal one if lactation and post partum abstinence are absent, and 0 if this occurs indefinitely).[15]

Hobcraft and Little measured the fertility effects of the intermediate variables by using multiplicative indices.[16] Women would achieve their maximum potential fertility if they spent all of their reproductive years in pregnancy or being infecund post-partum (that is all were married, did not contracept, nor aborted, nor experienced lactational infecundity). Fertility is lower than the potential maximum, because women increase the duration of time during which they are infecund (being celibate, contracepting, aborting, breastfeeding) and their actual fertility is the product of their potential fertility and the proportion of time spent in 'fertility-promoting' states.

However, both Bongaarts and Hobcraft and Little's methods yield poor estimates of the fertility inhibiting impact of delayed marriage, contraceptive use and induced abortion, when family building strategies are considered (for example, when women stop reproducing after achieving their desired family size, or when marriage is delayed.[17] In addition, the assumptions underlying the methods are too simplistic:[18] contraceptive use is not exogenous, abortions are not random, fertility of the unmarried may not be the same as those currently married. Specifically, Bongaart's C_c is a poor measure, when contraceptive use is concentrated in the older age groups (when desired family size is high), while Hobcraft and Little's C_c is good only in the absence of abortion and presence of universal marriage (index was intended to measure contraceptive impact irrespective of marriage delays or abortion). Bongaarts C_a is measured in the presence of non marriage and contraceptive use, not in their absence, while Hobcraft and Little's method underestimates C_a, in the absence of contraception and marriage delay (insufficient time is allocated to the exposure state).

---

[15] The period immediately following a birth during which the normal pattern of ovulation and menstruation is absent and thus a woman is infecund (unable to conceive).

[16] Hobcraft, J. (1992). Fertility Patterns and Child Survival: A Comparative Analysis. *Population Bulletin of the United Nations*, 33, 1-32.

[17] Reinis, K. (1992). The Impact of the Proximate Determinants of Fertility - Evaluating Bongaarts and Hobcraft and Little Methods of Estimation. *Population Studies*, 46(2), 309-326.

[18] Reinis, K. (1992). The Impact of the Proximate Determinants of Fertility - Evaluating Bongaarts and Hobcraft and Little Methods of Estimation. *Population Studies*, 46(2), 309-326.

Age is associated both with the proximate variables (menarche, marriage, coital frequency, fecundity, menopause) and with the socioeconomic variables (life cycle patterns (income, dependence on children) and development efforts (availability of education). The population age structure specifies the proportion of the population at risk of reproducing, thereby impacting on the society's aggregate birth rates. Within age stratified groups, differences in a woman's expected fecundity may stem from exogenous (regional health problems) or endogenous (prolonged lactation, induced abortion) factors. The probability of being sterile and time needed for fecund couples to reproduce increases systematically with age: proportion of women incapable of reproducing increases gradually after 20 years, sharply after 40, and reaches sterility by 50.[19] In non-contracepting populations of proven fecundity (i.e., couples subsequently reproduced successfully), birth intervals increase gradually from 24 months (for mothers aged 20-24), to 31 months (for those aged 35-39).[20] In addition, age at marriage is affected by expectations concerning fertility: women marrying before age 20 attain similar fertility levels, beyond this, each extra year of marriage is associated with an overall fertility reduction. Marriage at age 25 is universally associated with lower total fertility,[21] as such a delay implies certain structural changes and the emergence of new roles for single women (especially paid work outside the home).[22] Late age at marriage is associated with lower overall fertility, though marital fertility tends to be higher for couples marrying later.[23]

Mortality influences the population's age and sex structure (hence population at reproductive age), the number of children borne by a couple (through effects on child and infant mortality (positively associated with fertility to offset real/potential losses), and on parental life expectancy (probability that both spouses survive the full reproductive life span), and the length of birth interval (and hence fertility) through prematurely ending mother's lactation period after an infant's death. In addition, it affects fertility through modifying the environment in which fertility decisions are made (will be discussed more later).

---

[19] Schultz, P. (1976). Determinants of Fertility: A Microeconomic Model of Choice. In A.J. Coale (Ed.), *Economic Factors in Population Growth* (p. 89). London: Macmillan Press.

[20] Henry, L. (1961). Some Data on Natural Fertility. *Eugenics Quarterly*, 8(2), June, 81-91.

[21] McDonald, P.F., Ruzicka L.T., and J.C. Caldwell. (1981). Interrelations between Nuptiality and Fertility: Evidence form the World Fertility Survey. *World Fertility Conference 1980: Record of Proceedings 2*. See also Hobcraft, J. and J.B. Casterline. (1983). Speed of Reproduction. *World Fertility Survey Comparative Studies*, 25.

[22] McDonald, P.F. (1985). Social Organization and Nuptiality in Developing Societies. In J. Clelland. and J. Hobcraft (Eds), *Reproductive Change in Developing Countries: Insight form the World Fertility Survey*. Oxford: Oxford University Press.

[23] United Nations Population Division. (1985). Concise Report on the World Population Situation in 1983: Conditions, Trends, Prospects and Policies. *Population Studies*, 85, ST/ESA/SER.A/85. New York: United Nations.

The Impact of Modernization

Generally, it is argued that socio-economic modernization erode the benefits of having many children, labour, support, insurance, political influence, and which help to ensure that natural fertility reigns. Large scale production and compulsory education reduce children's labour productivity, new institutionalized and formal means of insurance diminish children's importance for old age (financial) security, and their political and legal functions. Hence, a lagged (rational) fertility decline occurs, at the same time as monetisation heightens awareness of children's cost (increased by education or opportunity cost of mother's time).[24] Furthermore, improving the quality of children incurs large sacrifices of current output: education withdraws them from the (paid) market labour force and the (household) non-market labour.[25] Parents will determine this allocation of their child's time, in response to perceptions of the returns accruing to educated, skilled, trained labour (rather than on criteria based on familial or class origins), where these returns are high (at the primary and secondary school levels) and the educational infrastructure can meet the demand, parents will increase investments in children's education and have fewer.[26]

New Home Economics Models[27] These analyze family decisions (fertility, marriage, female labour force activity) affecting demographic change, focusing on the efficiency of resource allocation, equality of income distribution and rapidity of growth and structural change. All household production models[28] include some element of income at the aggregate and individual levels. In any year t, couples are divided into those with a working wife (i.e., in the paid labour force), with fertility level F_t, and those with 'non-working wife' (not in paid labour force) with fertility level F_0. Both fertility levels depend on the husband's (real) income, Ym:

$$F_t^0 = a_0 + b_0 Ym_t$$

---

[24] Thompson, W. (1929). Population. *American Journal of Sociology*, 34, 959-979. Also, Davis, K. (1945). The World Demographic Transition. *Annals of the American Academy of Political and Social Science*, 273, 1-11. Also, Notestine, F.W. (1945). Population: The Long View. In T.W. Schultz (Ed.), *Food for the World*. Chicago: Chicago University Press.

[25] Birdsall, N. (1980). A Cost of Siblings: Child Schooling in Urban Columbia. *Research in Population Economics*, 2, 115-150.

[26] Bauer, J., and Andrew Mason. (1993). Equivalence Scales, Costs of Children and Poverty in Philippines and Thailand. In C.B. Lloyd (Ed.), *Fertility, Family Size, and Structure: Consequences for Families and Children*. New York: The Population Council.

[27] Butz, W.P., and M.P. Ward. (1979). *The Emergence of Counter-Cyclical US Fertility*. Santa Monica: The RAND Corporation. Also discussed in Murphy, M. (1992). Economic Models of Fertility in Post War Britain. *Population Studies*, 46, 235-258.

[28] Leridon, H. (1976). The Role of Economic Factors in Birth Rate Trends and Fluctuations. In A.J. Coale (Ed.), *Economic Factors in Population Growth*. (pp. 179-204). London: Macmillan Press.

But, the fertility of the couple with a working wife also depends on her real earnings, Yf.

$$F_t^1 = a_1 + b_1 Ym_t + c_1 Yf_t$$

The proportion of couples with a working wife is K_t, while that couples without a working wife is $(1 - K_t)$. Hence the observed overall fertility level:

$$F_t = (1 - K_t)(a_0 + b_0 Ym_t) + K_t (a_1 + b_1 Ym_t + c_1 Yf_t)$$

Therefore, given that b_0 and b_1 are positive, while c_1 is negative, then F would increase, if Ym increases, and would decline if K_t or Yf increase (the magnitude of this effect depends on K_t).

While statistically acceptable, this single functional form is inappropriate: it assumes that all fertility variation over time can be accounted for by the differential weighting of K. In a heterogeneous population (different elasticity, fecundity, views about child quality) fertility varies between groups defined by almost any criterion,[29] the same parameter values may not apply for all subgroups.[30] In addition, while the negative relationship between income and fertility holds at the aggregate level for a cross section of all countries, it does not, if only developing countries are considered, suggesting a non linear relationship at the aggregate level with fertility initially increasing with higher income and then declining.

Time Allocation Models[31] These emphasize 'family budgets' in terms of money and time.[32] Time, an input to the household production process, has value. Childbearing and rearing incur financial costs, especially the opportunity cost of time devoted to childcare by women, who tend to undertake the larger burden of childrearing (health costs, earnings foregone, future labour market prospects). Female labour force participation and decisions regarding time allocation are

---

[29] Murphy, M. (1992). Economic Models of Fertility in Post War Britain. *Population Studies*, 46, 235-258.

[30] Murphy, M. (1992). Economic Models of Fertility in Post War Britain. *Population Studies*, 46, 235-258. British fertility remained relatively unchanged for upper social classes lifestyles, while their labour force participation increased, whilst working class women's patterns of fertility had declined though their participation in the labour force had changed little. Werner, B. (1985). Fertility Trends in Different Social Classes: 1970-1983. *Population Trends*, 41, 5-13.

[31] Willis, R.J. (1973). A New Approach to the Economic Theory of Fertility Behaviour. *Journal of Political Economy*, 81(2), Mar-Apr, S14-S64.

[32] Schultz, T.P. (1969). An Economic Model of Family Planning and Fertility. *Journal of Political Economy*, 25(2), Mar-Apr. Also Willis, R.J. (1973). A New Approach to the Economic Theory of Fertility Behaviour. *Journal of Political Economy*, 81(2), Mar-April, S14-S64.

relevant to the wife's actual/potential earnings.[33]   The number of children is negatively related to the wage rate or other measures of value of time of wives and positively related to the wage rate or earnings of husband and that of children.[34]

Theories of Utility and Choice   Parents derive 'utility' from children: they are both consumption (parents derive 'intrinsic satisfaction' from family formation) and production goods (contribute with labour and support in old age).   But, childbearing and rearing incurs a 'price', diversion of household income (otherwise spent on other goods).[35]   Hence, parents choose an 'optimal' fertility level after evaluating their perceived costs (expenditures on food, clothing, education, medical care, dowry, cost of mother's time, reduction in child labour, and so on) and benefits (increased productivity, household income, old age support and so on),[36] which maximizes their 'utility function' (well being), subject to certain exogenously determined constraints (especially the 'budget constraint', which equates household expenses with income, and is determined by market wage, costs of child rearing and other expenses).[37]

---

[33] Sprague, A. (1988). Post War Fertility and Female Labour Force Participation Rates. *The Economic Journal*, 98, September, 682-700. Fertility and female work participation rates were affected by male and female earnings, income, real interest rates (determine least costly times to start childbearing), education, vacancies (result in greater female participation in paid work), and stocks of children. Earnings affect work activity and fertility to different degrees depending on the female age group.

[34] Willis, R.J. (1973). A New Approach to the Economic Theory of Fertility Behaviour. *Journal of Political Economy*, 81(2), Mar-Apr, S14-S64. Also Winegarden, C.R. (1984). Women, Fertility, Market Work and Marital Status: Test of New Household Economics with International Data. *Economica*, 51, 447-456. Increasing real wages for working women result in declines in fertility and propensity to be married, and increases female participation in the wage labour, while increasing male wages has opposite effects on female behaviour. Also, Birdsall, N., Fei, J., Kuznets, S., Ranis, G., and T.P. Schultz. (1979). Demography and Development in the 1980s. In P.M. Hauser (Ed.), *World Population and Development: Challenges and Prospects*. (pp. 211-295). New York: UNFPA.

[35] Liebenstein, H. (1967). *Economic Backwardness and Economic Growth*. New York: J Wiley and Sons. Also Becker, G. (1960). *Demographic and Economic Change in Developed Countries*. Princeton: Princeton University Press. Also Easterlin, R. (1969). Toward a Socioeconomic Theory of Fertility: a Survey of Recent Research on Economic Factors on American Fertility. *Fertility and Family Planning: A WorldView*. Ann Arbor: University of Michigan Press.

[36] Ohlin, G. (1976). Economic Theory Confronts Population Growth. In A.J. Coale (Ed.), *Economic Factors in Population Growth*. (pp. 3-16). London: Macmillan Press.

[37] Ohlin, G. (1976). Economic Theory Confronts Population Growth. In A.J. Coale (Ed.), *Economic Factors in Population Growth*. (pp. 3-16). London: Macmillan Press.

Chicago Columbia Model   Becker and Lewis formalized the demand aspect o childbearing with the 'quantity-quality' tradeoff.[38] Demand for children has quantit and quality aspects and is determined by economic factors and 'tastes' (function o family's religion, race, age, time period). Quality has a 'price' (determined by th amount of money spent on children). Hence, parents decide on the allocation o their limited resources. A modest increase in the fixed cost of quantity coulc greatly reduce the quantity of children and increase their quality. While childrei are not income elastic, total expenditures on them are. Children and goods are no substitutes per se, but time intensive children and goods intensive commodities ar indirectly so, as a change in the opportunity cost of commodity time, leads tc adjustments in consumption patterns according to relative cost changes. Witl higher income, a decline in work time accommodates increased direct time input: so the total parental time devoted to children (supplying goods for and actuall) producing them) need not decline.

Leibenstein[39] argued that couples exercised 'limited rationality' wher making fertility decisions. Before a 'threshold' number of children (determined b) preferences and varies across families and social groups) is reached, reproductive behaviour is not planned and irrational. Once this number is attained, the rationa decision-making level operates and decisions concerning the marginal child involve optimizing cost/benefit calculations. Socioeconomic development influences the family's social position, tastes for children and other consumption goods. But while the 'consumption utility' derived from the marginal child remains unchanged, the economic benefits decrease and the costs increase. Therefore, a family's threshold number of children may be redefined and fewer children may be favoured.

The Easterlin-Pollack-Wachter Model[40] This related actual fertility to changes in desired and natural fertility. It focused on natural fertility regimes, the transition tc fertility control and parental utility maximization (function of a vector oi commodities produced by the household using time and goods). Socioeconomic modernization and other basic determinants affect the fertility level through three core variables:

i.   Demand: total number of surviving children parents would have in the absence of fertility-regulation costs (determining only for modern societie:

---

[38] Becker, G.S. (1960). An Economic Analysis of Fertility. In A.J. Coale (Eds). *Demographic and Economic Change in Developed Countries.* Princeton: Princeton University Press.

[39] Leibenstein, H. (1975). The Economic Theory of Fertility Decline. *The Quarterly Journa of Economics,* 89, February.

[40] Easterlin, R.A. (1982). *Population and Economic Change in Developing Countries.* Chicago: University of Chicago Press.

with sophisticated contraceptives, high health standards and good nutrition).

ii. Supply: total number of surviving children parents would have in the absence of fertility regulation, influenced by uncontrollable biological (nutrition) and cultural (social control, lactation habits, sexual taboos, marriage customs) limitations affecting fertility and fecundity.

iii. economic, psychic, health and social costs of fertility regulation: the decision to regulate fertility is based on a comparison of strength of motivation (extent to which potential supply exceeds demand) and these costs.

These variables pass through three distinct phases during the development process: excess demand occurs when families bear fewer children than desired, and supply variables (health, IMR, nutrition) constrain the fertility level, there is no motivation for fertility regulation and the desired average family size is high. On the other hand, if the demand for children is less than the potential supply, the couple face the likelihood of bearing unwanted children and having a larger completed family size, a situation which arises when the trade-off indicates drawbacks to contraception.

'Taste' (indicated by a simplified taste function related to living standards) for children is a given, endogenous determinant: a function of the previous generation's averages. The preference hierarchy depends on past teenage experience whether as members of their parents' household (intrafamily model), or as members of a social group (socialization model) with set consumption and family size norms. Norms vary according to the 'budget' (time value, household technology) and 'multivariate' births and deaths (constrained by social variables, nutrition, health, reproductive span) constraints on the utility function. Changes in this and in income levels affect fertility behaviour: increases in the relative prices of children and mother's wage rates may result in children being raised in less time-intensive ways, or in declining fertility (taste norm parameters change with higher experienced consumption which accompany rising wages over time).

Easterlin's framework, because of its clarity and incorporation of key features of other fertility theories,[41] has been applied in the analysis of the determinants of contraceptive use (rather than of demand for children, or actual fertility) and of community level factors affecting children's supply and contraceptive costs. It has also been considered to have more application to the developing world than the Chicago Columbia Model (Becker, Willis et al).[42]

---

[41] Bongaarts, J. (1993). The Impact of Proximate Determinants of Fertility - A Comment. *Population Studies*, 47(3), 437-456.

[42] Behrman, J.R., and B.L. Wolfe. (1984). A More General Approach to Fertility Determination in Developing Countries: The Importance of Biological Supply Considerations, Endogenous Taste and Unperceived Jointness. *Economica*, 57, 319-339.

Bongaarts recently offered a simplified operational variant of Easterlin's model based on period measures.[43] The variables are:

i. supply of births F_n (natural total fertility) is lower than the biological maximum due to social norms, which unintentionally reduce fertility:

$F_n = F/C$ where C=index for proportional reduction in natural fertility attributable to birth control

F=observed fertility

$C = 1 - 1.02U$ where U=proportion of married women practicing contraception (excluding use during post partum infecundable period).

ii. demand for births F_w (wanted total fertility) is the childbearing rate achieved, if all unwanted births were eliminated:

$$F_w = F'_w + 1.09 - W_{m\,(40-44)}$$

F'_w = (total fertility) all births to women not wanting more children at time of survey

W_m = proportion of married women (40-44) who want more births

iii. degree of preference implementation I_p is the net result of the tradeoff between contraceptive costs and unwanted childbearing $\{=1\ (F_w)$, if no unwanted births occur; $=0\ (F_n)$ if all births are unwanted$\}$.

$$I_p = (F_n - F)/(F_n - F_w)$$

F_u (unwanted total fertility) is a function of the difference between supply and demand and the degree of preference implementation

$$F_u = \{(F_n - F_w)(1 - I_p)\}$$

Observed fertility $F = F_w + F_u$,

Hence $F = F_w I_p + F_n (1 - I_p)$

Increasing I_p will lead to increasing contraceptive prevalence (relationship is not fixed and not necessarily direct). With development, F_w and F decline, I_p increases, F_n is unchanged. Hence, changes in demand and I_p are the key factors for reducing fertility.[44]

---

[43] Bongaarts, J. (1993). The Impact of Proximate Determinants of Fertility - A Comment. *Population Studies*, 47(3), 437-456.

[44] Bongaarts, J. (1993). The Impact of Proximate Determinants of Fertility - A Comment. *Population Studies*, 47(3), 437-456.

The new household economics models have been adapted to reflect the conditions of the developing world:

i. the utility function now includes the number of surviving children, not the number of children ever born,[45] which increases the cost per child (includes resources allocated to children who have died). Fertility behaviour may be partially determined by a desire to offset (experienced or anticipated) child mortality.

ii. children are providers of consumption utility (parental satisfaction), consumption goods,[46] and producers or inputs into the household production function (engaged in housework, may enter the labour market at a young age), implying a high fertility strategy. Differences in child employment opportunities may contribute to fertility variation.

iii. children (especially sons) provide old age security and short run insurance against risk, provide income from diversified sources, offer political support in local disputes, maintain productive activities if household head is incapacitated, especially in uncertain environments where alternative formal institutions are lacking (positive effect on fertility).[47]

iv. view the relationship between fertility and the model (prices, income and factors working through these e.g., child mortality, productivity) within the context of the family's community, and as determining household level fertility.[48] Community level factors (schools, transport etc.) determine the value of these household variables and/or influence their impact on fertility.

---

[45] Schultz, T.P. (1976). Interrelationships between Mortality and Fertility. In R.G. Ridker (Ed.), *Population and Development*. Baltimore: John Hopkins University Press. Also Schultz, T.P. (1978). Fertility and Child Mortality Over the Life Cycle. *American Economic Review*, 68(2). Also Schultz, T.P. (1980). Interrelationship of Relations among Mortality, Economics of the Household, and the Economic Environment. In World Health Organization. *Socioeconomic Determinants and Consequences of Mortality*. Geneva: WHO.

[46] Rosenweig, M.R. (1977). The Demand for Children in Farm Households. *Journal of Political Economy*, 85(1). Also Rosenweig, M.R., and R.E. Evenson. (1977). Fertility Schooling and the Economic Contribution of Children in Rural India: An Econometric Analysis. *Econometrica*, 45(5).

[47] Cain, M.T. (1981). Risk and Insurance: Perspectives on Fertility and Agrarian Change in India and Bangladesh. *Population and Development Review*, 7(3). Also Cain, M.T. (1982). Perspectives on Family and Fertility in Developing Countries. *Population Studies*, 36(2). Also Cain, M.T. (1983). Fertility as an Adjustment to Risk. *Population and Development Review*, 9(4).

[48] Anker, R. and M. Anker. (1982). *Reproductive Behaviour in Households of Rural Gujurat: Social, Economic and Community Factors*. New Delhi: Concept Publishing. Also Entwisle, B., Hermalin, A.I., and W. Mason. (1982). *Socioeconomic Determinants of Fertility Behaviour in Developing Nations: Theory and Initial Results*. Washington, D.C.: National Academy Press. Also Bilsborrow, R.E. (1985). Collecting Community Level Data

The Response to Mortality Decline Mortality level changes affect family wealth, prices, risks and return on human capital, the real value of income streams and the relative value of human versus physical capital goods in parental investment decisions.[49] At the individual and cohort levels, the magnitude of direct association between child mortality and fertility (with a variable lag time) is larger than that which can be merely attributed to involuntary biological feedback mechanisms, suggesting that strong parental behavioural preferences are involved. But, there is little agreement on the causal relationship (if any), between them.[50] Choice Theory explains demand for births as a function of the optimal number of surviving children and the probability of a child to survive infancy: infant mortality rate is negatively related to demand for surviving children and positively to derived demand for births.[51] Child replacement hypothesis explains high fertility as a parental response to high infant mortality ('replacement strategy' to guarantee support in old age and backed by social and religious norms). Incomplete replacement results when high (financial and physiological) costs are incurred in rapidly increasing the pace of childbearing: IMR is inversely related to number of surviving children. Modern economic theories state that infant mortality and fertility are interdependent with feedback effects: parents invest resources (food, medical care) in their children, thereby determining the number that survive and their health.[52]

In the contemporary developing world, increased private material well being (individual wealth effects), transfer of medical knowledge and technology, effect of international agencies and foreign aid have led to rapid mortality declines,[53] particularly rapid in the below five age group and moderate in the older age groups. Any further declines are dependent on improving living and nutritional standards and female education. Yet, while mortality declines are a necessary and

for Fertility Analysis. In J. Casterline (Ed.), *The Collection and Analysis of Community Data.* Voorburg, Netherlands: International Statistical Institute. Also, Bilsborrow, R.E. and D.K. Guilkey. (1987). Community and Institutional Influence on Fertility: Analytical Issues. *Population and Labour Policies Programme Working Paper* No. 157. Geneva: International Labour Office.

[49] Birdsall, N., Fei, J., Kuznets, S., Ranis, G., and T.P. Schultz. (1979). Demography and Development in the 1980s. In P.M. Hauser (Ed.), *World Population and Development: Challenges and Prospects.* (pp. 211-295). New York: UNFPA.

[50] S. Kuznets, 1977. Recent Population Trends in Less Developed Countries and Implications for International Income Inequality. *Yale University Discussion Paper.* No 261.

[51] J.C. Caldwell, 1976. Toward a Restatement of Demographic Transition Theory. *Population and Development Review* (2) 3-4.

[52] A.R. Chowdry, 1988. Infant Mortality-Fertility Debate: Some International Evidence. *Southern Economic Journal* (54) January. pp. 666-673.

[53] Birdsall, N., Fei, J., Kuznets, S., Ranis, G., and T.P. Schultz. (1979). Demography and Development in the 1980s. In P.M. Hauser (Ed.), *World Population and Development: Challenges and Prospects.* (pp. 211-295). New York: UNFPA.

important precondition for fertility declines, they are not a sufficient condition and they certainly do not guarantee them.[54]

Women's Status Theoretically, improving women's status (measured by educational attainment and employment) and incorporating women in the development process would moderate fertility levels.[55]   This is achieved through increasing their resources (and hence the opportunity cost of their time),[56] enhancing their domestic decision making roles, exposing them to foreign ideals concerning family size, raising the age at marriage, facilitating access to contraceptive information and lowering mortality rates. With improved status, women would enjoy greater control over their own reproductive capacities, thereby lowering fertility levels (assuming that many of the children currently borne by women are 'surplus' or 'unwanted'). In addition, it would also attain other development objectives.

Formal education broadens one's horizons, increases one's knowledge, affects a psychological shift from fatalism to a sense of control over destiny, from passivity to the pursuit of achievement, from a religious, tradition bound and parochial world view, to a secular, cosmopolitan one where rationality reigns. For parents, education (through the spread of Western family formation values,[57] knowledge about and use of contraceptive methods)[58] encourages attempts at increasing control over fertility.[59]   It offers women alternative opportunities for status attainment and increases the opportunity cost of childbearing, thus reducing their motivation to have children.[60]   A positive association has been found between years of women's schooling and fertility limitation in societies already practicing

---

[54] Omran, A.R. and I.A. Salama. (1986). Micro-Analytic Study of Development and Fertility-Consideration of Transition Models. *Social Biology*, 33(3-4), 259-275.

[55] Farooq, G.M. and Deborah S. DeGraff. (1988). *Fertility and Development: An Introduction to Theory, Empirical Research and Policy Issues*. Paper No 7 (pp. 20-26). Geneva: International Labour Office.

[56] Mincer, J. (1963). Market Prices, Opportunity Costs, and Income Effects.   In Nick Eberstadt (Ed), *Measurement in Economics: Studies in Mathematical Economics and Econometrics in Memory of Yehuda Grunfeld*. Stanford: Stanford University Press.

[57] Caldwell, J.C. (1976). Towards a Restatement of the Demographic Transition Theory. *Population and Development Review*, 2(3/4), 321-366.

[58] Caldwell, J.C. (1982). *Theory of Fertility Decline*. New York.   Also, Caldwell, J.C., Reddy, P.H., and P. Caldwell. (1985). Educational Transition in Rural South India. *Population and Development Review* (11).

[59] Cochrane, S.H., Khan, M.A., and I.K.T. Osheba. (1990). Education Income and Desired Fertility in Egypt: A Revised Perspective. *Economic Development and Cultural Change*, 38(2).

[60] Notestine, F.W. (1953). Economic Problems of Population Change.   In *Proceedings of the Eight International Conference of Agricultural Economics*. London.

family planning, where a large proportion of women are exposed to schooling.[61] For children, education translates into Western family values and economic independence, both of which undermine the influence the older generation has over the younger and reduce the value of the younger generation to the older generation. Hence, parents have less incentive to have many children.[62]

Religious Theorie Three major hypothesis have been proposed to explain religious differences in fertility:[63]

i. characteristics or assimilation hypothesis: fertility differentials are due to differences in the demographic and socioeconomic attributes of a religion's followers.
ii. particularised theology proposition: religious differentials in fertility are due to doctrinal differences.
iii. minority group status: minority group's insecurities depress fertility below the majority group's level.

Chamie argued for the interactionist theory:[64] religious fertility differentials depend on the interaction of the socioeconomic levels within religious groups, and the local orientations (the current moral attitudes of the religious community) of these groups toward procreation and fertility control. Before the Demographic Transition, high fertility is appropriate for everyone, so religious affiliation does not differentiate. During the Transition, the influence of pronatalist religious values and orientations results in a lag in the adjustment of the adherents' fertility to the new conditions (for which low fertility is the expected response). After the Transition, the religious influence is eventually negated by the conditions of modern society.

---

[61] Cochrane, S.H. (1979). *Fertility and Education: What do We Really Know?* Baltimore. Also, Cochrane, S. (1983). Effects of Education and Urbanization on Fertility. In R.A. Bulatao and R.D. Lee (Eds), *Determinants of Fertility in Developing Countries* Vol. 2. New York.

[62] Axinn, W.G. (1993). The Supply Demand Framework for the Determinants of Fertility – An Alternative Implementation. *Population Studies,* 47, 481-493.

[63] El-Hamamsy, L. (1972). Belief Systems and Family Planning in Peasant Societies. In H. Brown and E. Hutchings (Eds.), *Are Our Descendants Doomed?* New York: Viking Press.

[64] Chamie, J. (1977). Religious Fertility Differentials: A Look at some Hypotheses and Findings. *Population Bulletin of the United Nations Economic Commission for Western Asia,* 13, July, 3-16.

Theories related to Timing of Fertility Decline

It is believed that the timing of fertility decline depends on socioeconomic development and other factors[65] given that

i.   culturally similar regions in Europe progressed through the transition at the same pace, despite economic differences,[66]

ii. fertility had declined prior to mortality changes in Southern and Eastern Europe,

iii. fertility declines varied as to whether they occurred before, during or after industrial development.[67]

Social history and modern anthropology consider changes over time in the definition and the role of family relevant to understanding interrelations between economic growth, population change and income distribution.[68] Therefore, fertility transition is a social phenomenon affected by the existence of extended family and reference groups, related to inter generational interdependence and survival, and to sociocultural values and norms (i.e., group behavioural change). Social values, beliefs and normative pressures therefore evolve towards encouraging a suitable level of fertility to counter changes in mortality levels. Declining mortality make such supports unnecessary and dysfunctional.

Social structures are boundaries within which innovation spreads: a priori constraints on the potential effect of diffusion on fertility decline. The 'Diffusion of Innovation' hypothesis[69] argues that the acceptability of ideas or innovations by individuals, groups or formal bodies (linked to the world by a structure of social relations, values and communication channels) depends on its perceived attributes and advantages, its compatibility with the sociocultural characteristics (moral

---

[65] Hauser, P.M. (1979). *World Population and Development: Challenges and Prospects* (p. 15). New York: UNFPA.

[66] Coale, A.J. (1975). The Demographic Transition. *The Population Debate: Dimensions and Perspectives, Papers of the World Population Conference* (pp. 347-355). New York: UN.

[67] Sweezy, A. (1973). Social and Economic Development and Fertility. In H. Brown (Ed.), *Population Perspectives* (p. 43). San Francisco: Freeman, Cooper.

[68] Birdsall, N., Fei, J., Kuznets, S., Ranis, G., and T.P. Schultz. (1979). Demography and Development in the 1980s. In P.M. Hauser (Ed.), *World Population and Development: Challenges and Prospects*. (pp. 211-295). New York: UNFPA.

[69] Rogers, E.M. and F.F. Shoemaker. (1971). *Communication of Innovations: a Cross Cultural Approach*. New York: Free Press. Also, Rogers, E.M. (1973). *Communication Strategies for Family Planning*. New York: Free Press.

values, social norms) of the adopting units, and the role of opinion leaders, social networks, inter spousal communication in its dissemination.[70]

Caldwell combined the economic demand for children and the cultural transmission of Western ideas and values that eventually undermine it into the inter generational wealth flows theory.[71] Marital fertility levels, being dependent on the direction and magnitude of inter generational wealth flows within families, can only (rationally) decline if the direction of wealth flows change from that of upwards (that is, from children to parents) to downwards (from parents to children). This shift occurs once the family becomes 'emotionally nucleated', i.e., when the emotional ties and commitments are stronger between married couples and their children than with the extended family. Exposure to Western ideas concerning the family (via education and the mass media) is the pivotal force behind the change.

Coale, on the other hand, identified three preconditions for fertility decline: fertility must be within the calculus of conscious choice, effective contraceptive techniques must be known and available, lower fertility must be considered advantageous.[72] The European decline started with a transition from no family limitation within marriage (pre-transition ASFRs were as those characteristic of natural fertility)[73] to rapidly increasing prevalence (diffusion of innovation hypothesis). Once fertility fell by 10 percent, it then almost always fell rapidly and continually, outpacing development.[74] Hence, contraceptive use could not have been an incidental adjustment to growing motivation for fewer children induced by slow developmental changes (in which case, contraceptive adoption and fertility declines would have been gradual). Given the presence of motivation, good family planning programmes (which disseminate concepts, means and services under medically optimal, culturally acceptable conditions) are related to fertility declines above and beyond development effects. Family limitation has an independent causal role in determining the timing and speed of fertility declines.[75] While,

[70] Hauser, P.M. (1979). *World Population and Development: Challenges and Prospects* (p. 63). New York: UNFPA.

[71] Caldwell, J.C. (1986). Routes to Low Mortality in Poor Countries. *Population and Development Review,* 12, 171-220.

[72] Coale, A.J. (1973). The Demographic Transition. *International Population Conference* Liege: IUSSP.

[73] Knodel, J. (1977). Family Limitation and the Fertility Transition: Evidence form the Age Patterns of Fertility in Europe and Asia. *Population Studies,* 31, July, 219-249.

[74] Freedman, R. (1979). Theories of Fertility Decline: A Reappraisal. In P.M. Hauser, *World Population and Development: Challenges and Prospects.* New York: UNFPA.

[75] Freedman, R. (1979). Theories of Fertility Decline: A Reappraisal. In P.M. Hauser, *World Population and Development: Challenges and Prospects.* New York: UNFPA.

historically, fertility declined without access to modern contraceptives, access to such facilities will accelerate them.[76]

In fact, family planning programmes have been instrumental in reducing fertility levels in the contemporary developing world.[77] It took the US 58 years (1842-1900) to make the transition from a TFR of six to 3.5. Columbia completed the same transition in 15 years (1968-1983) and Thailand in eight years (1969-1977). The fact that family size fell four times as rapidly in some countries with relatively good access to fertility regulation technologies as it did in nineteenth century America can be interpreted as strong evidence of the influence of effective choices in accelerating fertility decline.

Therefore, the prevailing view is that in the developing world, fertility decline has been influenced by the modernization level, country's income, effective family planning programmes (in combination with modernization accounted for 83% of total variance in decline) and time since their initiation, economic development, country's size, population policies, changes in age structure, age at marriage and marital fertility.[78]

Application of the Demographic Transition Theory to the Developing World?

The feasibility of certain of the assumptions underlying the Transition Theory can be doubted:

   i. TFRs will stabilize at replacement level (2.1 births per woman): Developed countries attained a below replacement level (1930s), a baby boom (1950s), then below replacement (1970s-1980s) and there are recent indications of it increasing again. Will similar mixed patterns occur in the Developing world upon completion of the Transition?
   ii. Development results in fertility decline: alternative responses may be made to the pressure of rapid population growth (e.g., migration), and development may even exert a positive influence on fertility (better health, female nutrition, less observance of breastfeeding and post partum abstinence, reduction in widowhood, higher income levels and shifts in income distribution).[79] In fact, the Transition preceded mortality declines

---

[76] Hajnal, J. (1965). European Marriage Patterns in Perspective. In D.V. Glass and D.E.C. Eversley (Eds.), *Population in History: Essays in Historical Demography* (pp. 101-143). London: Edward Arnold.

[77] Potts, M. (1997). Sex and the Birth Rate. *Population Development Review*, 23(1), March, 14.

[78] Hauser, P.M. (1979). Introduction and Overview. In P.M.Hauser (Ed.), *World Population and Development: Challenges and Prospects.* New York: UNFPA.

[79] Coale, A.J., Anderson, B.A., and E. Harm. (1979). *Human Fertility in Russia Since the Nineteenth Century.* Princeton: Princeton University Press.

and industrial development in certain areas of nineteenth century France and Hungary, and many culturally similar areas showed similar fertility patterns, irrespective of the socioeconomic developmental indices. In contemporary Developing countries, fertility decline has occurred despite a limited subset of development changes.

iii.   Fertility in traditional societies fluctuated around a biologically or culturally determined level then declined with modernization. Low fertility or small families are not a self-evident attribute of modernization itself, European marriage patterns kept a large part of the population single after puberty or forever and delayed family formation until access to property or position was gained.[80]

Furthermore, the demographic changes that the Developing countries are experiencing are different from those experienced during the European Transition. Fertility levels are higher than those in Europe; mortality levels were already low at the beginning of the Transition, have declined rapidly since[81] and the nature and pace of change during the Transition is different.   Rapid technological and communication innovations have speeded up the development process,[82] rendering it difficult to measure the extent of change that is necessary for motivating fertility declines.   Modern technology has facilitated the transfer of information (about Western history, development, technology and living standards)[83] to the Developing world, made parents aware of alternative lifestyles and has influenced the cultural milieu. However, such new ideas about the demand for children will only affect fertility if there is actual validation in change. Westernization is not a mandatory condition for fertility decline: parents in the developing world may be influenced by Western ideas, but this does not necessarily translate into wholesale adoption of these ideas: traditional familial values change very slowly and the benefits derived from children may be different,[84] though the costs may be similar.

Economic models continue to dominate the debate because of the inability of the other disciplines to propose a coherent explanation, and the intimidation of non-specialists from mounting a rigorous critique of the statistically sophisticated

---

[80] Hajnal, J. (1965). European Marriage Patterns in Perspective. In D.V. Glass and D.E.C. Eversley (Eds.), *Population in History: Essays in Historical Demography* (pp. 101-143). London: Edward Arnold.

[81] World Bank. (1994). *Development in Practice: Population and Development: Implications for the World Bank.* Washington, D.C.: World Bank.

[82] Hauser, P.M. (1979). Introduction and Overview. In P.M.Hauser (Ed.), *World Population and Development: Challenges and Prospects.* New York: UNFPA.

[83] Freedman, R. (1979). Theories of Fertility Decline: A Reappraisal. In P.M. Hauser, *World Population and Development: Challenges and Prospects.* New York: UNFPA.

[84] Freedman, R. (1979). Theories of Fertility Decline: A Reappraisal. In P.M. Hauser, *World Population and Development: Challenges and Prospects.* New York: UNFPA.

economic models.   However, while the application of such models may be relatively easier in the countries in which they were formulated (the West), where accurate longitudinal data is available, this is not the case in the capital deficient Developing world, where any data, let alone, detailed data, is difficult to get. Then, there is the issue of definition: how does one obtain quantitative measures of costs and benefits for children, value of time etc., in non-monetised economies where there is no corresponding market price?[85]   Or of household income levels (theoretical work is based on (current or past) lifetime family income) where in kind payments are made and consumption items are domestically produced? However, its main drawback is that it does not specify any assumptions (e.g. about the aspects of development to be measured, or length of lag times, changes mortality trends or the unit of analysis) that need to be made before meaningful research can be conducted.

The models were developed within the context of the industrialized West and thus take a Western perspective on family relations. The assumption that the household decision making unit is a functional, individual, nuclear family, with pooled economic resources or budget, ignores the importance of family structure and organization (individual preferences, economic constraints and role conflicts) in the decision making process and related intrahousehold dynamics[86] in the developing world.[87] In addition, they are based on rational decision making which may not be the case in the developing world.[88] Further, certain correlations are consistent with more than one model of fertility.

Quite apart from the question of the appropriateness of the supply-and-demand terminology to reproduction, it is unrealistic to assume that couples, early

---

[85] Nag, M. (1981). Economic Value and Costs of Children in Relation to Human Fertility. In N. Eberstadt (Ed.), *Fertility Decline in Less Developed Countries*. New York: Praeger Publishers.

[86] Fapohunda, E.R. (1988). The Non-Pooling Household: A Challenge to Economic Theory. In D.H. Dwyer and J. Bruce (Eds.), *A Home Divided: Women and Income in the Third World* Stanford: Stanford University Press.   Also, Boserup, E. (1985). Economic and Demographic Interrelationships in Sub-Saharan Africa. *Population and Development Review,* II(3). Also, Oppong, C. (1985). Parental Costs, Role Strain, and Fertility Regulation: Some Ghanaian Evidence. *Population and Labour Policies Programme Working Paper,* 134, Geneva: International Labour Office. Also, Farooq G. and M. Simmons. (1985). *Some Aspects of Anthropological Contributions. Fertility in Developing Countries: An Economic Perspective on Research and Policy Issues.* London: MacMillan Press.

[87] Ben Porath, Y. (1980). The F-Connection: Families, Friends, and Firms and the Organization of Exchange. *Population and Development Review,* 6(1).

[88] These include: Mincer's opportunity cost of time; Lewis and Becker's quality-quantity trade-off. For a full discussion refer Farooq, G.M. and Deborah S. DeGraff. (1988). *Fertility and Development: An Introduction to Theory, Empirical Research and Policy Issues.* Paper No 7 (pp. 20-26). Geneva: International Labour Office.

on in their reproductive life, reach a decision concerning desired family size, potential supply of children and contraceptive use and then adhere to this decision throughout their reproductive ages. Further, ignorance, uncertainty and risk mar all market performance, especially when infant mortality is high (when a minimum number of surviving children is needed, parents may seek more births).[89] Also, when parents do not bear the full costs of children (free education, medical care, various allowances), they will have more children than that they would normally be willing to pay for.[90] Finally, with changing preferences, couples make a series of short-term fertility decisions over their life cycle, thereby adjusting their behaviour[91] and contraceptive use to space births, especially during the demographic transition. The economic model's consistency may be preserved by explaining the observed variation by change in preferences, but nothing would be proved about the change.[92]

The other assumption of a couple's behaviour being affected only by their own circumstances does not allow for interaction between different groups in society, nor for changing attitudes towards appropriate male-female roles, population growth, shifts to post materialism and assertive individualism, improved contraceptive techniques and knowledge.[93] Calculations of children's costs and

---

[89] Ohlin, G. (1976). Economic Theory Confronts Population Growth. In A.J. Coale (Ed.), *Economic Factors in Population Growth* (pp. 3-16). London: Macmillan Press.

[90] Ohlin, G. (1976). Economic Theory Confronts Population Growth. In A.J. Coale (Ed.), *Economic Factors in Population Growth* (pp. 3-16). London: Macmillan Press.

[91] Heckman, J.T. and R.J. Willis. (1975). Estimation of Stochastic Model of Reproduction: An Economic Approach. In N.E. Terleckyj (Ed.), *Household Production and Consumption.* New York: NBER. Also, Newmen, J.L. (1984). *A Stochastic Dynamic Model of Fertility.* Paper presented at the Population Association of America Meeting in Minneapolis, Minn.. Also, Paqueo, V.B., Fabella, R.V., and A.N. Herrin. (1985). *On the Economic Theory of Prevention: The Case of Contraception and Choice of Methods.* A paper presented at the Seminar on Determinants of Contraceptive Method Choice, East West, Population Institute, Honolulu. Also, Rosenzweig, M.R., and T.P. Schultz. (1981). The Demand for and Supply of Births. *The American Economic Review,* 68(2).

[92] Leridon, H. (1976). The Role of Economic Factors in Birth Rate Trends and Fluctuations. In A.J. Coale (Ed.), *Economic Factors in Population Growth* (pp. 179-204). London: Macmillan Press.

[93] Preston, S.H. (1987). Changing Values and Falling Birth Rates. In K. Davis, M. Bernstam, and R. Ricardo Campbell (Eds), *Below Replacement Fertility in Industrial Societies: Causes Consequences, Policies.* New York: The Population Council.   Also Lesthaeghe, R., and J. Surkyn. (1988). Cultural Dynamics and Economic Theories of Cultural Change. *Population and Development Review,* 14, 1-45. Also Lesthaeghe, R. and D. Meekers. (1986). Value Changes and the Dimensions of Familialism in the European Community. *European Journal of Population,* 2, 225-268.

benefits should also consider the psychological and social aspects:[94] children are not homogenous and they do have productive value. Families have no market place, and using economic arguments is incorrect: the complex family interactions involve intense emotions which vitiate the use of standard theory. In addition, the models are based on incomplete operationalisation of the economic model, are inappropriately fitted and contain internal inconsistencies.[95]

Parental time can be invested in producing income or in childrearing. Increases in the wife's wage have two offsetting effects on fertility: positive income effects (more children can be afforded) and negative price effects (value of wife's time increases). Further, while price effects dominate in industrialized countries (negative relationship with fertility), in developing countries, women's work is not necessarily incompatible with childbearing (activities are engaged in simultaneously, help from extended family members). In addition, empirical specification for the variables (parent's lifetime wages, wealth, cost and quality characteristics of children and labour force participation rates over reproductive or work life) can only be roughly estimated. The woman with fewer children and more work may be reacting to an income constraint on living standards, rather than the opportunity cost of children.

Finally, the (expected) negative association between educational levels and fertility rates applies only at the secondary or higher levels of education (due to delayed marriage and greater contraceptive use). In fact, women with a few years of education have higher fertility than uneducated women, because of reduced breastfeeding and postpartum abstinence, while those with more than seven years of schooling have three fewer children than uneducated women.[96] Further, the (expected) negative relation between female employment and fertility is neither clear nor consistent. While Western working women tend to have fewer children than those at home, and having children tends to reduce the possibility that married women would work, a general pattern has not been found. European countries with the largest female labour forces do not have exceptionally low fertility and those with lower female participation do not have particularly high fertility. In addition, the nature of the causal relation between women and employment and its timing is unclear:[97] does employment have a fertility inhibiting effect, or does fertility have a

[94] Fawcett, J.T. (1983). Perceptions of the Value of Children: Satisfaction and Costs. In Bulatro, Lee (Eds.), *Determinants of Fertility in Developing Countries*. New York: Academic Press.

[95] Murphy, M. (1992). Economic Models of Fertility in Post War Britain. *Population Studies*, 46, 235-258.

[96] United Nations Population Division. (1985). Concise Report on the World Population Situation in 1983: Conditions, Trends, Prospects and Policies. *Population Studies*, 85, ST/ESA/SER.A/85. New York: United Nations.

[97] Bernhardt, E.W. (1993). Fertility and Employment. *European Sociological Review*, 9, May.

negative influence on workforce participation, or is it a mutual causation? Simultaneous causality may mean that increased female labour participation is a consequence and cause of fertility change, or both may be due to attitudes and contraception. In fact, the causality could work in the opposite direction if women with high fertility choose to remain outside the labour force. Subfecund women may be over represented in the labour market because of their lack of childcare responsibilities. Finally, micro level studies do not consider the social context (childcare facilities, labour market structure: jobs, work hours, conditions of work and pay, community structure, and contraceptive availability), despite these factors affecting an individual's decisions about number of children to have, timing of fertility and work participation.

Neither can the Demographic Transition Theory, nor any other social theory or model, be expected to explain all salient features and possible determinants of a dependent variable. They merely aim to isolate some strong relationships that are responsible for fertility and its trend.

Chapter 4

Gulf Fertility: Trends, Causes and Expectations

Gulf Crude Birth Rates (CBRs) have been declining: from an estimated average of 47 to 34 per 1000 population between 1950 and 1990. Of the six Gulf States, Oman and Saudi Arabia had the highest initial levels of CBRs, whilst Bahrain and Kuwait had the lowest. The rate of decline varied as well: Oman and Saudi Arabia experienced the slowest rates of decline in CBR (0.2 percent and 0.4 percent per annum, respectively), whilst UAE enjoyed the most rapid rate of decline (1.3 percent per annum).

However, these estimates do not differentiate between the national and non-national populations. While the total CBR for Kuwait declined by 1 percent per annum between 1965 and 1990, that for Kuwaitis declined by 1.3 percent per annum in two stages: an increase of 4 percent per annum between 1970 and 1974, followed by a decline of 2 percent per annum between 1974 and 1989. In addition, Crude Rates, despite being commonly used to show fertility trends, do not necessarily reflect changes in fertility: they may be due to the age structure, the marital fertility rates and so on.

Total Fertility Rates (TFRs) on the other hand, are a more accurate reflection of fertility trends.[1] These declined by 2 percent per annum in Bahrain between 1980 and 1991, and more gradually by 0.1 percent per annum in Kuwait between 1980 and 1989. The Age Specific Fertility Rates (ASFR) yields even more information.[2] As Figure 4.1 shows, between 1957 and 1985, Kuwaiti fertility declined amongst the younger age groups (by 2.5 percent per annum for those aged 15-19 and by 0.6 percent per annum for those aged 20-24, and increased for all the other age groups: by 0.1 percent for those aged 25-29 as well as those aged 40-44, by 0.3 percent for those aged 30 to 39, and by 7 percent per annum for those aged 45-49.

---

[1] The Total Fertility Rate (TFR) is the number of births a woman would have, were she to experience the age-specific rates of a given period. The equation for the TFR is: (ΣASFR x 5).

[2] Age Specific Fertility Rate (ASFR) is the number of births in a year, to women of each age group. The equation for the ASFR is:
(the number of births in a year to women aged (x) to (x+5)/(Total women aged x to (x+5)) x 1000.

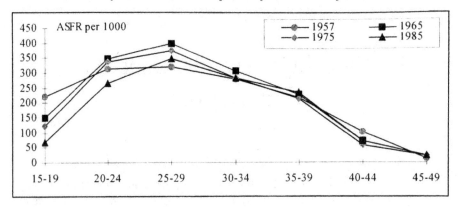

Figure 4.1　Kuwaiti Age Specific Fertility Rates (ASFR): 1967-1989
Source: Kuwaiti Statistical Abstracts, various years

Similarly, Bahraini fertility declined across the age groups between 1983 and 1990 (Figure 4.2): the greatest annual decline was by 7 percent amongst the 15-19 year olds, and the slowest annual decline was by 1 percent for those aged 30-39, and those over 45. The fertility rates for other age groups also decreased: by 4 percent for those aged 20-24, by 2 percent for those aged 25-29 and by 3 percent for those aged 40-44.

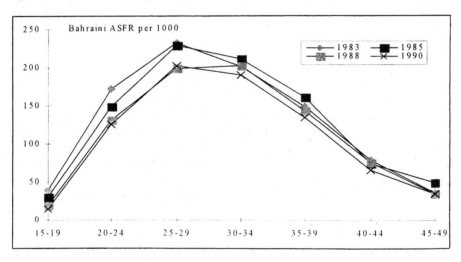

Figure 4.2　Bahraini Age Specific Fertility Rates (ASFR): 1983-1990
Source: Kuwaiti Statistical Abstracts. various years

Yet, while Gulf fertility trends have been declining, current fertility levels are still high. The average TFR of 4.8 children per woman is especially striking when compared to TFRs from other countries in the same 'income' category.[3] Figure 4.3 shows that all countries with per capita GNPs over $5000 register TFRs of at or below replacement level.

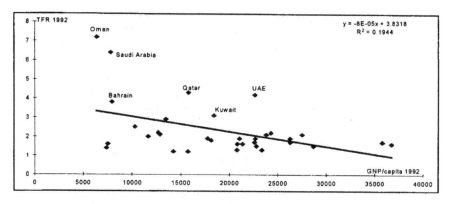

Figure 4.3 Association between TFR and GNP per Capita
Source: World Bank 1993. All countries of the world with GNP/capita higher than $5000 that have TFR registered have been included in chart, though not necessarily labeled, includes mainly developed countries.

Furthermore, the Gulf States are relatively 'modern', in terms of educational attainment, infrastructural development, living standards (Table 4.1). If the Demographic Transition theory applied in the Gulf States, then their fertility levels should be lower.

Table 4.1 Comparative Development Indicators

	Bahrain	Kuwait	Qatar	UAE	Saudi	Oman	High Income
Life Expectancy	77	76	74	75	72	73	78
Urban population	88	100	91	86	86	72	79
Primary School Enrollment (net)	98	87	94	98	n/a	86	97
Improved Sanitation	100	98	100	n/a	n/a	92	100
GDP Growth (% annual)	3	n/a	n/a	10	1	n/a	2
Paved Roads (% of total)	77	81	90	100	30	30	91

Source: UNICEF Statistical Abstract. World Bank Database, 2000

---

[3] World Bank. (2000). World Economic Datasheets. Internet url: www.worldbank.org.

Explaining Gulf Fertility Anomalies

Bongaart's Proximate approach quantifies the individual level variables, contraception, marriage and breastfeeding, involved in Gulf fertility. Since abortions are illegal in the Gulf, unless it is considered to seriously affect the mother's physical health, the Gulf Family Health Surveys did not incorporate any information about it, and it is assumed to be non-existent (=1) in this analysis. Table 4.2 highlights that in most of the Gulf States, post-partum abstinence is an important variable. Contraceptive use is significant particularly in Oman, Qatar, Saudi Arabia and the UAE. Marriage levels are important in Oman, Saudi Arabia and the UAE.

Table 4.2 Proximate Determinants of Gulf Fertility

	TFR	Marriage[4]	Contraception	Post Partum Infecundability
Bahrain	3.2	0.47	0.49	0.63
Qatar	3.9	0.49	0.60	0.83
Kuwait	4.1	0.56	0.54	0.90
UAE	4.9	0.60	0.76	0.72
Saudi Arabia	5.7	0.61	0.69	0.70
Oman	7.1	0.74	0.80	0.46
Average	4.8	0.58	0.65	0.71

Furthermore, the index of Contraception, C_c, highlights another paradox (Figure 4.3): Bahrain with the highest level of contraceptive prevalence[5] (evidence of a motivation for fertility regulation), has the lowest use effectiveness[6] (evidence of either continual contraceptive failure, or reliance on traditional or ineffective techniques).

---

[4] Bongaarts identified five countries with 'exceptionally high' C_m proportions: Pakistan (0.79), Syria (0.73), Turkey (0.76), Kenya (0.77), Jordan (0.75), and Hutterites (0.73). Bongaarts, J. (1987). The Proximate Determinants of Exceptionally High Fertility. *Population and Development Review*, 13(1), March, 133-139.

[5] Proportion of currently married women currently using contraceptives.

[6] The reduction in the monthly probability of conception due to the use of contraceptives. Since estimates of e are difficult to obtain, and rarely available, the standard method-specific values (adapted from data from the Philippines) are used in the calculation of average effectiveness levels in developing countries: Sterilisation 1, IUD 0.95, Pill 0.9, Other 0.7, Withdrawal 0.7, Condom 0.616. Bongaarts, J. (1982). *Studies in Family Planning*, 13(6/7), June-July, 187.

Table 4.3 Contraceptive Use Effectiveness and Prevalence (2000)

	Use effectiveness (e)[7]	Prevalence (u)[8]
Bahrain	0.76	0.62
Qatar	0.85	0.43
Kuwait	0.86	0.50
UAE	0.87	0.26
Saudi Arabia	0.88	0.33
Oman	0.84	0.22
Average	0.84	0.39

Further clues to the factors underlying Gulf fertility levels are obtained through quantifying the proportion of 'wanted' births. Bongaarts' operationalization of the Easterlin model shows that of the 4.19 observed births in Bahrain, 2.9 were wanted and 1.29 were unwanted. The proportionate reduction from the natural fertility level of 9.29, that was due to contraception was 0.45, with a I_p index of 0.79.[9] However, Bongaarts warned that errors of the order of 0.1 or 0.2 births per woman in observed total fertility are common, and errors of similar magnitude for wanted fertility. Errors are larger for natural fertility due to natural fertility being calculated from observed fertility by dividing by a factor C which is always smaller than 1. I_p also contains errors because it is derived form natural observed and wanted fertility: the second decimal is less than fully reliable.[10] Despite this, the Author's Survey support this finding in Bahrain (Figure 4.4): Bahraini women tend to plan their first four births only. After this threshold, few births seem to be planned.[11]

---

[7] The reduction in the monthly probability of conception due to the use of contraceptives. Average (e) is estimated as the weighted average of the method specific use effectiveness levels e(m) with the weights equal to the proportion of women using a given method $u_{(m)}$: $e = \Sigma e_{(m)} u_m/u$

[8] Proportion of currently married women currently using contraceptives.

[9] $C = 1 - 1.02$(percent women contracepting = 53.8 percent) = 0.45124
F_n = Observed Fertility/C = 4.19/0.45124 = 9.286
Wanted fertility = (Births to women not wanting more = 2.33) + 1.09 - (women wanting more births = 0.52) = 2.9
$I_p = (F_n-F)(F_n-F_w) = (9.286-4.19)/(9.286-2.9) = 0.798$
Unwanted Fertility = $(F_n-F_w)(1-I_p) = (9.286-2.9)(1-0.7979) = 1.29$

[10] Bongaarts, J. (1990). The Measurement of Wanted Fertility. *Population and Development Review*, 16(3), 487-506.

[11] This finding could be a function of the age of the mother: those women with fewer than four children were of the older age groups.

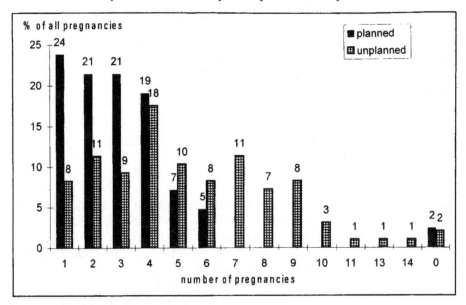

Figure 4.4 Relationship between Planning and the Number of Births in Bahrain (1994)
Source: Nadeya Mohammed, Bahraini KAP Survey, 1994

Human fertility is controlled by cultural norms about family size and other related matters (for example, marriage, abortion, contraception) which correspond to the number which maximizes the net utility to be derived from having children.[12] This depends on the socioeconomic and political structure, and family organization patterns.

Islamic Influence

Gulf marriage and fertility rates are closely related, since it is only within the institution of marriage that childbearing can occur: theoretically, to ensure a secure, stable system in which childrearing can occur. Islam commends the virtues of marriage, regarding it as 'sunna', the way of the Prophet, as protection against illicit sexuality, and completion of half of the religion. The median age at marriage in the Gulf States averaged 17.3 years: 20 in Kuwait, 19 in Bahrain and Qatar, 16 in Saudi Arabia and UAE, 15 in Oman.[13] The median age at first birth averaged 19

---

[12] Freedman. R. (1975). *The Sociology of Human Fertility.* New York: John Wiley and Sons.

[13] Rashood, R., Alnesef, Y., and Farid, S. (2000). *Kuwait Family Health Survey.* Council of Health Ministers of GCC States. Naseeb, T., and S. Farid. (2000). *Bahrain Family Health*

years: 17 in Oman, 18 for Saudi Arabia, 21 for Bahrain and Qatar, 19 in UAE. This implies that nearly all Gulf women are at risk of pregnancy for all their reproductive lives.

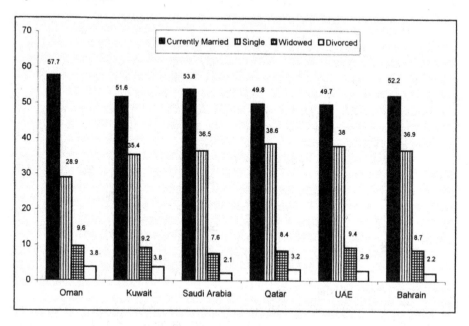

Figure 4.5 Marital Distribution of Gulf Women aged 15+
Source: Gulf Family Health Surveys, 2000

Further, to ensure that marriage as an institution prevails even in adverse conditions, war, famine, or other disasters when the probability of a demographic imbalance and hence the single state increases (specifically, when the ratio of females to males increases), Islam has allowed polygamy:

> And if you fear that you will not deal justly with the orphans, then marry what women are pleasing you: two, three, or four; and if you fear that you will not deal fairly, then take one or what your right hand owns (i.e., slaves).

Survey. Council of Health Ministers of GCC States. Suleiman, A.J.M., Al Riyami, A., and S. Farid. (2000). *Oman Family Health Survey.* Council of Health Ministers of GCC States. Fikri, M., and S. Farid. (2000). *United Arab Emirates Family Health Survey.* Council of Health Ministers of GCC States. Khoja, T.A., and S. Farid. (2000). *Saudi Arabia Family Health Survey.* Council of Health Ministers of GCC States. Jaber, K.A., and S. Farid. (2000). *Qatar Family Health Survey.* Council of Health Ministers of GCC States.

In fact, polygamy is higher in the Gulf than anywhere else in the Middle East: of all married women aged less than 50, nine percent in Kuwait, 19 percent in Saudi Arabia, eight percent in Bahrain and Qatar, 11 percent in Oman, 14.5 percent in the UAE were in polygamous relationships (that is, they had at least one co-wife).

Divorce is 'the most detested of all the permitted' rulings, and is a prolonged and expensive process (as the dowry is lost to the woman), ensuring that time is 'bought' for reconciliation. The mean age of the 'Widowed/Divorced' female population in Bahrain was 29 years, in Kuwait it was 27, and in Oman it was 32. For a marriage to be revoked, the husband must repudiate his wife thrice: he is encouraged to reconcile with his wife on the first two occasions when there is a delay of three months. After the third time, the woman has to remarry and then be divorced before she can return to her first husband.

Finally, Islam encourages remarriage: the Prophet was the prime example of this: all but one of his nine wives were divorcees or widows. Of those Gulf women whose first marriages were dissolved, 70 percent in Oman, 65 percent in Saudi Arabia, 54 percent in Bahrain and the UAE, 44 percent in Qatar and 39 percent in Kuwait remarried. Therefore, Islam ensures that young people get married young, and stay married for the larger proportion of their lives.

Yet, while Islam supports marriage, Islamic teachings per se, have little in them that would prohibit fertility regulation. While many interpretations, some less liberal than others, of Islam's stance on fertility regulation and birth control exist,[14] nearly all theologians agree that the question of birth control depends on circumstantial necessities. If an individual's circumstances warrant its practice, then Islam does not object to its adoption, so long as the practice of family planning is voluntary, optional and not achieved by compulsion, and only safe, legal methods are used. Further, it is recommended that once the family's circumstances improve, contraceptive use should be abandoned.[15] Therefore, family planning in Islam is an individual, personal matter, and can be defined as maintaining intervals between conceptions under valid conditions that necessitate it. The techniques should not be harmful, constitute abortion and nor mean the permanent cessation of procreation.[16]

The Fatwa (Islamic ruling) on 'Birth Control if Advantageous' referred to Hadiths which permitted coitus interruptus, and allowed the usage of oral

---

[14] We will only highlight those views on which there is universal agreement.

[15] Omran, A. (1992). *Family Planning in the Legacy of Islam*. London, New York: Routeledge. Omran, A. (1973). Islam and Fertility Control. In A. Omran (Ed.), *Egypt: Population Problems and Prospects*. Chapel Hill: University of North Carolina, Carolina Population Centre. Also, Sabiq, S. (1957). *Fiqh al Sunnah*. Cairo: House of Arab Writers Press (Arabic).

[16] Lenski, G. (1961). *The Religious Factor*. New York: Doubleday/Anchor Books. Also. Sabiq, S. (1957). *Fiqh al Sunnah*. Cairo: House of Arab Writers Press (Arabic).

contraceptives, especially when there is a pressing necessity for their use.[17] Other theologians have permitted usage of contraceptives

> if the woman is too weak or has been continually delivering children or if the person is poor.[18]

Imam Ghazali further added the case of a woman who fears damage to her beauty.[19] Others argue it is 'preferable' referring to the Quranic verse

> He hath not laid upon you any hardship in religion.[20]

Sheikh Nadeem Al Jasr, the Grand Mufti of Tripoli, and member of the Islamic Research Academy, Al Azhar, Cairo, upheld the freedom of married couples in controlling the number of children they want, as long as they were satisfied and mutually agreed upon their action. The Prophet (PBUH) actually mentioned birth control, and specifically coitus interruptus.[21]

However, with respect to abortion the views are more contentious. Sunnis permit abortion, which they consider 'disliked though permissible', under certain restrictions of the conditions under and timing at which it can be performed. Some theologians permit it to within 120 days before 'life is instilled into the foetus',[22] others before any foetal movement (that is, within the first 40 days) and in certain cases, within the first trimester.[23] All approve of abortion if the mother's life or health are endangered by the pregnancy. Other more liberal Imams allow abortion if the pregnancy affects the health of a woman's other children, or to ensure better living standards for the family.[24] All agree that abortion cannot be used as a means of birth control: the pregnancy must have occurred by mistake and cannot be used

---

[17] 'El Liwa al Islam' fatwa (130 Hijri (1951)).

[18] Sabiq, S. (1957). *Fiqh al Sunnah*. Cairo: House of Arab Writers Press (Arabic).

[19] 'El Liwa al Islam' fatwa (130 Hijri (1951)).

[20] Ali, Y. (1975). *The Holy Qur'an*. New York: Islamic Foundation and the Muslim Student's Association. Sura 23: Verse 78.

[21] An example of one such Hadith is: A man who went to the Prophet and claimed that 'I have a slave girl and I practice withdrawal with her. I dislike her becoming pregnant, yet I have the desires of men. The Jews believe that withdrawal constitutes killing a life in miniature form.' The Prophet (PBUH) replied 'If God wishes to create it you can never change it'.

[22] Sheikh Ahmed Ibrahim in International Planned Parenthood Federation, Arab World Region. (1992). *Unsafe Abortion and Sexual Health in the Arab World: the Damascus Conference* England: KPC.

[23] Roudi, N. (1988). Demography of Islam. *Population Today*, 16(3).

[24] Goldziher, I. (1981). *Introduction to Islamic Theology and Law*. Princeton: Princeton University Press.

in the case of criminal activities or adultery.[25] Shi'as, on the other hand, prohibit it in every case.[26]

Islam's stance on sterilization is similarly contentious.   Most Sunni theologians forbid its use[27] mainly because it constitutes disabling or ending the continuity of human progeny. Others believe that sterilization is permissible if a woman's husband approves.[28] Shi'as permit it for persons suffering from incurable mental, psychological and sexual diseases, especially if they are infectious and/or hereditary.

Therefore, Islam contributes to Gulf fertility indirectly through its support for early marriage which has the effect of frequently exposing Gulf women to the risk of repeated pregnancies, over their entire reproductive lifespan. However, it cannot be argued that Islam contributes to high fertility through imposing restrictions on the use of family planning. Therefore, further explanations must be sought in the social and economic context.

Tribal Politics

The Proximate variable approach identified marriage as a significant determinant of Gulf fertility, particularly for Oman and Saudi Arabia:[29] the more tribal of the six Gulf States.[30]

The rulers and the majority of the population in the Gulf States trace their lineage to one tribe or the other. The 'Utub confederacy comprised many tribes (including al Sabah, al Khalifa, al Jalahima, Dawasir, Ben Ali) who were descendant from Jamilah, a branch of the Great Anazah tribe. In the seventeenth century, severe drought forced their migration from the Southern Central Arabia to

[25] Dr. Mohammed Said Ramadan Al Boutti in International Planned Parenthood Federation, Arab World Region. (1992). *Unsafe Abortion and Sexual Health in the Arab World: the Damascus Conference.* (p. 10). England: KPC.

[26] Moomen, M. (1985). *An Introduction to Shi'i Islam.* Oxford: George Ronald. Stubbs, G.M. (1980). Population Policy in the Arab Countries. In A. Omran (Ed.), *Population in the Arab World.* New York: UNFPA.

[27] Nazer, I. (1974). *Induced Abortion: A Hazard to Public Health?* (p. 490). Beirut: Aleph Publishers.

[28] Omran, A. (1992). *Family Planning in the Legacy of Islam.* London, New York: Routeledge.

[29] Registered for other countries listed by Bongaarts: Pakistan (0.78), Syria (0.73), Turkey (0.76), Kenya (0.77), Jordan (0.74), and Hutterites (0.73). Bongaarts, J. (1987). The Proximate Determinants of Exceptionally High Fertility. *Population and Development Review,* 13(1), March, 133-139.

[30] Al Baharna, H. (1968). *The Legal Status of the Arabian Gulf States.* Manchester: Manchester University Press.

the Gulf coasts near Qatar, and then on to Kuwait where they remained until 1766. The Khalifa branch then migrated and established themselves in Zubara (Qatar). In 1782, the 'Utub of Zubara and Kuwait attacked Bahrain and took over from Shaikh Nasr Al Madhkur (the Persian Empire governor) and hence the Khalifas became established in Bahrain. Disputes amongst the Khalifas led to a branch returning to Zubara and ruling as the Khalifa al Thanis in what later became known as Qatar. The Qawasim of the Emirates were the pirates, merchants and smugglers of the Trucial Coast,[31] whilst the Bu Said dynasty (to which Qaboos belongs) headed the large maritime force which conquered Zanzibar over a hundred years ago. As for Saudi Arabia: it is the only State in the world to be named after the ruling family: the Al Sauds who conquered the main towns of the Arabian Peninsula from the Ibn Rashid tribe in the 1800s.[32]

Within this tribal social context, marriage is a critical means of strengthening intertribal alliances, and used regularly by the ruling Sheikh families. Ibn Saud, the founder of Saudi Arabia, used marriage as a political strategy to ensure the support of the dominant tribes in the Peninsula whilst he was trying to unite it under his rule in the early 1900s. More recently, the ruling family of the UAE has intermarried with that of Qatar, and the al Sabahs of Kuwait with the al Sauds of Saudi Arabia, the al Khalifas of Bahrainis with the al Maktoums of the UAE. The leading merchant families also have members dispersed across the six States: the Kanoos belong to the Hawala tribe and have members in Bahrain, Saudi Arabia, Emirates; the Dawasir have family members in Bahrain, Kuwait, Qatar and Saudi Arabia.[33] Sharing common desert boundaries, which are still disputed, intensifies the need to strengthen ties through marriage to minimize the risks of confrontation.

At the 'non-sheikh' (general populace) level, this underlying ideology – of using marriage to strengthen familial alliances and extended family network – prevails. The proportion of consanguineous marriages is high: on average, 42 percent of all married couples in the Gulf States are related to each other: 54 percent in Oman, 52 percent in Saudi Arabia, 45 percent in Qatar, 40 percent in UAE, 36 percent in Kuwait, 31 percent in Bahrain.[34] Such unions reinforce the

---

[31] Heard-Bey, F. (1982). *From Trucial States to United Arab Emirates: A Society in Transition.* Longman Group Ltd, Essex.

[32] Abu-Hakima, A.M. (1972). The Development of the Gulf States. In Derek Hopwood (Ed.), *The Arabian Peninsula: Society and Politics* (pp.41-44). London: George Allen and Unwin Ltd.

[33] Field, M. (1984). *The Merchants: The Big Business Families of Arabia.* London: John Murray (Publishers) Ltd.

[34] Rashood, R.. Alnesef, Y., and Farid, S. (2000). *Kuwait Family Health Survey.* Council of Health Ministers of GCC States. Naseeb, T., and S. Farid. (2000). *Bahrain Family Health Survey.* Council of Health Ministers of GCC States. Suleiman, A.J.M., Al Riyami, A., and S. Farid. (2000). *Oman Family Health Survey.* Council of Health Ministers of GCC States.

solidarity of the extended family and imply that couples will marry young as they know each other already. It also translates into a lower probability of marital disputes and disruption through divorce, given that the marriage would involve other family members.

This tribal ethic also underlies the patrimonial social system prevalent across the Gulf States. None of the Gulf States have enforced a minimum legal age for marriage (other than the Shari'a minimum of 'at puberty' or 'first means'), and the UAE and Kuwait encourage marriage and high fertility through their many pronatalist policies: allowances for dowries, fully paid honeymoon vacations, child and maternity benefits, subsidized housing and loans for marriage.

Such a pronatalist framework positively impacts fertility, through its implication for accessibility to family planning, and to an extent explains the low contraceptive prevalence rates identified by the proximate approach. Bahrain and (since 1990) Oman are the only Gulf States that lend direct official support for contraceptive usage. Hence in most Gulf States, only a limited range of contraceptives are available in commercial outlets (since 1976, none have been available in Saudi Arabia) and known about. The morning-after Pill, diaphragms, sponges and Norplant are not available. There is limited (if any) family planning counseling or support facilities: the only Family Planning Association in the Gulf (in Bahrain), merely trains nurses at the local College of Medicine and Nursing and its major activity has been educating mothers and pregnant women about nutrition, rather than fertility regulation.[35]

Therefore, while some information about family planning may be disseminated, it is irregular, biased and may fail to reach the majority of the population. The scarcity of family planning information, implies that Gulf couples may not always appreciate the mechanism by which contraceptives work (which is vital for their proper usage), as any knowledge that they may have on family planning would have been gleaned from other peers or their mothers:[36] 93 percent of the Author's Survey respondents in Bahrain obtained information through family and friends rather than doctors or medical personnel.[37] Therefore, it is questionable that their appreciation of the mechanism by which contraceptives work (which is vital for their proper usage) is precise. For example, usage directions on condom packs are in English, a language that few are fully proficient in (97.4 percent of Bahrainis purchased condoms from commercial outlets, where usage instructions are not

Fikri, M., and S. Farid. (2000). *United Arab Emirates Family Health Survey*. Council of Health Ministers of GCC States. Khoja, T.A., and S. Farid (2000). *Saudi Arabia Family Health Survey*. Council of Health Ministers of GCC States. Jaber, K.A., and S. Farid. (2000). *Qatar Family Health Survey*. Council of Health Ministers of GCC States.

[35] *Gulf Daily News*. 13 January 1992.

[36] The impact of the internet on this has yet to be ascertained.

[37] Mohammed, Nadeya. (1994). The Effect of Fertility on the Development of Bahrain. Unpublished M.Phil. Dissertation, Oxford University.

usually given). The main problem that the Survey respondents complained about were of condoms splitting (indicative of improper use, not unfortunate mishap) and of getting pregnant while being on the contraceptive Pill (most of whom had stopped taking the pill in the middle of the cycle, then practiced rhythm or withdrawal).[38]

Disillusionment with contraceptives, due to recurring failure of the methods used, may actually reduce motivation, especially as contraceptives are used primarily to minimize the health risks posed by successive pregnancies, to provide higher standards of living and care for the other children rather than to achieve a particular desired Completed Family Size. Such factors may to a large extent, explain the contraceptive ineffectiveness identified in Bahrain.

Social Context: Gendered Inequalities

The third key feature of the Gulf States, with a direct impact on fertility, is the Gendered stratification system.

Reproduction lies at the core of the gender stratification system in the Gulf, since it defines the identity of both men and women. Underpinning the desire for children is the completion of the self, given that children serve as primary ego extension for fathers and mothers, who view their children as their memory in life and after death. Motherhood is a woman's most important role and primary mission in life, at the very essence of her identity, stemming from the God given maternal instinct: the primordial 'natural' drive fuelling her maternal desires and her capacity to care for and love her children for her entire life. Only through motherhood can a woman achieve a complete social construction/identity, as a whole person with a productive worthwhile status, with a sexual identity as a female, with the proper parts, processes, and inclinations, and a gender identity as a woman who has passed beyond the transitional state of newlywedness to assume the normal rights duties and responsibilities of womanhood: Omani post partum visiting rituals have been found to encourage reproduction because they ensure continued social interest in a woman.

Furthermore, the Gulf production or budgetary unit includes a wide group of relatives: household income is not merely that earned by the household head, but also monies contributed by other employed family members, even those not necessarily physically residing in the same house (a family is an economic entity not a residential one).[39] Even among urban business families, successful

---

[38] Mohammed, Nadeya. (1994). The Effect of Fertility on the Development of Bahrain. Unpublished M.Phil. Dissertation, Oxford University.

[39] Caldwell, J. (1993). Routes to Low Mortality in Poor Countries. *Population and Development Review*, 12(2), 171-220.

commercial enterprise is often structured on the extended family.[40]   Therefore, fertility control remains improbable as long as the nuclear family remains a subunit of a larger economic unit: relatives may regard it as their right to exert effective pressure towards higher fertility or against fertility limitation.

Such is the social significance of reproduction, that spinsters and infertile women are pitied and marginalized, and infertility is sufficient justification for remarriage and/or divorce.   Of all the Bahraini divorces in 1992, 56 percent occurred within two years, and 76 percent of these were amongst childless couples.[41]   This threat of divorce, given that a man has the right to repudiate a marriage and/or remarry, is sufficient reason to reduce motivation to contracept (Figure 4.6).[42]   The Author's survey found that of currently married non-contracepting Bahraini women who did not intend to use contraception because their husband opposed, 12 percent were less than 25 years, 33 percent were 25-34, 49 percent were 35-44, and 7 percent were 45-49.[43]

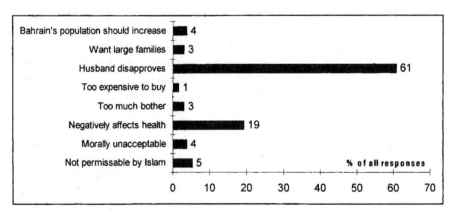

Figure 4.6 Reasons for Bahraini Women not Using Contraceptives (1994)
Source: Nadeya Mohammed, Bahraini KAP Survey, 1994

---

[40] Field, M. (1984). *The Merchants: The Big Business Families of Arabia*. London: John Murray (Publishers) Ltd.

[41] *Bahrain Statistical Abstract.* (1991).

[42] Mohammed, Nadeya. (1994). The Effect of Fertility on the Development of Bahrain. Unpublished M.Phil. Dissertation, Oxford University.

[43] Rashood, R., Alnesef, Y., and Farid. S. (2000). *Kuwait Family Health Survey*. Council of Health Ministers of GCC States. Naseeb, T., and S. Farid. (2000). *Bahrain Family Health Survey*. Council of Health Ministers of GCC States. Suleiman, A.J.M., Al Riyami, A., and S. Farid. (2000). *Oman Family Health Survey*. Council of Health Ministers of GCC States. Fikri, M., and S. Farid. (2000). *United Arab Emirates Family Health Survey*. Council of Health Ministers of GCC States. Khoja, T.A., and S. Farid. (2000). *Saudi Arabia Family Health Survey*. Council of Health Ministers of GCC States. Jaber, K.A., and S. Farid. (2000). *Qatar Family Health Survey*. Council of Health Ministers of GCC States.

As Figure 4.7 illustrates, the distribution of contraceptive use by years since first marriage reflects this relationship: recently married women, and those who have been married for less than five years, and hence need to 'confirm' their identity, are least likely to use contraception.

Furthermore, the ideology of 'motherhood' may also affect the type of contraception that a woman may choose. Not only are abortions shunned for religious reasons, but the social stigma that would be attached to a mother who would resort to such measures is a strong deterrent. That abortions are not a contraceptive option is demographically important, because it implies that if 'accidental' pregnancies were to occur, they cannot be terminated.[44]

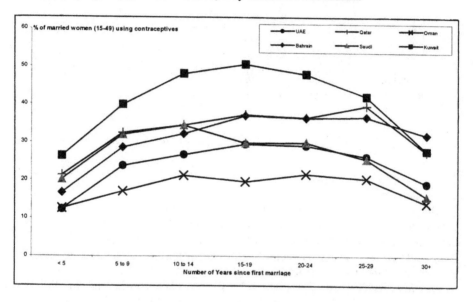

Figure 4.7 Age Specific Contraceptive Use Amongst Married Gulf Women
Source: Gulf Family Health Survey, 2000

The Author's survey discussed the circumstances under which Bahraini women could contemplate aborting a fetus (Figure 4.8).

---

[44] Regardless of Abortion's legal and religious status, it does exist in the Muslim/Arab world. Illegal (and hence unsafe) Abortions in the Arab World was the subject of major IPPF conference held in Damascus in December 1992. Gulf women will resort to abortion (using abdominal massages, herbal or spicy drinks) if they feel compelled to terminate a pregnancy though usually as a last resort. The fact that it is not publicized (for social and legal reasons) does not negate its importance as a factor in fertility regulation. Refer International Planned Parenthood Federation Arab World Region. (1993). *Unsafe Abortion and Sexual Health in the Arab World.* England: KPC.

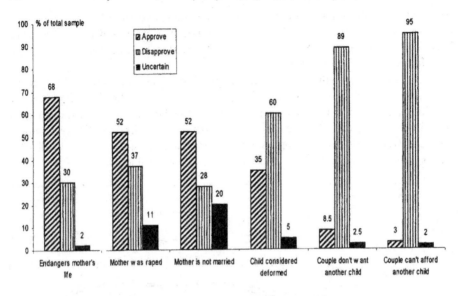

Figure 4.8 Circumstances Under Which Bahraini Women Approve of Abortion

Source: Nadeya Mohammed, Bahraini KAP Survey, 1994

Finally, given that Gulf States lack the formal institutions and facilities for caring for the aged, it is a universal expectation that it is the children's duty to take care of their aged relatives. Hence, women particularly gain from having many children, as they would ensure a means of support in old age. Children are essential to parental security in other ways: financial support in old age, physical security, enhance social status and authority. Therefore, for a large proportion of Gulf families, the direction and magnitude of the inter generational wealth flows[45] is upwards. If Caldwell's theory applies in the Gulf, then we would expect the fertility to decline only when the balance shifts from this upward flow regime to net flows of wealth from parents to children, since only under these conditions can fertility decline be economically rational. This shift can only occur if the social transition to the emotional nucleation of the family takes place or a 'modern' view of the family is adopted: when the emotional bonds and obligations are stronger between conjugal partners and their offspring than with other relatives, acquaintances or institutions.

Therefore, relative to the benefits of family planning, the costs of contraception and fertility regulation in the Gulf States are much higher than the benefits derived from reproducing – therefore contributing further to the explanation of high Gulf fertility.

---

[45] Caldwell, J.C. (1982). *Theory of Fertility Decline.* London: Academic Press.

Rentier Economics

There are few individual level costs to child bearing and rearing in the Gulf States, given the generous welfare system, free health and education services, tax-free status and allowance structure. Within such a context, Gulf nationals may not feel the need to limit fertility.

The oil price hike of 1973-1974, and the governments' equity participation in oil production, laid down the foundations of the rentier States of the Gulf.[46] Rentier economies depend on external sources of income, oil 'rent'[47] as oil fields (found in certain geographical regions only) are not open to the market for purchase and sale, are subject to monopoly ownership and are ultimately fixed in supply. Therefore, national income is procured by selling a commodity at prices above production costs, rather than being produced by the population. Hence, national income is determined by decisions beyond the population's control,[48] and its increase does not reflect a strengthening of the domestic economy. Gulf economic growth was 'bought' with oil income, depends on international oil prices and its rate is independent of the relationship existing between investment and output (marginal or incremental capital to output ratio). In fact, the oil sector adds considerably to the GDP[49] and GNP[50] without any additional fixed investment (small capital to output ratio or capital coefficient) so long as the extra production falls within its production capacity.[51] Therefore, increases in GDP or GNP do not reflect rapid progress up the (usually slow) 'development' hierarchy.[52]

Such an economic system relates to Gulf fertility in many ways. First of all, Gulf governments managed, within a short span of time to convert their barren

---

[46] Beblawi, H. (1987). The Rentier State in the Arab World. In H. Beblawi and G. Luciani, (Eds.), *The Rentier State* (pp. 49-52). Kent: Croom Helm Ltd.

[47] Marshall, A. (1984). *Principles of Economics* (p. 350). London: Macmillan.

[48] Chatelus, M. (1987). Policies for Development: Attitudes Toward Industry and Services. In Hazem Beblawi and G. Luciani (Eds.), *The Rentier State* (pp. 108-138). Kent: Croom Helm.

[49] Gross Domestic Product: the total final output of goods and services produced by residents and non residents within the State territories, regardless of its allocation between domestic and foreign claims.

[50] Gross National Product: the total domestic and foreign output claimed by residents of a State. GNP= GDP + {(factor incomes accruing to residents from abroad for factor services eg labour and capital) - (income earned in the domestic economy accruing to foreign persons)}. It is the total domestic and foreign value added, claimed by a country's residents, without deducting for depreciation of the domestic capital stock.

[51] Luciani, G. (1987). Allocation vs. Production States: A Theoretical Framework. In H. Beblawi and G. Luciani (Eds.), *The Rentier State* (pp. 69-70). Kent: Croom Helm.

[52] Sayigh, Y.A. (1991). *Elusive Development: From Dependence to Self Reliance in the Arab Region.* London, USA and Canada: Routledge, Chapman and Hall, Inc.

desert landscapes into modern urban cities. This entailed, with some lag time, changes in lifestyle, previously not experienced in the precarious environment of pearl diving and smuggling: urbanization, better nutrition, salaried employment, economic security, subsidized utilities, generous allowances and welfare systems.

On the one hand, this has had a positive impact on fertility, through the effect of such changes on breastfeeding patterns. Increased urbanization and education has worked to reduce the duration of breastfeeding: the difference in breastfeeding duration between rural and urban mothers averaged 3.7 months across the Gulf States in the 1989 Survey, and this reduced to 1.4 months by the 2000 Survey.[53] Figure 4.8 shows the difference by education: illiterate Gulf mothers breastfed their children for 14 months, while those mothers with secondary school and above level education breastfed their children for 10 months.[54]

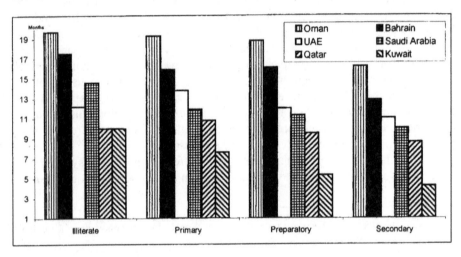

Figure 4.9 Mean Duration of Breastfeeding by Maternal Education Level
Source: Gulf Family Health Survey, 2000

---

[53] Rashood, R., Alnesef, Y., and Farid, S. (2000). *Kuwait Family Health Survey*. Council of Health Ministers of GCC States. Naseeb, T., and S. Farid. (2000). *Bahrain Family Health Survey*. Council of Health Ministers of GCC States. Suleiman, A.J.M., Al Riyami, A., and S. Farid. (2000). *Oman Family Health Survey*. Council of Health Ministers of GCC States. Fikri, M.. and S. Farid. (2000). *United Arab Emirates Family Health Survey*. Council of Health Ministers of GCC States. Khoja, T.A.. and S. Farid. (2000). *Saudi Arabia Family Health Survey*. Council of Health Ministers of GCC States. Jaber, K.A.. and S. Farid. (2000). *Qatar Family Health Survey*. Council of Health Ministers of GCC States.

[54] The Authors' KAP Survey obtained similar results for Breastfeeding: on average Bahraini women breastfed for 10 months. Of those women who breastfed for 10+ months, 64 percent were aged 30-49 and 78 percent of them were educated up to intermediate school level. Mohammed, Nadeya. (1994). The Effect of Fertility on the Development of Bahrain. Unpublished M.Phil. Dissertation, Oxford University.

The provision of public sector employment as a means of distributing the oil rent and incorporating the populace into the system, created a large middle 'class'[55] with significant disposable and tax-free income, while the generous welfare system reduced the costs of living: with free education and health care, subsidized food and utilities.[56] Such an economic system has made the costs of childbearing and rearing to parents minimal.

More specifically, the opportunity costs of child bearing and rearing to women are minimal. Gulf women are, on the whole, voluntarily unemployed: of Bahraini women over the age of 15, 61 percent were classified as housewives, and two percent had no desire to work.[57] For the employed few, maids (employed at salaries averaging $163 per month, primarily as domestic servants and as nannies for any children still at home), minimize the costs of childbearing. For those employed women who cannot afford maids, the extended family network (mainly other females in the family or in-laws) provides the necessary free nursery service. Further, no costs are incurred with respect to career opportunities lost: female employment is primarily in the public sector at the administrative level where salary increases and promotions are virtually guaranteed and various benefits are accorded to mothers, 100 days fully paid maternity leave and six months of breastfeeding time allowances after the maternity leave.

On the other hand, this transition of the Gulf States to modern economies, with its associated increases in education, health status and employment levels, has been the main driving force underlying Gulf fertility declines, limited though these may have been. Higher education[58] reduces fertility levels through broadening ones' horizons, increasing knowledge and breaking down traditional attitudes and beliefs. Theoretically, it affects fertility through delaying the age at marriage, thereby reducing the total possible number of childbearing years. Already this relationship seems clear in the Gulf States where illiterate women have the lowest SMAMs, averaging 18 years, whilst those educated to above intermediate level

---

[55] 'Class' relations in the GCC States are very different from Marxists ones and are therefore placed within inverted commas. As production relations are centred around the exploitation of natural resources by society, the social structure is determined by the relations of the different groups with those who receive the rent (oil revenues): power and wealth can only be acquired through access to oil revenues. Therefore, those who control the source of rent can shape the emerging social stratification structure, as the position of individuals and groups in the social strata is defined by the closeness to the source of rent. Longueness, E. (1984). Petroleum Rent and the Class Structure in the Gulf Countries. *Mediterranean People*, 26.

[56] Economic Intelligence Unit. *Annual Report 1995.*

[57] Bahrain Census, 1991.

[58] Mean schooling quantity attained to be an undifferentiated mass with known and similar influence across all levels and situations, as this would be a fair indicator of fertility, idealized family size, family planning attitude and contraceptive use.

have the highest SMAMs, averaging 23 years.[59] In addition, the mean number of children borne by illiterate women (who are older as well) is on average 2.7 times the number borne by those women educated to secondary+ level.[60] The Author's Survey similarly found that Bahraini women with below secondary school level education were likely to have 3.5 times more, and those educated up to secondary school level were likely to have 2.2 times more children than those educated at above secondary school level.

Furthermore, higher maternal education has worked to lower infant and child mortality rates, and hence, lower overall reproductive levels.[61] The average Gulf infant mortality rate is 18.6 for those with mothers educated up to primary level, as against a rate of 11 for those with mothers with a secondary+ level of education.[62]

---

[59] Rashood, R., Alnesef, Y., and Farid, S. (2000). *Kuwait Family Health Survey*. Council of Health Ministers of GCC States. Naseeb, T., and S. Farid. (2000). *Bahrain Family Health Survey*. Council of Health Ministers of GCC States. Suleiman, A.J.M., Al Riyami, A., and S. Farid. (2000). *Oman Family Health Survey*. Council of Health Ministers of GCC States. Fikri, M., and S. Farid. (2000). *United Arab Emirates Family Health Survey*. Council of Health Ministers of GCC States. Khoja, T.A., and S. Farid. (2000). *Saudi Arabia Family Health Survey*. Council of Health Ministers of GCC States. Jaber, K.A., and S. Farid. (2000). *Qatar Family Health Survey*. Council of Health Ministers of GCC States.

[60] Rashood, R., Alnesef, Y., and Farid, S. (2000). *Kuwait Family Health Survey*. Council of Health Ministers of GCC States. Naseeb, T., and S. Farid. (2000). *Bahrain Family Health Survey*. Council of Health Ministers of GCC States. Suleiman, A.J.M., Al Riyami, A., and S. Farid. (2000). *Oman Family Health Survey*. Council of Health Ministers of GCC States. Fikri, M., and S. Farid. (2000). *United Arab Emirates Family Health Survey*. Council of Health Ministers of GCC States. Khoja, T.A., and S. Farid. (2000). *Saudi Arabia Family Health Survey*. Council of Health Ministers of GCC States. Jaber, K.A., and S. Farid. (2000). *Qatar Family Health Survey*. Council of Health Ministers of GCC States.

[61] This association is not expected to be clear in the Gulf States, as it may also be due to illiterate Gulf women being generally older. Therefore, they would have completed their reproductive cycle, and would have had more children, in contrast to those who are more educated and who would be younger and would not have attain their complete family size yet. In addition, older women would have had children at a time when the medical facilities were not as developed as they are now, whereas the younger ones (who happen to be more educated) have access to closer and better facilities.

[62] Rashood, R., Alnesef, Y., and Farid, S. (2000). *Kuwait Family Health Survey*. Council of Health Ministers of GCC States. Naseeb, T., and S. Farid. (2000). *Bahrain Family Health Survey*. Council of Health Ministers of GCC States. Suleiman, A.J.M., Al Riyami, A., and S. Farid. (2000). *Oman Family Health Survey*. Council of Health Ministers of GCC States. Fikri, M., and S. Farid. (2000). *United Arab Emirates Family Health Survey*. Council of Health Ministers of GCC States. Khoja, T.A., and S. Farid. (2000). *Saudi Arabia Family Health Survey*. Council of Health Ministers of GCC States. Jaber, K.A., and S. Farid. (2000). *Qatar Family Health Survey*. Council of Health Ministers of GCC States.

Higher educated couples are more likely to use contraceptives correctly, have more information regarding contraceptives, and communicate with their spouse regarding fertility regulation and childbearing more openly and be more exposed to mass media and printed materials concerning family planning.[63] Higher educated Gulf women are more likely to be currently using contraceptives than those who are less educated, and were more likely to discuss family size with their husbands (Figure 4.10). Similarly, educated men are less likely to merely value the reproductive role of their wives: Omani women with educated husbands (secondary+ level) were seven times more likely to use contraception, have half the number of children and tended to have gotten married two years later than those with below primary level schooling.[64] In the Author's survey, women with secondary school level husbands were four times more likely than those with illiterate husbands to use contraception.[65]

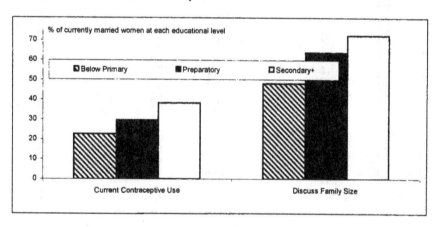

Figure 4.10 Family Planning Usage and Decision Making by Education Level
Source: Gulf Family Health Survey, 2000

---

[63] Freedman, R., Coombs, L.C., Chang, M., and T. Sun. (1974). Trends in Fertility, Family Size Preference, and Practice of Family Planning: Taiwan, 1965-1973. *Studies in Family Planning*, 5(9), September, 270-288.

[64] Rashood, R.. Alnesef, Y., and Farid, S. (2000). *Kuwait Family Health Survey*. Council of Health Ministers of GCC States. Naseeb, T., and S. Farid. (2000). *Bahrain Family Health Survey*. Council of Health Ministers of GCC States. Suleiman, A.J.M., Al Riyami, A., and S. Farid. (2000). *Oman Family Health Survey*. Council of Health Ministers of GCC States. Fikri, M., and S. Farid. (2000). *United Arab Emirates Family Health Survey*. Council of Health Ministers of GCC States. Khoja, T.A., and S. Farid. (2000). *Saudi Arabia Family Health Survey*. Council of Health Ministers of GCC States. Jaber. K.A., and S. Farid. (2000). *Qatar Family Health Survey*. Council of Health Ministers of GCC States.

[65] Mohammed, Nadeya. (1994). The Effect of Fertility on the Development of Bahrain. Unpublished M.Phil. Dissertation, Oxford University.

Education also increases couples' aspirations for upward mobility and wealth accumulation thereby reducing the attraction of large families. Such change also enhances women's prospects for obtaining paid employment, which offer satisfactions alternative to children (for example, companionship, recreation and creative activity or financial remuneration). Educated Gulf women are more likely to be employed, and have fewer children: working Bahraini women had on average three children, whilst non-working women had a mean number of five children (Figure 4.11).

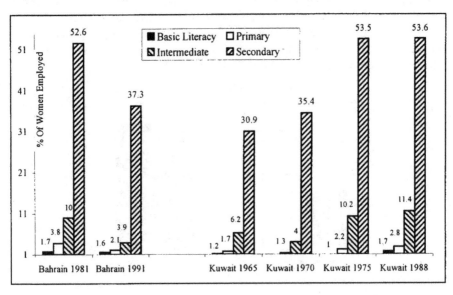

Figure 4.11 Educational Status of Employed Gulf Females
Source: Statistical Abstracts

Concluding Remarks

The changes that the oil wealth instigated, in terms of urbanization, education, employment, contributed towards a reduction in Gulf fertility levels. However, the other associated changes, greater wealth, better health and nutrition, in combination with the social, political and religious norms which lie at the very core of Gulf cultures, have slowed the decline, and to keep fertility levels higher than would be expected for countries at this income and development level.

          The social and cultural system that being 'Islamic' as defined by the patriarchal Gulf governments have built a pronatalist framework, one that promotes the role of a woman as a mother who does not mind sacrificing her life for the benefit of her family, obedient and patient wife. The individualistic career seeking ambitious female who is independent is not encouraged, and both the single woman and the childless wife are openly pitied. The education systems of the Gulf States support this framework, reproducing gender divisions and power relations through a dual system of completely segregated male and female education, a gender specific education policy, that emphasizes women's domestic functions and gender,[66] and curriculum differentiation at the various educational levels.[67]

Therefore, it would be surprising if the pace of fertility decline increased. Any change in attitudes would have to evolve with the next generation that may be more open minded and exposed. In the mean time, marriages continue to be arranged, brides relatively young, bridegrooms up to five years older, and couples tend to be related. Society emphasizes the sexual purity of females, their remaining within the home as mothers and wives. There is strong resistance to the 'emotional nucleation' of the conjugal couple, to changing the old order to a new one and great respect for the family. This is a social context conducive to high fertility which can only change very slowly.

---

[66] The policy issued in 1970, specifies that the 'object of educating a woman is to bring her up in a sound Islamic way so that she can fulfill her role in life as a successful homemaker, an ideal wife, and a good mother, and to prepare her for those jobs which suit her nature, like teaching. nursing and medicine'. Item 53, of the *Educational Policy of Kingdom of Saudi Arabia*. 1970.

[67] El-Sanabary, N. (1994). Female Education in Saudi Arabia and the Reproduction of Gender Divisions. *Gender and Education*, 6(2), 141-150.

PART II
PUBLIC SERVICES AND EMPLOYMENT IN THE ARAB GULF STATES

Chapter 5

Public Services in the Gulf States

Becker called the twentieth century the Age of Human Capital, since that is when development economists recognized a country's success in developing and utilizing the skills, knowledge, health, and habits of its population was the primary determinant of its standard of living. Many studies have shown a close association between growth in per capita incomes since 1960 and human capital measures (e.g., the proportion of the population with elementary school, high school, and higher education, life expectancy, initial per capita incomes in 1960, investments in physical capital). In particular, although on average, developing countries grew a little less rapidly than richer ones, poorer nations with more educated and healthier populations managed to grow faster than the average.[1] Human capital (education, on-the-job and other training and health) has been found to comprise about 80 percent of the capital or wealth in the United States and other advanced countries. Hence, inadequate investment in human capital formation has serious consequences: future productivity losses in agriculture and industry, persistent high fertility, high infant and maternal mortality (especially given low female education levels).[2] This Chapter will consider the human capital achievements of the Gulf States: specifically the trends in various quantitative and qualitative indicators of education and health care.

Educational Achievements of the Gulf States

There are four main reasons for the provision of education services. First, education is a fundamental human right as it encourages individual creativity and improves participation in the socio-economic and cultural roles in society.

---

[1] Becker, G.S. (December 16, 1994). A lecture presented at the World Bank on December 16th. *Human Capital and Poverty Alleviation.*
http://www.worldbank.org/html/extdr/hnp/hddflash/workp/wp_00052.html.
[2] Cochrane, S. (1986). *The Effects of Education on Fertily and Mortality.* Education and Training Paper, EDT 26. Washington D.C.: World Bank.

Education is a pre-requisite not only for the full excise of the individual rights, but also for understanding and respecting the rights of others.[3]

Hence, its role should not be limited to producing skilled manpower, or to judging educational success by the number of children and adults who have 'efficiently consumed a learning package'.[4]

Second, education contributes to improving parental and children's health and nutrition status, thereby reducing (child and maternal) mortality and increasing life expectancies. Such benefits accrue indirectly through increased paternal income, the development of 'modern' attitudes and rationality,[5] and directly through improved access to health care and information regarding preventative medicine. In particular, maternal education is strongly related to infant mortality rates and nutritional status: on average, each maternal schooling year translates into nine per 1000 fewer infant and child deaths.[6] Further, female education influences fertility through its effect on the age at marriage and family planning practices.[7] Educated women marry later, use contraceptives more frequently, want and have fewer children and lose fewer children in the first years of life (through better child spacing, nutrition, hygiene, use of modern health systems and programs (for example, immunization)) more than their uneducated peers.[8] Therefore, women's education is the key to population control, progress along the demographic transition, family health and hygiene, nutrition and children's education.[9]

Third, there are close connections between human resource development or education and economic growth,[10] though this is difficult to demonstrate. In the agricultural sector, primary education has been found to exert an impact on economic productivity[11] through:

---

[3] Address to the International Round Table on 'Today's Children: Tomorrow's World'. Paris, UNESCO. 1989 Mimeo DG/89/12.

[4] Hallak, J. (1990). *UNDP: Investing in the Future: Setting Educational Properties in the Developing World* (p. 45). International Institute for Educational Planning. Pergamon Press.

[5] Inkeles, A. and D. Smith. (1984). *Becoming Modern: Individual Change in Six Developing Countries.* Cambridge, Ma: Harvard University Press.

[6] World Bank. (1986). *Poverty and Human Development.* New York: Oxford University Press.

[7] Cochrane, S. (1986). *The Effects of Education on Fertily and Mortality.* Education and Training Paper, EDT 26. Washington D.C.: World Bank.

[8] United Nations. (1981). *Women's Education and Fertility Relationships in Fourteen World Fertility Survey Countries: Meeting of Experts in Factors Relating to Family and Fertility.* Geneva: United Nations.

[9] Cochrane, S. (1986). *The Effects of Education on Fertily and Mortality.* Education and Training Paper, EDT 26. Washington D.C.: World Bank.

[10] Tilak, J.P.G. (1988). *Education, Economic Growth, Poverty and Income Distribution: a Survey of Evidence and Further Research.* Washington D.C.: World Bank.

[11] Jameson, K.D. (1988). Education's Role in Rural Areas of Latin America. *Economics of Education Review,* 7(3).

   i.   increasing production or interacting with other production factors.
   ii. improving marketability of products through application of effective techniques.
   iii. application of modern practices.

When direct productivity measures are unavailable, earnings could serve as proxy: in developing countries, returns to primary schooling average 27 percent and those to secondary around 15 to 17 percent.[12] Literacy and numeracy alone explain differences in wages of those who have completed secondary school. Historical evidence shows that only after attaining universal primary education (UPE) could the industrialized countries achieve significant economic growth.[13] In addition, the newly industrialized countries (Korea, Singapore, and Hong Kong) and those with fastest growing GNPs (Thailand, Portugal, and Greece) had UPE and near universal literacy just before their economic ascent.[14]

     Finally, participation in the benefits of technological progress and active contribution to technological innovation depends on trained and effectively utilized researchers, engineers, and technicians, without whom assessment of alternatives, appropriate selection and/or application of such choices to their context would not be possible. However, sound and sustained economic development also requires socio-economic regulation, land reform, economic management (for example, in the case of Japan and Korea). Education is therefore, a necessary, through insufficient condition for economic development.

     To develop human resources in the near future, today's instruction and literacy efforts cannot be left to deteriorate. Sustained effort is necessary to increase enrollment and to achieve universal primary education.

Quantitative Educational Achievements

From a long term and quantitative perspective, the story of educational development in the Gulf has been a success. As Table 5.1 reveals, the stock of human capital (that is, the number of literate people) has increased dramatically especially between 1960 and 1970 and amongst the female population:

---

[12] Psacharopoulos, G. (1985). Returns to Education: a Further International Update and Implications. *Journal of Human Resources*, 20(4), 584-604.
[13] Peasle, A. (1965). Elementary Education as a Prerequisite for Economic Growth. *International Development Review*, 7.
[14] World Bank. (1987). *World Development Report*. Oxford: Oxford University Press.

Table 5.1 Per Annum Increases in Literate Population (aged 10+)

Bahrain	Total	Males	Females	Kuwait	Total	Males	Females
1965-71	23.9	19.6	35.7	1957-70	35.6	28.8	62.2
1971-81	17.7	17.9	17.4	1970-75	8.8	7.2	12.2
1981-91	7.3	6.4	8.9	1975-80	12.3	12.5	11.6
UAE				1980-85	8.2	7.2	10.0
1968-75	12.3	11.4	18.1				

Source: UN Demographic Yearbooks (DSSD)

Since 1965, illiteracy rates have also declined, by an average of 25 to 50 percent across the Gulf States (Figure 5.1).

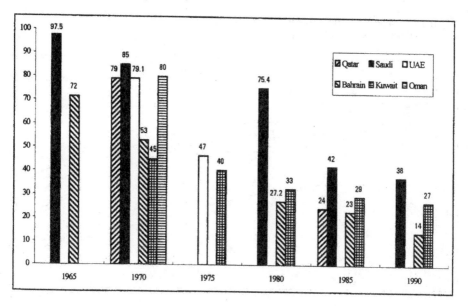

Figure 5.1 Illiterate Population in the Gulf States
Source: UNESCO Statistical Yearbooks

The age specific literacy rates of Bahrainis and Kuwaitis further illustrate the educational achievements over time (Figures 5.2 and 5.3): those aged 10 to 14 enjoy the highest literacy rates (averaging 99 percent in 1990s in comparison to 66 percent in 1970s in Bahrain, and 94 percent verses 78 percent in Kuwait), whilst those aged 40 and above show the lowest rates (averaging 58 percent in 1990s in Bahrain, and 50 percent in Kuwait).

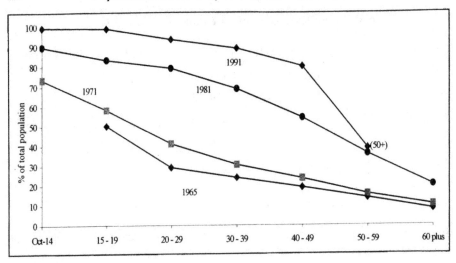

Figure 5.2 Age Specific Literacy Rates in Bahrain
Source: UNESCO Statistical Yearbooks

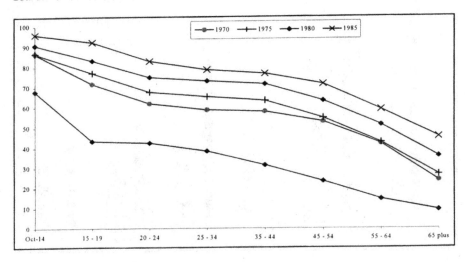

Figure 5.3 Age Specific Literacy Rates in Kuwait
Source: UNESCO Statistical Yearbooks

Another quantitative indicator of educational attainment is school enrollment ratios. While literacy rates essentially measure the effects of the educational system as it was in the past, school enrollment ratios are a measure of the coverage of the system in the present, and represent the additions made to the human capital stock.

Figure 5.4 indicates that First Level Gross Enrollment Ratios (GERs) for both sexes
have attained near universal level in all the Gulf States except for Saudi Arabia.[15]

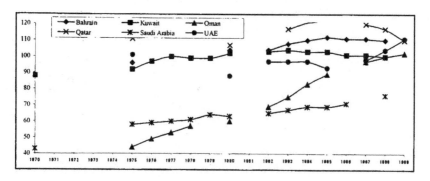

Figure 5.4 First Level Gross Enrollment Ratios in the Gulf States
Source: UNESCO Statistical Yearbooks

In addition, Second Level Enrollments (includes general education, teacher training
and all other second level education), increased by an average of 1 percent per annum
between 1975 and 1993, with Oman attaining the most dramatic increase, at 3 percent
per annum, and Qatar experiencing the lowest increase, at 0.05 percent per annum
(Figure 5.5).

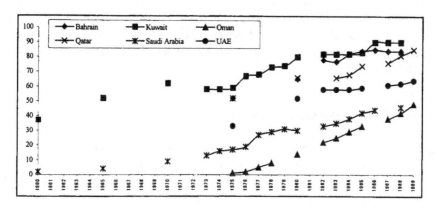

Figure 5.5 Second Level Gross Enrollment Ratios in the Gulf States
Source: UNESCO Statistical Yearbooks

At the third level,[16] the GERs increased by an average of one percent per annum
between 1975 and 1990 (Figure 5.6).

---

[15] The Gross Enrollment Ratios (GERs) exceed 100 percent because the formula includes all
pupils for the numerator and the population in the official school age range for the
denominator: the actual pupil's age distribution spreads over outside the official school ages.

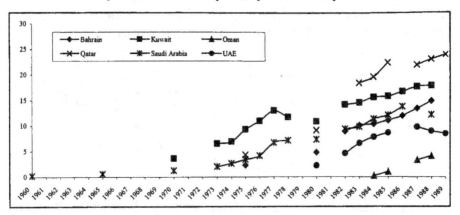

Figure 5.6 Third Level Gross Enrollment Ratios in the Gulf States
Source: UNESCO Statistical Yearbooks

However, education cannot be measured simply in quantitative terms. Unless educational quality is maximized, human resource development is impeded, schooling demand is discouraged, efficiency is lowered and resource wastage occurs. Yet, the quality of a country's school system is difficult to measure and define. A priori one might expect a decline in the standard of education in a situation in which popular pressures and questions of international prestige make governments answerable regarding the expansion of school places but not regarding the quality of education provided. Also, parents with little or no school experience themselves have little basis for evaluating the standard of education their children are receiving.

Qualitative Educational Achievements

However, such expectations should not lead to an exaggeration in the belief that there may be a tendency for educational standards to fall. A more objective view, though still limited, of what has been happening can be obtained by studying trends in certain measurable variables that can be expected to either to influence or reflect the quality of educational system. Educational wastage is the incidence in a country's educational system, from the point of view of its efficiency, of factors such as premature school leaving and retardation or repetition. Other variables that may be measured include pupil teacher ratios, teacher qualifications and expenditure on education per pupil, rates of non-attendance, total number of pupil years spent in school for every pupil who successfully graduated from primary school.

---

[16] The population base on which Third Level GERs are calculated is: all population aged 20-24.

Table 5.2 Student Teacher and School Ratios

	Years	Pupil Teacher Ratio*		Pupil Teacher Ratio**		Pupil School Ratio	
		Primary	Second	Primary	Second	Primary*	Second**
Bahrain	1965-88	27.0	14.1	31.6	16.5	451.1	607.5
Kuwait	1965-88	21.4	14.9	18.0	12.6	635.4	624.5
Oman	1973-89	30.3	8.7	27.5	15.1	332.9	580.1
Saudi	1965-88′	22.4	14.7	16.0	14.3	192.3	196.3
UAE	1970-89	27.3	12.7	18.1	12.6		
Qatar	1965-89	19.5	8.9	12.3	8.6	149.2	337.8
Arab States	1990			26.0	18.0		

All ratios in actual numbers *data for earliest year **data for latest year

Source: UNESCO, Statistical Yearbooks 1970-1995

Table 5.2 details various ratios for the six Gulf States. Between 1965 and 1988, the student-teacher ratios at the primary level were reduced by an average of one percent per annum in all Gulf States, except for Bahrain, where it increased by 0.8 percent per annum. At the second level, pupil teacher ratios were maintained at an average of 12.8 in Saudi, Qatar and the UAE, though they increased in Bahrain (by 0.73 percent per annum) and Oman (by three percent per annum), and reduced in Kuwait (by 0.7 percent per annum). Overall, and in comparison to the Arab States average, Gulf pupil-teacher ratios are relatively good, except for Bahrain and Oman, both of which seem to be struggling to maintain the primary level ratios (which is where the strain of high fertility would be first felt). The pupil-school ratio has increased in all, but Kuwait, indicating an expansion in the physical infrastructure. However, given the larger number of students per teacher in Bahrain and Oman, it is likely that in these two States, class sizes are increasing.

The annual growth rates, calculated in Table 5.3, indicate that second level students have increased faster than primary level students (averaging 263 percent at the second, in comparison to 23 percent at the primary level). Similarly, increases in the second level teachers have been more rapid than in primary level teachers (averaging 176 percent verses 33 percent for primary teachers). Oman has shown the most dramatic increase in its second education level, whilst the UAE has witnessed the most rapid growth in its primary education level. However, with the exception of Kuwait, the growth rate in primary schools has not kept pace with the growth in the numbers of students. In addition, Bahrain and Oman have not balanced the increase in the students and teachers – the growth rate in students has been more rapid than that of teachers.

Table 5.3 Per Annum (%) Change in Education Indicators

	Years	Primary Level			Second Level	
		Schools	Students	Teachers	Students	Teachers
Bahrain	1965-88	2. 1	4.4	3.1	20.0	16.5
Kuwait	1965-88	12.2	11.9	15.0	31.7	38.6
Oman	1973-89	18.9	37.5	41.9	n/a	n/a
Saudi	1965-88	23.9	24.4	35.9	80.4	82.7
UAE	1970-89		46.3	72.6	103.7	105.1
Qatar	1965-89	4.0	14.9	26.2	78.4	81.7

Source: UNESCO, Statistical Yearbooks 1970-95

One explanation for this could be that Gulf States schools have become larger and therefore, they have managed to incorporate the increase in student numbers. However, in Bahrain and Oman, neither school nor teacher numbers have increased as rapidly, hinting at potential overcrowding. Therefore, in those States with relatively less oil income, some difficulty may have been experienced in dealing with the rapid growth rate in the student population. However, those States with relatively larger oil reserves have succeeded in minimizing this effect through recruiting larger teaching forces, and constructing larger or more schools.

Another measure of school quality is the repeater levels for first and second level education (Figure 5.7). The actual number of repeaters at the first levels have tended to increase in Saudi Arabia, Oman and the UAE (by an average of 14 percent per annum), remained relatively constant in Bahrain (at an average of 5000 per year) and declined in Kuwait and Qatar (by an average of 0.7 percent per annum). This would be expected given the growth in total student numbers. In terms of proportions of total primary school level children, Oman and Saudi have the highest proportion of repeaters (averaging 13 percent), and Kuwait has the lowest (averaging seven percent).

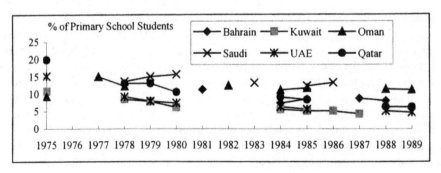

Figure 5.7 Repeaters in Primary Schools across the Gulf States
Source: UNESCO Statistical Yearbooks

At the second level, repeaters have increased in all the Gulf States at an average of ten percent (Figure 5.8), except for Bahrain, which has witnessed a decline averaging eight percent.

However, it is problematic to analyze educational wastage, mainly because little is known of its causes, particularly, measuring the extent which is attributable to supply factors (schools not offering grades to the end of the primary school course, schools with poor teachers, facilities), or to demand factors (lack of interest among parents in providing their children with a basic education) or to an interaction of both. Overall, the indicators point to a relatively good basic education service in the Gulf States, with the exception of Bahrain and Oman both of which may be experiencing some strains.

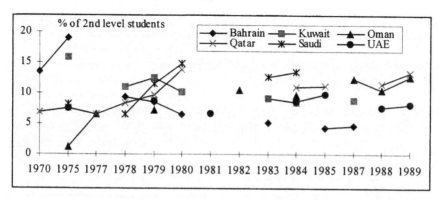

Figure 5.8 Repeaters in Second Level Education across the Gulf States
Source: UNESCO Statistical Yearbooks

The final aspect of the analysis of Gulf States educational quality is examining the public expenditure for educational provision. Despite education being a fundamental human right, and a key to economic development, governments need to weigh its claim on the limited resources, against the need for other investments. They also need to develop the criteria to guide the allocation of educational resources among the different kinds of education. There is also a potential conflict between investment- and consumption-oriented education, though both are desirable. How governments resolve this conflict has grave consequences for the educational status of their populations, as in most settings, as it is in the Gulf, the central government is the primary source of funds for education.

In the struggle to expand the coverage of their educational systems, all Gulf States have doubled or even trebled their actual educational expenditures within a short period of time (Figure 5.9). The share of public educational expenditure as a proportion of GNP has risen in Kuwait and Qatar (by 0.05 percent per annum), Oman and UAE (by 0.08 percent per annum), though it has declined in Saudi Arabia and Bahrain (by 0.13 percent and 0.02 percent per annum, respectively). However, as a proportion of the GNP, educational expenditures have remained at an average of 4.8 percent for all Gulf States. This contrasts to 6 percent of the GNP which the industrial world allocates to education,[17] despite their population age structure being older than that in the Gulf.

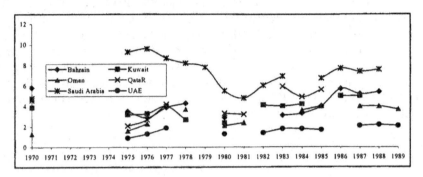

Figure 5.9 Share of Education Expenditures in GNP
Source: UNESCO Statistical Yearbooks

However, it is not merely the amount of money that is spent on education that is important, the purpose to which that amount is allocated determines the State's educational development. Between 1975 and 1989, an average of 82 percent of each Gulf State's educational budget was allocated to current expenditures (Figure 5.10). This increased to an average of 94 percent by 1988-89.

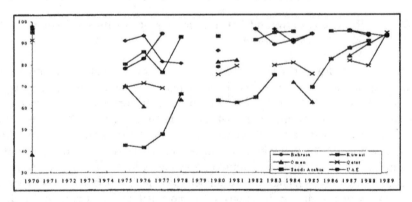

Figure 5.10 Proportion of Current Expenditures in the Education Budget
Source: UNESCO Statistical Yearbooks

As Table 5.4 details, of this current expenditure, on average of 81 percent is allocated to paying the salaries of the increasing large teacher forces.

[17] United Nations Development Program. (1995). *Human Development Report 1995: Gender and Human Development.* Oxford: Oxford University Press.

Table 5.4 Distribution of Current Education Expenditures

State	Year	Salaries	Teaching Materials	Welfare/Others
Bahrain	1984	87.5	6.2	6.3
Kuwait	1986	74.6	1.1	8.5
Oman	1989	79.9	3.7	14.4
Qatar	1989	79.2	1.7	19.5
Saudi	1987	81.7	n/a	n/a
UAE	1989	80.4	3.5	16.1

Source: UNESCO, Statistical Yearbooks, 1970-95

Therefore, less than an average of seven percent is spent on teaching and learning materials or maintenance, inputs that are critical to the learning process.

In addition, different age structures and income levels impose different levels of additional strain. A developing county that matches the share of GNP invested in education to that of developed countries, might fall well short of matching them in terms of the share of GNP on education per head of the school age population.[18] While the Gulf school age population has been increasing by an average of six percent per annum, the proportion of educational expenditures of the total GNP has been declining (by an average of one percent per annum) in Bahrain, Kuwait, Saudi Arabia, Qatar and Oman (Table 5.5). The only increase has been in the UAE: by 0.7 percent per annum.

Table 5.5 Comparison of Education Expenditures with School Age Population

	1975	1980	1985	1992	1975	1980	1985	1992
	Bahrain				Oman			
Education as % of GNP	40.4	30.5	27.9	29.0	36.4	35.1	35.6	31.0
5-19 as % of total population	3.5	2.9	4.0	5.0	1.6	2.1	4.0	3.9
	Saudi Arabia				UAE			
Education as % of GNP	36.2	34.9	34.9	33.5	23.6	20.8	24.5	26.7
5-19 as % of total population	4.3	5.5	6.7	9.4	0.9	1.3	1.7	2.0
	Qatar				Kuwait			
Education as % of GNP	29.2	28.7	22.8	20.3	35	33.3	31.1	30.9
5-19 as % of total population	2.1	3.3	5.6	3.4	3.2	2.4	2.0	6.4

Source: UN Demographic Yearbooks, UNESCO Statistical Yearbooks

---

[18] For example: in 1965, the UK was spending six percent of its GNP on education, while Ghana was spending 5 percent. The proportions of school age population was 22 percent for the UK and 37 percent for Ghana. Hence UK was spending twice as high a percent of GNP per head of the school age population as was Ghana.

Finally, differences are greater when the proportions are converted into actual expenditures per head of population, because per capita GNP is so much higher. When per capita income and the larger proportion of the total population in school going ages are both taken into account, a wide gulf appears between the Gulf and other countries in the same income bracket, in terms of the expenditure on education per head of the school age population (Table 5.6). [19]

Table 5.6 Per Head Education Expenditures (US $)

	1975	1980	1985
Bahrain	175.9	250.8	226.2
Kuwait	358.5	324.8	356.6
Oman	179.7	185.8	176.2

Source: World Bank, UN DSSD

A Qualitative Survey of Bahraini Schools

To further shed light on the quality of education in the Gulf States, the author conducted focus group discussions with Bahraini school teachers from Bahraini primary schools in the summer of 1995. These teachers averaged 25 years of experience, and were in the 40-50 age group. They were all certified teachers and had rotated around various primary schools around Bahrain over the course of their careers.

All respondents agreed that overall the education system was well provided for: education was free for nationals, the school buildings were well maintained (all schools were renovated every three years, with regular maintenance as and when required), and the class sizes were relatively small – averaging 30 to 40 students at the primary level. Teachers would have a maximum of 180 students in their care. School teachers were mainly Bahraini, though one in every 30 teachers was Egyptian, recruited by the Saudi Arabian government to work in Bahrain (another example of Saudi Arabian aid contribution to Bahrain). While in the 1940s to 1950s, students went to school on a shift basis (that is, in the afternoons, or mornings), as there were insufficient schools and teachers, today, this is not the case.

The education system in Bahrain has undergone various changes. In the 1950s to early 1970s, the system was modeled along the Egyptian education system. The curriculum was structured and covered a range of topics that were

---

[19] Whereas France spent $341 and Japan $187 per head of the population, Ghana spent $35 and India $8 per head.

culturally biased towards the West (that is, not particularly relevant to the situation in the Gulf). Regular tests were conducted and promotion was based on satisfying the examiners (during an examination) that the curriculum was learnt (this was assumed to imply 'understanding' the subjects). However, in the late 1980s, the modular system was introduced, with a change to the content of the curriculum to subjects that were more culturally relevant.

While this fundamental change was necessary, the respondents thought that there were various disadvantages to the current system. First of all, despite being culturally based, the curriculum was 'weaker' and less informative. While the benefits of individual coursework were appreciated, the topics on which this was based, were not thought-provoking. This rendered the project too simple and an exercise in plagiary from various reference books. Therefore, the respondents doubted whether it actually contributed towards extending or developing the critical and analytical skills of the students.

This 'weak' information base was further illustrated in the examination method: final exams were based on multiple choice questions: one line responses, rather than long essays that would display depth of information, while granting the student the right of creative expression. In addition, they believed that the new system made repeating a class very difficult. Examinations contribute towards merely 30 percent of the final grade, and continual assessment throughout the year (including easy coursework and regular class attendance) contributing towards 70 percent. This was rationalized as a necessary measure to reduce pressure on student numbers and class sizes. Further, the new system allowed students to fail (that is receive grades that were below the 35 percent passing rate) in up to five subjects (that is the entire curriculum), and yet be allowed to re-sit the exams before the new year, and be promoted to the next class. Therefore, they believed that Bahraini students graduated from high school 'literate', though not necessarily 'educated'.

The Health Services Achievements of the Gulf States

Nutrition and health programs are generally considered to be desirable because of their contribution to a population's welfare and happiness. However, instead of viewing them as a sine qua non of development, many economists see them either as a form of lower priority consumption, which ought to give precedence to infrastructural or industrial investment, or as merely 'welfare-istic', bringing superficial and temporary relief to the structural problems of the poor. Both views have some elements of truth: some expenditures (for example, excessive drug treatment, or cosmetic or unnecessary surgery) are neither productive nor safe, and public expenditure may be used by governments to placate the poor. However, both views ignore the important contribution that appropriate interventions in health, nutrition, water supply and health awareness make to population growth, economic performance and redistribution.

Good health services are conducive to a reduction in fertility larger than the corresponding decline in infant mortality, thus reducing population pressure on resources. In addition to this, there are other economic viewpoints (short and long term and intergenerational effects and re-distributive effects) and growing empirical evidence advocating better and increased investments in human resources.[20] The most important of these are:

i. Improving (adult) labor productivity and performance,[21] through the alleviation of illness, physical and mental growth retardation. Malnutrition at an early age caused by dietary deficiencies, infection or lack of sensory stimulation leads to impairment of cognitive capacity and physical performance in the long term.

ii. Reducing absenteeism, and thereby reducing work losses. In addition, children's illness adversely affects adult productivity and family production, particularly in agriculture, as parental time is shifted to nursing care, or to the pursuit of health care.

iii. Increasing public resource savings. Good primary health care networks reduce the demand for expensive hospital staff inputs and infrastructure, resulting in savings, which would potentially offset the costs incurred for establishing the primary care system: hospitalization is more expensive than outpatient care by a factor of two to 20. In addition, a lack of adequate health care at an early age can cause greater demand for health services and substantial outlays in the long term. Early interventions are more effective and efficacious from a health perspective than subsequent treatments in adolescence and adulthood.

iv. Improving household level savings, as cost-effective basic services reduce the household's need to purchase drugs and health services from private providers at prices up to 20 times higher than those charged by the public health sector.[22]

---

[20] Cornia, G.A. (1989). Investing in Human Resources: Health, Nutrition and Development for the 1990s. *Journal of Development Planning*, 19.

[21] Rau, M.N. (1979). Nutrition and Labour Productivity. *International Labour Review*, 118(1), January-February, 1-12.

[22] UNICEF considers that the introduction of Oral Rehydration Therapy in Developing Countries would prevent unnecessary deaths and reduce occupancy of hospital beds and generate savings of $600 million on private and public purchases of inappropriate and misuse anti-diarrhoeal drugs.

The Provision of Public Health Care in the Gulf States

In all the six Gulf States, public health services are either provided free, or at a nominal charge for certain prescriptions and specialist consultations. In addition, the Ministries of Health are responsible for formulating the national health policies, developing the appropriate strategies, supervising their implementation and evaluation, and measuring the impact of these strategies on the population's health status. Assessing the health resources, as measured by ratio of medical personnel and beds to population, would indicate access to public health care services[23] and therefore, the 'quantity' aspect of the public health care system. Table 5.7 indicates the basic indicators of public health services across the Gulf States.

Table 5.7 Basic Indicators of Public Health Services in the Gulf States (per 10,000 population)

Indicator	Bahrain	Kuwait	UAE	Saudi Arabia	Qatar	Oman
Hospital Beds	30.1	28.3	17.0	22.9	n/a	22.2
Doctors	17.1	18.9	18.1	16.6	12.6	13.4
Nurses	47.6	47.5	34.1	33.0	28.9	32.6
Dentists	1.8	2.6	2.6	1.6	2.1	0.9
Bed/Doctor Ratio	2.1	1.4	n/a	1.4	n/a	1.7
Bed/Nurse Ratio	0.8	0.6	n/a	0.7	n/a	0.7

Source: Ministries of Health, Annual Statistics Reports

The oil revenues of the 1970s resulted in increases in the provision of beds, and employment of medical personnel in all three Gulf States. Figure 5.11 charts the different indicators of the public health care system over time in Bahrain, Oman and Kuwait. Between 1970 and 1980, the proportion of medical personnel increased by an average of 0.14 percent per annum in Bahrain and Oman, and 0.09 percent per annum in Kuwait. On the other hand, that for beds increased only in Oman (by eight percent per annum), and declined by an average of 2.3 percent per annum in both Bahrain and Kuwait. Since the 1980s, the increases have either been small or reversed: Kuwait's ratio of doctors to population has stabilized at 15 per 10000 population, and that of Bahrain's has stabilized at ten per 10,000 population,

---

[23] McGranahan, D., Scott, W., and C. Richard. (1990). *Qualitative Indicators of Development. UNRISD Discussion Paper,* November.

as has the ratio of beds to population in Oman at 25 per 10,000. However, the ratio of nurses to population in Oman increased by 94 percent between 1980 and 1989, from 18 to 33 per 10,000 population.

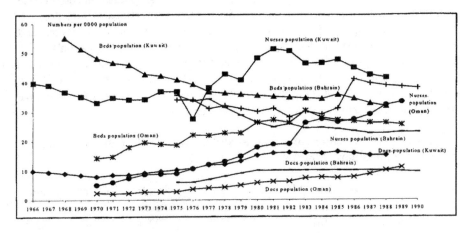

Figure 5.11 Provision of Health Resources in the Gulf States
Source: Statistical Abstracts, various years

However, despite the continued increase in the number of beds, and medical personnel, it is clear that its growth rate is not keeping pace with the increase in population numbers. In fact, in Bahrain, while the ratio of beds to population in the public sector declined by seven percent (from 41 to 38 per 10000), that in the private sector increased, thereby maintaining a stable overall ratio of 41 per 10000 population. This also suggests that more people are now resorting to using private health services than have been in the past.

Table 5.8 Comparison of Health Expenditures across the Gulf States

	National Health (% of GNP)	Proportion of national health in local health care	Government health expenditure as % of total Government expenditures
Bahrain	6.7	24	7
Kuwait	6.0	21	n/a
Oman	2.1	· 60	9
Saudi Arabia	8.0	24	n/a
Qatar	2.7	39	6
UAE	9.0	n/a	n/a
Similar Income	4.0	16	13

Estimates refer to years between 1989-94 for central health expenditures

Source: WHO, various years

Table 5.8 compares public health expenditures across the Gulf States with those in countries with a similar level of income. The Gulf States allocate a relatively low level of public expenditure to health care provision, when this is considered as a proportion of total government expenditures. Further, while it may be expected that the proportion spent on local health services would be relatively small for the smaller States of Bahrain, Kuwait, Qatar and the UAE, that in Oman and Saudi Arabia which have large and dispersed rural populations, should not be.

Yet, while the above data on health resources indicate the quantitative change in health care provision, it does not suggest reasons for the changes, nor does it reflect on the quality of health care provided: for example, what is the point of having a hospital bed if it is left unattended? Expenditures made to meet the needs of the population should also be distinguished from those made merely because it was necessary to spend public revenue. Therefore, to adequately appreciate the public provision of health care, an evaluation of the health services aspect[24] is necessary. This can be measured by the proportion of population immunized, maternal health care registration, access to primary health services, drug availability (for example, the proportion of children at risk fully immunized against major infectious diseases of childhood), proportion of households within a given distance of primary health care centre and proportion of households at risk who can purchase or obtain drugs free of charge.[25]

The proportion of children immunized against the major infectious diseases of childhood (mainly tuberculosis, diphtheria, pertussis (whooping cough), tetanus, polio and measles) is one of the key indicators of primary health care coverage and of child health status. All Gulf States have an Expanded Program of Immunization aiming at immunizing all children aged less than one against TB, polio and measles, and all children aged three against TB. With the system of health cards, each of a Gulf child's vaccinations are registered and recorded.[26] Over 98 percent of Bahraini, Kuwaiti and Saudi children, 89 percent of Qatari, 95 percent of Emirati and Omani children are registered (and hence vaccinated) and drop out rates are relatively low.[27] However, a delay of about a year in acquiring these immunizations as compared to the

---

[24] Those aspects for which information is available will be reviewed, based on the findings of the Gulf Family Health Surveys of 1990, and 2000, and WHO estimates.

[25] McGranahan, D., Scott, W., and C. Richard. (1990). Qualitative Indicators of Development. *UNRISD Discussion Paper*, 15, November.

[26] 99.4 percent of Kuwaitis aged six, had a health card, as found by the Kuwait Family Health Survey, 2000.

[27] Rashood, R., Alnesef, Y., and Farid, S. (2000). *Kuwait Family Health Survey*. Council of Health Ministers of GCC States. Naseeb, T., and S. Farid. (2000). *Bahrain Family Health Survey*. Council of Health Ministers of GCC States. Suleiman, A.J.M., Al Riyami, A., and S. Farid. (2000). *Oman Family Health Survey*. Council of Health Ministers of GCC States. Fikri, M., and S. Farid. (2000). *United Arab Emirates Family Health Survey*. Council of Health Ministers of GCC States. Khoja, T.A., and S. Farid. (2000). *Saudi Arabia Family Health Survey*. Council of Health Ministers of GCC States. Jaber, K.A., and S. Farid. (2000). *Qatar Family Health Survey*. Council of Health Ministers of GCC States.

schedule has been consistently found in all Gulf States. Except for Bahrain, children in rural areas were less likely to be immunized, as were children born to mothers who were illiterate or only had primary level education. In Kuwait, the proportion of children immunized against TB averaged 23 percent, just short of the complete coverage recommended for the below six age group. Oman and Saudi Arabia showed the greatest need for improvement in their immunization programmes, especially in the rural outskirts of the South and the Central areas. Despite this, the age specific immunization rates indicate an improvement over time: the proportion of children immunized against all six diseases was 90 percent for those aged six, 94 percent for those aged four and 96 percent for those aged two.

At the macro-level, the declared cases of such infectious diseases could be taken as a proxy indicator for vaccination coverage. TB, tetanus and polio cases in Kuwait have fallen amongst the 0-4 year olds since 1983 by an average of 9.6 percent per annum,[28] with most gains being made against Polio (averaging 14 percent per annum). In Oman, while TB was reduced by 10.5 percent per annum between 1989 and 1993, measles continued to be a leading infectious disease. Further, the proportion of immunization cases were highest in Muscat and lowest in Al Wusta (Central): averaging 23 percent verses 0.6 percent for TB, Tetanus and Polio, and Measles vaccinations (1991).[29]

However, the cross-country comparisons detailed in Table 5.9 indicate that overall, the Gulf States have achieved high immunization levels, despite Bahrain, Qatar and the UAE tending to have slightly lower proportions of immunization than the Gulf average. Such high rates could be suggestive of a relatively well-supported public health system.

Table 5.9 WHO Estimated Immunizations (1996)

Country	BCG	DPT	Polio	Measles	Tetanus	HBV
Bahrain		92	90	89	45	89
Kuwait		100	100	93	21	94
Oman	96	99	99	98	95	99
Qatar	96	91	91	86		90
Saudi Arabia	93	97	97	94	62	94
UAE	98	90	90	90	...	90
GCC States	96	95	95	92	56	93
Arab States	82	79	79	78	50	74
Similar Income	82	83	85	82		
LDCs	89	82	84	79	43	

Source: WHO International Estimates, 1996

---

[28] Kuwait Statistical Abstract, various years.
[29] Oman Statistical Yearbook, 1993.

Finally, the prevalence of private hospital care is another indicator of quality of public health services. Patients will resort to private care only if they perceive the public health services to be offering a mediocre coverage, and/or not containing the necessary expertise to treat their ailments. Since 1966, the Kuwaiti private sector has witnessed a dramatic expansion (Figure 5.12): 30 percent per annum increase in nurses, six percent in doctors, five percent in dentists.

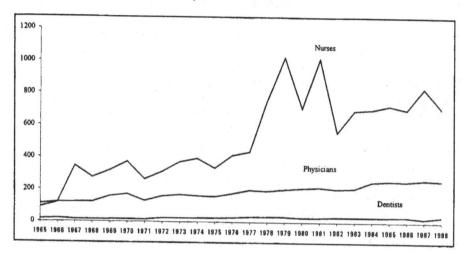

Figure 5.12 Kuwaiti Private Health Service
Source: Kuwaiti Statistical Abstracts

Bahraini private hospitals increased their number of beds by three percent per annum between 1986 and 1991. Between 1990 and 1991, the number of dentists increased by 40 percent, that of nurses by five percent, whilst the number of physicians increased by 282 percent. Bahraini outpatient attendance at private hospitals increased by an average of two percent per annum.[30] The number of private Omani health clinics being established has been increasing by 14 percent per annum since 1990.[31]

While this increased reliance on the private sector health care may imply higher living standards and the exercise of increased choice in a more capitalistic economy, it may also reflect a lack of confidence in the public sector services due to a decline in its 'qualitative' standards. In addition, while it is feasible that in Kuwait, the UAE and Qatar, this is an indicator of greater affluence, this is a weak argument in the case of the less wealthy Bahrainis and Omanis.

---

[30] Bahraini Statistical Abstracts, various years.
[31] Omani Statistical Abstracts, various years.

Case Study: Assessing the Quality of Bahraini Health Service Provision in the 1990s

The author conducted two in-depth focus group discussions, in the summer of 1996, to assess the quality of the Bahraini health service. A total of 16 female Bahraini General Practitioners, aged between 27 and 35, with at least four years of working experience in the Health Clinics around Bahrain, as well as the main Salmaniya Hospital in Manama were involved. A discussion guide was used in the moderated sessions.

Overall, the health service provision was believed to be adequate, with well-equipped medical facilities (state of the art diagnostic equipment, clean hospitals and clinics) and a well-organized administrative system. The Clinics were accessible to all Bahrainis, and there were mobile camps for those in more remote villages. Services were offered free to nationals in the morning clinics and in the hospital. A small fee was levied in the afternoons against the nationals, and against non-nationals at all times. In compliance with the Health for All by 2000, it is the Ministry of Health's policy not to turn away any patient that comes to the clinic, regardless of the triviality of the case.

However, there were certain weaknesses in the system. On the one hand, were issues related to the quality of the training that GPs received, which will in turn, affect the quality of care provided. Limited attempt was made to train GPs or update them on the new developments in their field. Few public seminars are held, and any conferences attended had to be funded for by the doctors themselves. Scholarships for further specialization were rare: a reflection of the capacity of the system to absorb Specialists, rather than the need or demand for them. The seven Consultant positions in the Ministry were already filled by young GPs who would have at least another 20 years of service left before retiring. Therefore, the career development route open to an aspiring GP was to rotate in the Family Health Program in the Health Clinics for four years, before being promoted to Senior Resident. No encouragement was given to submit for medical qualifying examinations, or professional associations, and promotion was neither based on performance, or participation in and publication of research papers.

On the other hand, the quality of service provided in the Clinics, has been deteriorating, due to time constraints. Officially, a doctor in Bahrain had to spend eight minutes per patient.[32] In reality, doctors could only afford to spend five minutes per patient.[33] In addition 'urgent' or 'emergency' cases had to be seen after the daily appointment schedule was completed. Such was the pressure on the

---

[32] Many studies agree that consultations lasting less than 10 minutes do not have a significant effect on health promotion. Wilson, A.D. (1985). Consultation Length: General Practitioner's Attitudes and Practices. *British Medical Journal*, 290, 1322-1324.

[33] This compares with six minutes in Saudi Arabia. Al Shammari, A.A. (1991). Factors Associated with Consultation Time in Riyad Primary Health Care Centers, Saudi Arabia. *Saudi Medical Journal*, 12, 371-375.

system that by 8:30 am, the daily appointment schedule of all doctors in any given Health Clinic is fully booked. Overall, respondents believed that they were under increasing pressure to increase the number of patients they saw on a daily basis.

Another feature of the Bahraini medical service, not quantitatively captured, is the change in the quality of the medication that is being dispensed free of charge to patients. In the past, medication was imported from world-renowned pharmaceutical firms: Sandoz, Welcome, Bayer and so on. Over time, these have been replaced by drugs manufactured by the new pharmaceutical firms, based in the Levant. The GPs doubted the quality and effectiveness of these medications, not merely because they were cheaper in cost, but also because the drugs were less potent, because they were constituted of chemicals that were similar, though not identical in effect to the other brands, and because they were not subject to rigorous testing prior to their distribution. In addition, patients continually complained that the drugs were not curing their symptoms, hence the Physicians usually prescribed other brands that patients would then have to purchase from commercial outlets. Finally, while theoretically, all medication is provided free of charge under the Bahraini Health System, in reality, most drugs were regularly out of stock, so patients had to purchase them from commercial outlets anyway.

Operating parallel with the free public health service is the private service, which operates under two optional arrangements:

i.   Independent private Clinics managed by Physicians who may or may not be employed as GPs in the public sector,

ii.   Private Clinics operating in a Ministry of Health owned Polyclinic, where GPs (who work in the Public Health Clinics in the mornings) benefit from well-equipped surgical facilities, and pay a proportion of their profits to the Ministry of Health, towards the rental of the premises.

The arrangement is beneficial to the GPs as it enables them to earn two incomes, and it generates revenue for the Ministry of Health, to help subsidize its public sector. In addition, it offers additional choice to patients, thereby reducing the strain on the public sector. However, all surgery continues to be performed in the Ministry of Health's Salmaniya Hospital in Manama.

Despite the advantages of this arrangement, various kinds of abuse were possible. First of all, there were no regulations on the fees that could be levied on a patient: the current average is $128 per visit (since quality is perceived to be a function of how expensive the Clinic is), additional to the cost of any medication that would be prescribed, and which would have to be purchased either from the Clinic's or commercial pharmaceutical outlet. Second, privately practicing GPs take advantage of their access to the public sector facilities, by ensuring their private patients obtain surgery appointments ahead of the public sector referrals (in some cases replacing a previously scheduled appointment with their own patients).[34] The reputation a GP thereby earned (for managing to arrange surgeries quickly) secured the GP a long list of patients. In addition, there have been cases of privately practicing GPs trying to prolong the treatment period necessary for a particular condition, through a phased multiple treatment course. This guaranteed that a patient would need more than one consultative visit to obtain a complete cure.

Concluding Remarks

Overall, the public education and health care systems in the Gulf States seem to be adequate. However, there is a need for improvement in the rural areas, especially in Oman, and Saudi Arabia where access to such facilities is limited. In addition, the Bahraini case studies have indicated that increasing demand and/or financial constraints have stimulated the establishment of an alternative private-public health sector, with loopholes opening the way to various abuses, and in the case of education, increasing class sizes and alternative shift structures.

---

[34] This is usually ordered by senior GPs and hence the nurses are not in a position to question their decision.

Chapter 6

The Gulf Labour Force

Demography plays an important role in manpower determination. At a fundamental level, the number of people seeking work depends primarily on the size and age composition of the population, and each change in fertility, mortality and migration affects the labour force to different extents.

Fertility exerts the most obvious impact on labour force size and age structure, though this operates with very long lags. Underlying this is the momentum of population growth, that everyone who will enter the labour force within the next 15 years has already been born and the size of the labour force two decades hence is largely determined by current fertility rates. Therefore, today's birth rate reductions can only reduce the number of youths entering working age 15 to 20 years hence. Mortality's effect is more subtle: while birth rates merely influence the numbers of those newly born, death rates affect all age groups unevenly, and improving life expectancies increases the number of adults available to work across the spectrum of working ages. If increased life expectancies are associated with reductions in morbidity and disability, then the potential pool of workers, especially at the older ages will increase. And when people expect to live longer, they are more likely to stay in education for a longer time, thereby foregoing current earnings for better job opportunities in the long run. Migration can also directly influence the labour forces' size and characteristics: most migrants tend to be young adults, therefore, lowering the average age of a mature labour force. In the case of the Gulf States, migration amongst the national populations is insignificant, while the issue of non-national workers has been discussed in Chapter One.

Therefore, regardless of the overall magnitude of the population growth rate, crude birth and death rates jointly determine the labour market. This is because the population's age structure differs for a high birth and death rate economy, from that for a low birth and death rate one, even though the natural rate of increase may be the same for both. High birth and death rates are more likely to produce a population structure with a larger dependent age group, aged below 15, than that found in a low birth and death rate situation. Low death rates in combination with persisting high fertility rates will increase the size of the present labour force, whilst simultaneously generating high current dependency ratios and rapidly expanding future labour forces.

In addition to these 'accounting' effects of population growth and age structure, behavioural and structural changes directly bear upon the labour force's size and profile. For example, smaller proportions of young people work as they spend more years in school and overall education attainment increases. Likewise, a smaller percentage of elderly people work as they acquire the financial means to retire. Structural changes emerge as the proportion of agricultural labour force is reduced and that in industry and services is expanded. Shifts from agricultural occupations to service and manufacturing jobs enable increases in per capita incomes whilst simultaneously absorbing expanding labour forces.

Factors Affecting Labour Force Size in the Gulf States

While retirement ages vary and many individuals work before the age of 15 or after the age of 65, the majority of the labour force in every country is between the ages of 15 and 64. Table 6.1 highlights that this (potential) working age population has been increasing over time in the Gulf States, though at a slower pace since the 1970s.

Table 6.1 Change in Working Age Population Size

Period	Kuwait Per annum Increase	Period	Bahrain Per annum increase
1957-65	12.4	1971-81	5.2
1965-70	11.1	1981-91	3.6
1970-75	7.9	Oman[1]	
1975-80	4.1	1990-95	0.5

Source: Statistical Abstracts

Yet, not every Gulf national of working age may be in the labour force. The actual labour force consists of those people who are counted as 'economically active' although definitions of economic activity may differ.[2] The Refined[3] and Crude[4] labour force participation rates take this into account. Table 6.2 shows that the

---

[1] Detailed data for Oman is not available, though official estimates claimed that in 1990, the 15-64 age group, accounting for 44.5 percent of the total population, was expected to grow to 47.1 percent by 1995. Ministry of Development and Planning. (1995). *Fourth Five Year Development Plan, 1991-5,* Sultanate of Oman.

[2] Students, housewives and disabled people may be excluded, while those who are not working, but are actively seeking jobs, may be included.

[3] Refined Labour Force Participation Rate is the proportion of labour force in the economically active population.

[4] Crude Labour Force Participation Rate is the proportion of labour force in the total population.

proportion of working adults (in the actual labour force) in the Bahraini population has increased slowly, by around 12 percent (1959 and 1991), whilst that in Kuwait has declined by around 10 percent (1957 and 1985).

Table 6.2 Labour Force Participation Rates and Per Annum Changes

			Kuwait				Bahrain
Year	Crude LFPR	Refined LFPR	Annual Increase	Year	Crude LFPR	Refined LFPR	Annual Increase
1957	22.3	46.9		1959	25.0		
1965	18.2	39.5	7.5	1965	22.0		0.9
1970	17.1	37.7	9.7	1971	21.3	43.2	3.1
1975	18.4	39.4	9.3	1981	25.7	46.0	6.1
1980	18.6	26.9	7.6	1991	28.0	58.1	4.8
1985	20.0	40.3	6.2				**Oman**
				1990-95	17.8		22.2

Source: Statistical Abstracts, various years

Figures 6.1 and 6.2 further breakdown the labour force trends in Kuwait and Bahrain. While the proportion of employed Kuwaitis remained constant, that for Kuwaiti females increased dramatically, particularly after 1970. A similar increase can be seen for Bahraini females.

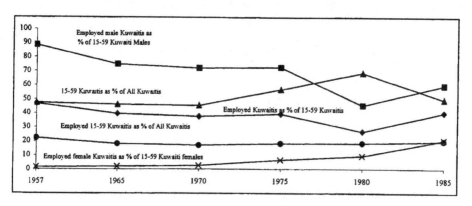

Figure 6.1 Kuwaiti Labour Force Details since 1957
Source: Statistical Abstracts, various years

Detailed data is not available for the Omani labour force, however, official estimates show that the proportion of Omanis in the workforce has declined at a rate of three percent per annum between 1975 and 1990, from 64.5 percent to 39 percent. This was attributed to decreased participation of women in the labour force and the decrease in the average age of the workforce, which has withdrawn the population into education.[5]

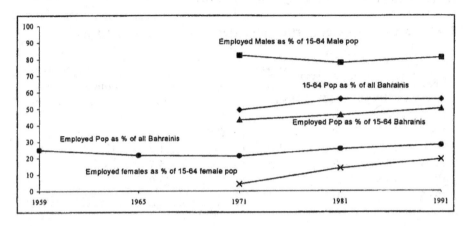

Figure 6.2 Bahraini Labour Force Details
Source: Statistical Abstracts, various years

Dependency Ratios[6]   These demographic dynamics also affect the dependency burden borne by the working age population. Theoretically, the population outside of the labour force (that is, those who are too young or too old to work) are usually supported by working adults directly, as in the case of children or elderly parents living within a household, or indirectly, through social security and other taxes paid by the employed persons. High births rates, and to some extent, shorter life expectancies produce a high child dependency ratio and a low old-age dependency ratio.

Table 6.3 Child Dependency Ratios

Kuwait		Bahrain	
Year	Ratio	Year	Ratio
1957	186	1971	291
1961	162	1981	315
1965	181	1991	348
1970	200		
1975	324		

Source: Statistical Abstracts, various years

---

[5] Ministry of Development and Planning. (1995). *Fourth Five Year Development Plan, 1991-5*, Sultanate of Oman.
[6] Dependency Ratios = {Population aged 0-14/Population aged 15-64} x 100.

While generally a 100 percent is considered to be a relatively high dependency situation, where every adult is supporting one child, Table 6.3 indicates that the dependency ratios of the Gulf States, are exceptionally high, reflecting the underlying young population age structure. Furthermore, these dependency ratios are increasing over time; especially after oil revenues facilitated better health services and thereby rapidly reduced infant mortality rates.

Labour Force Age Structure Behavioural factors also affect the labour force size in the Gulf States. Table 6.4 reflects a general trend across the Gulf States: Gulf nationals are entering the labour force at an older age, and retiring at a younger age.

Table 6.4 Age Specific Labour Force Participation Rates

	Bahrain						Kuwait	
	1981			1991			1975	1988
	Male	Female	Total	Male	Female	Total	Totals	
	s	s		s	s			
15-19	20.7	3.7	12.1	10.1	0.9	5.6	7.8	4.4
20-24	74.1	24.5	48.8	58.5	12.6	35.6	38.9	42.6
25-29	91.9	36.7	65.3	86.6	25.3	55.3	48.5	70.9
30-34	95.7	15.3	58.1	92.5	27.3	58.5	50.2	68.1
35-39	95.7	7.2	48.5	93.9	23.4	59.8	51.1	51.6
40-44	95.9	4.7	47.3	94.7	16.6	59.2	50.5	42.9
45-49	94.4	3.8	48.9	94.3	8.1	48.6	49.5	27.9
50-54	89.5	2.8	47.8	88.4	4.1	43.6	41.9	18.2
55-59	83.6	1.6	47.6	79.2	2.3	40.6	38.7	15.3
60-64	64.9	0.9	35.9	52.7	0.6	27.1	20.8	5.0
65+	43.2	0.4	22.4	32.6	0.2	17.4		

Source: Statistical Abstracts, various years

As Figure 6.3 illustrates, the median age of the Bahraini labour force averaged 29.8 years in 1981 (31.8 for males, and 25.6 for females). This increased to 33.1 by 1991 (33.7 for males, and 31.1 for females).

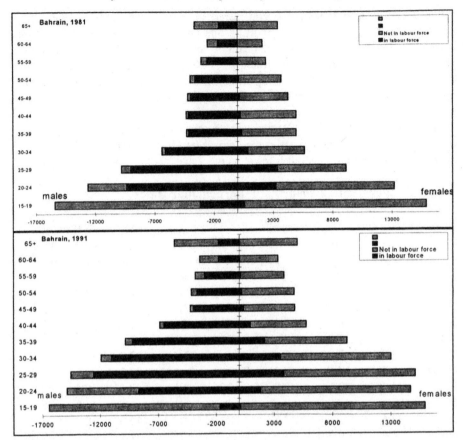

Figure 6.3 Bahraini Labour Force Pyramids in 1981 and 1991

Figure 6.4 shows that in Kuwait, the reverse was true: the median age declined from 31 in 1975, to 29.3 by 1988.

Because young adults represent a greater share of the working age population in Gulf countries, the declining participation of the younger age groups has a significant impact on the labour forces of the Gulf States.

National Female Labour Force Participation   In addition to the age structure differences, the labour force behaviour is very different, the most obvious is the low propensity of Gulf women to work outside the home. Table 6.5 also highlights the increase in the proportion of working national women, averaging 35 percent amongst Kuwaiti women, between 1957 and 1985, and 18 percent amongst Bahraini women, between 1971 and 1991.

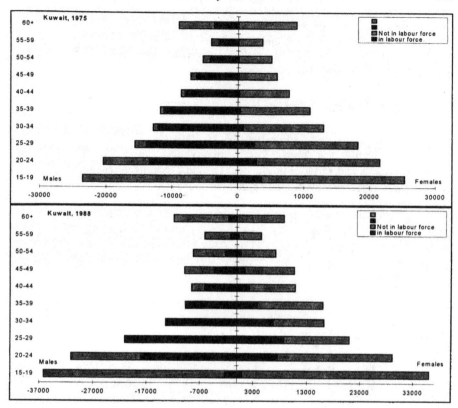

*1988 results are from a Labour Survey, not a Census

Figure 6.4 Kuwaiti Labour Force Pyramids in 1985 and 1988

Table 6.5 Proportion of Employed Gulf Women (aged 15-64)

Year	Kuwait	Year	Bahrain
1957	1.6	1971	4.2
1965	2.0	1981	13.7
1970	2.6	1991	19.4
1975	6.6		
1980	9.4		
1985	17.0		

Source: Statistical Abstracts, various years

Despite these dramatic increases, the low female labour force participation levels compound the effects of the young age structure, they are widening the gap in labour force size.   Hence, it is not surprising that Gulf States depend disproportionately on non-national workers.

The Quality of the National Labour Force

While the size of a labour force may be an important determinant of a State's productive capacity, the labour force's quality also determines the value and quantity of goods and services produced. The education experience and skill level of its workers represent this human capital.

Education   As the number of educated and trained people increases, so does the potential stock of labour services, and hence the Gulf's productive capacity. In both Bahrain and Kuwait, the proportion of illiterate workers has declined: by 60 percent in Bahrain between 1981 and 1991, and by 30 percent in Kuwait between 1965 and 1975 (Table 6.6).

Table 6.6 Labour Force by Education Level

	Bahrain		Kuwait		
	1981	**1991**	**1965**	**1970**	**1975**
Illiterate	24.8	9.9	51.6	44.7	35.9
Read/write	18.6	11.1	39.0	31.2	23.5
Primary	13.0	13.3	3.6	10.3	14.2
Preparatory	11.1	13.8	3.2	6.5	11.9
Secondary	27.5	38.7	1.4	5.0	10.6
Bachelors	4.4	9.5	1.2	2.1	4.0
High diploma	0.5	2.3			
Masters	0.0	1.0			
Doctorate	0.0	0.3			

Source: Statistical Abstracts, various years

Table 6.7 Education Levels of Employed Gulf Women

	Bahrain		Kuwait		
	1981	1991	1965	1970	1975
Illiterate	8.1	3.5	48.9	44.7	10.1
Read/write	3.7	2.1	16.7	31.2	3.2
Primary	5.6	3.2	7.7	10.3	7.8
Preparatory+	8.1	5.1	10.0	6.5	20.2
Secondary+	63.0	57.2	11.6	5.0	44.8
BSc	11.1	22.3	5.0	2.1	13.9
High diploma	0.5	4.9			
Masters	0	1.2			
Doctorate	0	0.4			

Source: Statistical Abstracts, various years

The data above suggests a quantitative increase, or a widening, in the human capital due to rising levels of education. Expanded education over the past decade has nearly wiped out illiteracy among the younger generations. Over time, the Gulf's human capital stock will continue to increase, as better-educated younger workers replace their less-educated older co-workers. These trends are particularly well illustrated, in Table 6.7, which details the educational distribution of female workers, most of whom are educated to above secondary level.

Skills   In terms of the skill level of the labour force, Table 6.8 shows that the administrative functions, in which one would expect relatively literate workers, have been increasing, by 12.7 percent per annum in Bahrain and 25 percent per annum in Kuwait, whilst that for labourers has been declining, by an average of three percent per annum in Bahrain and Kuwait.

Table 6.8 Skills Distribution of Gulf National's Labour Force

	Bahrain			Kuwait			
	1971	1981	1991	1957	1965	1970	1975
Professional	7.7	14.0	27.4	2.0	4.4	6.2	11.2
Administrative	1.5	1.5	11.3	2.2	4.2	1.0	1.2
Clerical	10.5	19.3	17.9	13.5	22.1	19.2	20.5
Sales	10.8	8.7	3.2	15.3	13.3	10.9	7.1
Service	12.3	14.3	16.8	17.7	14.6	38.8	37.8
Hunting/fishing/farming	8.4	4.9	1.5	2.6	3.9	1.5	4.5
Labourers[7]	48.8	37.3	22.0	46.7	37.5	22.4	17.6

Source: Statistical Abstracts, various years

The rates of change indicate the speed at which the younger more educated cohorts are emerging (Table 6.9).

---

[7] Includes miners, quarriers, transport and communication, labourers and operators.

Table 6.9 Rate of Change in Skill Distribution (per annum)

	Bahrain		Kuwait		
	1971-81	1981-91	1957-65	1965-70	1970-75
Professional	18.0	18.2	26.9	29.0	32.0
Administrative	5.3	10.2	22.3	-12.0	14.0
Clerical	18.2	3.4	17.2	9.8	11.0
Sales	2.3	-4.7	3.4	8.3	-1.1
Service	7.9	7.0	2.5	72.0	8.3
Hunting/Fishing/Farming	-1.0	-5.6	26.0	-19.0	67.0
Labourers	-0.3	-8.1	-12.0	326.0	2.9

However, the picture in Oman is entirely different (Table 6.10): in 1990, 82 percent of the Omani labour force ranged from unskilled to semi-skilled, a reflection of poor educational achievements of the past.[8] This is also mirrored in the sectoral distribution of the Omani workforce: 57 percent are in the agricultural sector. In contrast, the sectoral distribution of the Bahraini and Kuwaiti workforce indicates a shift from a more mining based economy to that which is more service oriented though the government sector continues to dominate.

Table 6.10 Sectoral Distribution of the National Workforce

	Bahrain			Kuwait			Oman
	1971	1981	1991	1965	1970	1975	1990
Agriculture/Fishing	8.0	4.4	2.6	1.7	1.4	4.6	57.4
Mining/Quarrying	15.0	13.4	13.0	3.4	2.8	2.1	)
Manufacturing	n/a	n/a	n/a	4.6	10.3	2.6	13.1*
Electricity, Gas, Water	4.0	3.3	1.3	3.2	3.7	2.0	)
Construction	15.1	7.0	3.6	4.1	3.6	2.3	2.9
Sales, Restaurants, Hotels	13.0	10.5	9.0	10.8	10.6	7.3	)
Transport/ Communication	13.6	15.6	10.6	6.5	4.0	5.3	2.6
Finance, Insurance	2.0	5.0	7.6	2.0	1.7	0	)
Social Services	29.2	40.4	53.2	63.8	62.0	73.9	24.0
Unknown	0.2	0.3	0.2	n/a	n/a	n/a	n/a

* Includes mining, industry, electricity/water, tourism, transport/communications, banking

Source: Statistical Abstracts, Oman 4th 5 Year Development Plan

---

[8] Ministry of Development and Planning. (1995). *Fourth Five Year Development Plan, 1991-5* (p. 148). Sultanate of Oman.

The rates of change in the distribution reflect the pace at which the economy is evolving (Table 6.11): the Kuwaiti economy is rapidly moving towards a service oriented economy, given the rapid increase in social services and transport and communication sectors, while the Bahraini economy's early gains in the service sector are beginning to slow down.

Table 6.11 Rate of Change in Sectoral Distribution (per annum)

	Kuwaiti			Bahraini	
	1957-65	1970-65	1970-75	1971-81	1981-91
Agriculture/Fishing/Hunting	1.5	3.8	79.3	-1.9	-1.8
Mining/Quarrying	1.4	4.8	1.2	3.3	2.3
Manufacturing	9.7	47.0	-12.6		
Electricity, Gas, Water	29.3	14.6	-3.9	-3.1	-2.9
Construction		5.9	-0.9	2.0	1.8
Sales, Restaurant, Hotel	0.5	9.1	0.2	7.1	-0.6
Transport/Communication	9.1	-1.9	18.7	27.7	11.0
Finance, Insurance		5.1	-20.0	10.5	8.2
Social Services	9.2	8.9	14.9	13.5	-0.1

Source: Statistical Abstracts

Unemployment   Census data indicate relatively low levels of national unemployment in Kuwait, averaging 4.8 percent for males and 0.13 percent for females. Slightly higher levels have been recorded in Bahrain: averaging seven percent for males and 3.4 percent for females. However, Figure 6.12, indicate an upward trend in unemployment in Bahrain, and a negative trend in Kuwait.

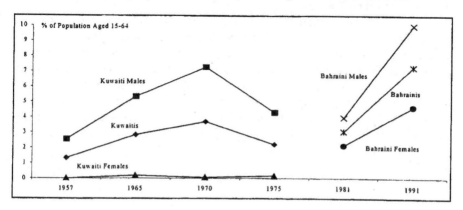

Figure 6.5 Unemployed Bahraini and Kuwaiti Males and Females
Source: Statistical Abstracts, various years

The exclusion of the categories of 'student' and 'housewife' from the populations, further refines the official unemployment, and gives a 'not-formally-working' proportion (Figure 6.6), which is relatively significant, and rising.

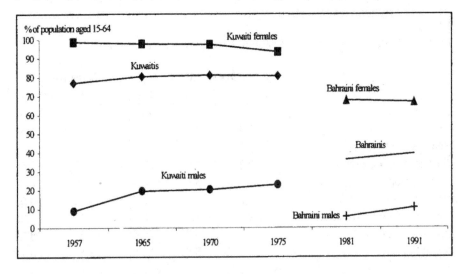

Figure 6.6 Non-Working Population in Kuwait and Bahrain

Certainly, Bahraini unemployment has increased even according to official sources.[9]   Since the 1990s increasing numbers of educated, unskilled young nationals have been joining the labour market, at a time when government oil revenues have been declining. That all the Gulf States have been advocating the policy of nationalisation, and training of the youth, is indicative of a new pressure being faced by the governments.

So far, the national labour market in the Gulf has been tight, as exemplified by rising returns to labour and low unemployment. Rapid economic growth kept labour demand buoyant while constraints on female labour market participation limited labour supply to some extent. However, there are indications of increasing labour surpluses. While theoretically, labour surpluses should not pose a problem so long as appropriate macro and sectoral policies are devised that ensure rapid economic growth, the nature of the Gulf political system thwarts any attempt at managing the migrant subpopulation.

---

[9] *Akhbar al Khaleej*, 13 September 1994.

PART III
TOWARDS 2025: THE
ALTERNATIVE SCENARIOS

Chapter 7

Alternative Scenario Projections: Underlying Assumptions

While the methods and tools for projecting population size and structure are relatively easy, establishing the assumptions on likely future fertility, mortality and migration trends, on which to base scenarios, tends to be difficult, as it requires substantive interdisciplinary knowledge.

The Alternative Scenarios generated here differ from the projections made by the United Nations and other international organizations, in specification, justification and combination of assumptions. While the UN projections, try to forecast future demographic trends as accurately as possible, at any given moment in time, the Alternative Scenarios have been generated to merely illustrate certain likely future demographic developments to demonstrate a particular outcome. Specifically, they were chosen to:

  i.   chart the different paths that the Gulf Demographic Transition could take by 2025
 ii.   illustrate the implications of specific fertility and mortality trends
iii.   determine the potential alternative of future population growth rates based on implausibly rapid/slow assumed trends of fertility decline
 iv.   highlight the importance of integrating population matters in Gulf development planning, through outlining the implications of variant scenarios on public services provision, should they be realized.

Hence, rather than generating one most probable variant based on a complex set of assumptions, the scenario projections, are based on some relatively simple assumptions, for each of fertility and mortality levels, for the national and non-national populations in Bahrain, Kuwait and Oman. These three States have been selected because they are the only States, from amongst the six, to have complete demographic data sets. The scenario projections have been generated for the national and the non national populations separately, because the non-nationals have their own demographic characteristics, and that while they are an integral part of Gulf economies, they are not settlers in the Gulf societies, they are subject to different socioeconomic conditions and make unique demands on these economies. Hence, while nationals have three alternative scenario projections, the non-nationals have only one illustrative scenario.

Through a comparison of the realistic and unrealistic options, feasible future trends are outlined. The results of the scenarios are then compared, and their impacts assessed.[1] To this extent, this approach may be closer to sensitivity analysis of assumptions in population projection.[2]

Time Frame

The first problem to be tackled in any projection is the selection of an appropriate time frame. Of all socioeconomic trends, those related to population are the most stable, though this does not necessarily mean they are totally certain. In fact, the uncertainty increases with time because of the greater probability of structural changes.[3] In particular, predicting future fertility levels are extremely problematic: while future births is a function of birth rates, the numbers of potential parents is itself a function of past demographic rates, a feedback feature well illustrated by baby booms and bust echoes (it takes 25 to 30 years, approximately the mean age of childbearing, for a boom to echo). Beyond this, the uncertainty about the number of potential mothers is added. Further, demographers can only have first hand knowledge about their own generation and that of their children as they are not likely to be able to even guess the potential social changes that may occur to, and due to, individuals they will never know (their grandchildren and great grandchildren). Predicting migration levels is similarly difficult, not because of cohort size, but because of unpredictable government policy changes. In fact,

> Relatively short term forecasts, say up to 10 or 20 years, do tell us something, but that beyond a quarter century or so we simply do not know what the population will be.[4]

The risk of projecting too far into the future is the loss of legitimacy (believability) mainly because the assumptions would rest on shaky foundations. Therefore, the projection horizon should represent a compromise between the advantages of providing more information, and the dangers of making false forecasts: 30 to 40 years is considered a threshold beyond which projections become less reliable.[5]

---

[1] Lutz, W. (1994). *The Future Population of the World: What Can We Assume Today?* London: IIASA, Earthscan Publications.

[2] Lutz, W. (1991). *Future Demographic Trends in Europe and North America: What Can We Assume Today?* (pp. xi-xx). London: IIASA, Academic Press, Ltd.

[3] Lutz, W. (1994). *The Future Population of the World: What Can We Assume Today?* London: IIASA, Earthscan Publications.

[4] Keyfitz, N. (1985). *Applied Mathematical Demography.* Springer Texts in Statistics.

[5] Lutz, W. and J.R. Goldstein. (1991). Alternative Approaches to Population Projection. In W. Lutz (Eds.), *Future Demographic Trends in Europe and North America: What Can We Assume Today?* London: IIASA, Academic Press, Ltd.

Given this, each of the Alternative Scenarios project the population from 1990 to 2025: corresponding to an 80 to a 90 percent confidence interval of an intuitive probability distribution where on each side, only five to ten percent of all possible cases should lie outside the values considered.[6]

Base Year Population Characteristics

The second issue to resolve in any projection, is the demographic characteristics of the population in the base year. This is rendered particularly difficult in the case of the Gulf States, because of the inadequacy and recency of Census taking. International organizations tend to adjust Gulf government's population estimates to different degrees based on their individual assumptions about the inadequacies suffered in that State.

Total Population Size Estimates   Generally, these tend to be based on Census results (for example, Kuwait), or projections based on them with adjustments for under-enumeration (as in the case of Bahrain).

For those Gulf States with limited, dated, or inaccurate Censuses, guestimates tend to be smoothed for age misstatement, missing children and/or under enumeration: the UN projected the 1980 UAE Census population to 1985 based on natural increase plus estimate of naturalized population, and the 1975 to 1980 population was assumed to be the difference between the national 1980 population and that projected from 1975 on basis of natural increase. Oman's population size in 1992 was based on Bahrain's projected population for 1991-1992, adjusted for migration. UNESCWA projected the 1974 Saudi Census population, adjusted by an error rate equal to that in the 1986 Egyptian Census, to obtain a size for 1992, and then adjusted that by sex to the 1992 Census.

---

[6] Lutz, W. (1994). *The Future Population of the World: What Can We Assume Today?* London: IIASA, Earthscan Publications.

Table 7.1 Base Year National Population Distribution (1990)

1990	Bahrain			Kuwait			Oman*		
	Males	Females	Total	Males	Females	Total	Males	Female	Total
0-4	23864	22699	46563	83765	79614	163379	13021	12541	25562
5-9	21739	21101	42840	71415	68741	140156	13626	13240	26866
10-14	19941	19662	39603	59979	58177	118156	12296	11789	24085
15-19	16836	16145	32981	49658	48032	97690	9032	8499	17531
20-24	17816	16625	34441	40791	40294	81085	5792	5249	11041
25-29	13403	14387	27790	32634	34528	67162	4064	4014	8078
30-34	10461	11345	21806	26234	28783	55017	3199	3311	6510
35-39	9153	8312	17465	20432	23098	43530	2830	3241	6071
40-44	5557	6394	11951	14843	18073	32916	2332	2358	4690
45-49	5067	5595	10662	12230	13904	26134	2133	2097	4230
50-54	4904	4636	9540	10886	10888	21774	2111	1955	4066
55-59	4740	4796	9536	8728	8139	16867	1344	1100	2444
60-64	3923	3037	6960	6218	5680	11898	1495	1212	2707
65-69	2615	2238	4853	4303	4083	8386	686	592	1278
70-74	1471	1279	2750	2879	2895	5774	695	721	1416
75+	1961	1599	3560	2909	3205	6114	856	893	1749

*in multiples of 10

The Alternative Projections in this Book are based on the total national and non-national population counts of Bahrain, Kuwait and Oman as obtained from the latest official estimates (Table 7.1, above).[7] The age and sex distribution of the Omani and Bahraini populations were based on the Census age distributions, whilst that for Kuwait was based on the 1992 estimate of the UN's Economic and Social Commission for Western Asia (UNESCWA).

Non-National Population Estimates   International estimates of non-national populations resident in the Gulf States tend to be based either on past estimates, if available, or on the difference between Census estimates of the total population in the most recent year and that projected to that year based on natural increase alone.

---

[7] Bahrain Census, Kuwait Preliminary Census Results, Oman Preliminary Census Results.

Table 7.2 Non-National Population Characteristics (1990)

	Bahrain			Kuwait			Oman		
	Male	Female	Total	Male	Female	Total	Male	Female	Total
0- 4	6242	5871	12113	41553	27663	69216	37814	36584	74398
5-9	5198	4871	10069	46710	31413	78123	39204	38456	77660
10-14	3439	3146	6585	44945	30456	75401	34498	33856	68354
15-19	2234	2070	4304	39644	25358	65002	24870	23373	48243
20-24	10002	6116	16118	26424	20881	47305	23105	16473	39578
25-29	22836	9399	32235	34335	22110	56445	33054	16206	49260
30-34	30211	9268	39479	63170	25659	88829	32626	13853	46479
35-39	23580	6326	29906	78509	26147	104656	28989	11981	40970
40-44	13712	3382	17094	69061	21422	90483	20485	8451	28936
45-49	6865	1554	8419	51154	14843	65997	12569	6793	19362
50-54	3653	868	4521	35843	9410	45253	8986	5509	14495
55-59	1684	424	2108	23270	5477	28747	4760	3102	7862
60-64	733	242	975	12796	2906	15702	4600	3263	7863
65-69	245	122	367	5392	1455	6847	1925	1605	3530
70-74	119	93	212	1694	711	2405	1979	2032	4011
75+	140	87	227	713	711	1424	1925	1925	3850

Table 7.2 outlines the base year non-national population distribution used in the projections. These were based on the UNESWA estimates for each of the three Gulf States for 1990.

Fertility Level Estimates International organization use fertility estimates, based on the vital registrations: registered births by mothers age, of Bahrain, Kuwait and the UAE, and then adjust these with regression curves. Age Specific Fertility Rates have also been drawn from the 1989 Maternal Child Health Surveys. For Qatar, UNESCWA used the birth registration for 1984 to 1991, and pro-rated the population from 1982. The 1986 Census population was then fitted with an exponential regression to obtain the ASFR.

In the Alternative Scenarios, TFR estimates were obtained from the 1989 Maternal Child Health Surveys of Bahrain, Oman and Kuwait: 4.19 for Bahrainis, 6.51 for Kuwaitis and 7.86 for Omanis. For the non-nationals, a TFR of 2.1 was assumed.

Mortality Estimates Given the overall inadequacy of Gulf States' death registration systems, international organizations tend to develop mortality estimates, drawn from life tables, and the Maternal Child Health Surveys, and adjusted with correction factors, obtained after applying different regression models. UNESCWA applied a three year moving average to Bahraini death registration data. The population was then pro-rated from the 1981 Census to 1990, and Age Specific Death Rates were adjusted by 0.859 (median estimate of completeness of death registration). The UN used the 1979 to 1981 Kuwaiti lifetables based on life expectancy (based on registered births and deaths, age and sex structure, and the trend of deaths through 1987).   The UN calculated Omani IMR by applying survival ratios to the 1986 births (estimated from clinic and hospital surveys), while UNESCWA applied Kuwaiti sex differentials to determine Omani IMR by sex.

For the Alternative Scenarios, UNESCWA's 1992 estimates of Kuwaiti, Omani and Bahraini life expectancies were accepted for 1990: 68.7 for Bahraini males, 72.8 for the females; 74.3 for Kuwaiti males and 78.1 for the females, and 69.8 for Omani males and 72.6 for Omani females. For the non-nationals, life expectancies of 71 were assumed.

Future Trends

The third issue to address in a population projection exercise involves devising the assumptions for a (positive or negative) change in the demographic rates: a task rendered particularly difficult in the case of the Gulf States, given the dearth of data about past trends, the lack of demographic studies or surveys that may indicate future trends and the recency of the changes in these trends.

Theoretically, there are three main ways of making these assumptions, the choice depending on the amount of data available. Generally, fertility, mortality and migration assumptions tend to be based on the extrapolation of past trends, using linear or other functional forms of extrapolation or a combined trend with superimposed cycles (if periodicity is assumed).[8] This approach rarely takes into account the broader socioeconomic and cultural context within which demographic changes occur, and consequently fails to anticipate major behavioural changes in nuptiality and marital fertility.[9]   Further, it is an approach appropriate when absolutely no information is available about likely future trends (that is, disregarding the demographic transition theory, any information about desired family size and surveys on family planning demands). Another approach is that of variance from history, which combines external substantive information about likely future trends with past information.[10] The average level is determined externally and only the likely variance from the past is derived. Hence, it sets future upper and lower bounds to the level of fertility, but derives from history the proportion by which fertility rates change between periods. The final approach is

---

[8] Lutz, W. (1994). *The Future Population of the World: What Can We Assume Today?* London: IIASA, Earthscan Publications.

[9] Lutz, W. (1991). *Future Demographic Trends in Europe and North America: What Can We Assume Today?* (pp. xi-xx). London: IIASA, Academic Press, Ltd.

[10] Lutz, W. (1991). *Future Demographic Trends in Europe and North America: What Can We Assume Today?* (pp. xi-xx). London: IIASA, Academic Press, Ltd.

through studying past time series to gain knowledge concerning the process and its structure, and then integrating outside knowledge derived from other sources.

The UN's projection assumptions are based on the long term trends in the more developed world,[11] and are divided into low, medium and high population variants. Low population variants are based on a rapid fertility decline towards a TFR rate of 1.6 to 1.7 per woman, and population growth rates of 0.6 percent per annum. Medium population scenarios assume that by 2025, the average annual growth rates would be one percent per annum (1.7 percent for Western Asia), while the TFR would stabilize at replacement level (around 2.1 children per woman). The high population variant assumes the slowest fertility decline, with average annual population growth rates declining to 1.4 percent, and TFRs stabilizing at 2.5 children per woman by 2025. The long range projections have only one mortality variant (expressed in terms of life expectancy at birth (e^0) by sex), as it is believed that the effect of variant mortality assumptions are small in comparison to those of fertility. No area in the world is projected to reach the ultimate e^0 of 85 prior to 2075.[12]

UN's assumptions for the Gulf States, show a population of relatively high fertility, and long life expectancies, reaching near replacement levels in about 30 to 50 years. The median variant assumes that replacement level fertility would be achieved by 2025 by all Gulf States, except for Oman and Saudi Arabia, which would achieve TFRs of 3.94 and 3.8 respectively. Such assumptions project an average total decline in TFR of 44 percent for UAE, Bahrain and Kuwait, 41 percent for Oman and Saudi Arabia and 52 percent for Qatar. On the other hand, mortality decline between 1990 and 2025, averages 57 percent for Kuwait and Bahrain, and 64 percent for UAE, Oman, Saudi Arabia and Qatar. Total life expectancy is expected to increase by an average of 8 percent for Bahrain, Oman, Qatar and UAE, 6 percent for Kuwait, and 9 percent for Saudi Arabia. Finally, the net migration rate is expected to reach zero by 2010 in UAE, Kuwait and Qatar, by 2015 in Saudi Arabia, and by 2025 in Bahrain.

Chapters 1 to 4 analyzed the main determinants of population growth in the Gulf States – migration, mortality and fertility, and developed some qualitative expectations of future trends. In line with the expectations of the Demographic Transition, fertility can be expected to continue declining in all the Gulf States, even in those States (for example, Oman and Saudi Arabia), where the fertility transition may have just started. To obtain quantitative estimates of this decline, an extrapolation of past demographic trends for each demographic variable, using a linear equation was conducted. Assuming a symmetric distribution, the central values (the mean of the high and low assumptions) should be the most likely Scenario. Table 7.3 identifies the three levels that could be attained by the year

---

[11] United Nations. (1992). *Long Range World Population Projections: Two Centuries of Population Growth 1950-2150.* New York: UN. ST/ESA/SER.A/125.
[12] United Nations. (1992). *Long Range World Population Projections: Two Centuries of Population Growth 1950-2150.* New York: UN. ST/ESA/SER.A/125.

2025: TFR would decline to 2.7 (slow variant), 2.5 (median variant) and 2.1 (fast variant).

Table 7.3 Total Fertility Rate Assumptions for the Alternative Scenarios

Scenarios	Bahrain			Kuwait			Oman		
	One	Two	Three	One	Two	Three	One	Two	Three
1990	4.2	4.2	4.2	6.5	6.5	6.5	7.9	7.9	7.9
1995	3.9	3.9	3.9	5.9	5.9	5.9	7.0	7.1	7.1
2000	3.6	3.7	3.7	5.3	5.4	5.4	6.2	6.3	6.4
2005	3.3	3.5	3.6	4.6	4.7	4.9	5.4	5.6	5.7
2010	3.0	3.2	3.3	3.9	4.2	4.3	4.6	4.8	4.9
2015	2.7	2.9	3.1	3.4	3.6	3.8	3.8	4.0	4.2
2020	2.4	2.7	2.9	2.7	3.1	3.2	2.9	3.3	3.4
2025	2.1	2.5	2.7	2.1	2.5	2.7	2.1	2.5	2.7

As Chapter 2 highlighted, mortality levels have already been dramatically reduced. In 1990, Kuwaitis, from amongst the Gulf nationals, expected to live the longest: 78.11 years for Kuwaiti females and 74 years for Kuwaiti males, levels that are comparable with those found in the West. Since the other Gulf States lag behind Kuwait, it is feasible to expect that Bahrain and Oman would achieve these life expectancies by 2025 (Table 7.4). On the other hand, it is assumed that Kuwait would maintain them, since any further improvement would be difficult, given the nature of the diseases that would be expected to increase amongst an ageing population: circulatory, cancers, diabetes. The United Nation's West Model Life Tables were also applied. Only one variant of life expectancy was assumed, given its negligible impact on overall population growth rates.

Table 7.4 Life Expectancy Assumptions for the Alternative Scenarios

	Bahrain		Kuwait		Oman	
	Males	Females	Males	Females	Males	Females
1990	68.68	72.85	74.29	78.11	69.81	72.65
1995	69.47	73.60	74.29	78.11	70.44	73.43
2000	70.26	74.35	74.29	78.11	71.07	74.21
2005	71.05	75.10	74.29	78.11	71.70	74.99
2010	71.85	75.86	74.29	78.11	72.33	75.77
2015	72.64	76.61	74.29	78.11	72.96	76.55
2020	73.43	77.36	74.29	78.11	73.59	77.33
2025	74.22	78.11	74.29	78.11	74.22	78.11

Finally, given that emigration by Gulf nationals is limited, the projections assume a 0 net migration rate.

Assumptions for Public Health Services Projections

The Alternative Scenarios highlight the implication of different age and sex structures on Gulf health care and education needs. This is because changes in the size and composition of the population are an important determinant of the demand for health care and education services and the resources required by the public service system. Through this, the extent of the strain that Gulf governments can expect to face would be identified.

Health Care

The level of health service demand in the projections has been measured through a consideration of the proportion of the population with access to such services (the health service coverage ratio (HSCR)),[13] which is simplified into:

$$HSCR = NHC_t/POP_t$$

where NHC_t = persons in the population with access to health services
where POP_t = total population at time t

To take into account the effect of changes in the size and structure of the population on the total demand for health care, four major health coverage groups (k) 1 to 4[14] have been identified:

  total population, comprising all those above age 0,
  mothers, consisting of women aged 15 to 49,
  children, comprising children of both sexes aged 0 to 4 and
  infants, including those aged below 1.

Using this aggregation, the HSCR can be written in terms of group-specific health service coverage rates.

$$HSCR = NHC_{tk}/POP_{tk}$$

where NHC_k is the number covered in each coverage group.

The coverage ratios for each group represent assumptions about the proportion with access to health care in each of the groups, their specific needs as well as the overall level of health care available. The health needs of the 'total population' category are primarily curative and include treatment for acute diseases and injuries. The needs of the mother-and-child population are primarily preventative, limited family planning service, pre and post natal care for pregnant women (such

---

[13] Green, G. (1986). Planning for Population, Labour Force and Service Demand: A Microcomputer based Training Module. In ILO, *Background Papers For Training In Population, Human Resources and Development Planning*. Geneva: ILO.

[14] The aged population group has not been included as it is not sufficiently large enough numerically to require separate analysis, and is not a group that the public sector caters to currently.

as check ups and anti-tetanus vaccinations), the immunization of children against childhood diseases (such as diphtheria, pertrussis, typhoid (DPT) and measles), and nutritional supplements.[15]

Table 7.5 Health Service Coverage Ratios Assumed (Linear) Under Alternative Scenario Projections

	Bahraini Coverage Ratio			Kuwaiti Coverage Ratio			Omani Coverage Ratio		
	Infant	Child	Maternal	Infant	Child	Maternal	Infant	Child	Maternal
1990	85.0	84.0	97.0	75.0	80.0	97.0	92.0	82.0	82.0
1995	87.1	86.3	97.4	78.6	82.9	97.4	93.1	84.6	84.6
2000	89.3	88.6	97.9	82.1	85.7	97.9	94.3	87.1	87.1
2005	91.4	90.9	98.3	85.7	88.6	98.3	95.4	89.7	89.7
2010	93.6	93.1	98.7	89.3	91.4	98.7	96.6	92.3	92.3
2015	95.7	95.4	99.1	92.9	94.3	99.1	97.7	94.9	94.9
2020	97.8	97.7	99.6	96.4	97.1	99.6	98.9	97.4	97.4
2025	100.0	100.0	100.0	100.0	100.0	100.0	100.0	100.0	100.0

As Table 7.5 outlines, the alternative projections assume a linear increase in coverage ratios to total coverage by 2025. Also incorporated into the model is the number of health care personnel, doctors, nurses and dentists, and facilities, hospital beds, that would be required (per 10,000 population) to meet the needs of the growing population (Table 7.6). The model assumes that the current ratios of personnel and services to population are maintained to 2025. If,

$$HCPP_{tk} = NHCP_{tk}/NHC_{tk}$$

where   HCPP is the coverage group (k) at time (t), and

NHCP$_{tk}$, is the number of health care personnel specializing in treatment of group k and

NHC$_k$, is the size of the covered population in this group.

Then, the total number of health care personnel can be calculated in terms of the demographic structure of the covered population

$$NHCP_t = HCPP_{tk}*NHC_{tk}   \text{for } k=1 \text{ to } 4.$$

---

[15] Because virtually all mother and child category population groups require access to these treatments, the coverage ratio for this group tends to be somewhat higher than that of the other groups. Conversely, because the general population group has the lowest incidence of morbidity, the coverage rate for this group tends to be lower than the other two.

Table 7.6   1990 Estimates for Health Personnel/Facilities per 10,000 Population (including non-nationals)

	Bahrain	Kuwait	Oman
Hospital Beds	1.23	3.13	2.01
Doctors	0.88	1.51	0.58
Dentists	0.06	0.16	0.06
Nurses*	3.32	3.08	3.00
Cost/head $	220.10	311.80	N/a

*nurses per doctor.
Bahrain's dentist to population proportions were assumed for Oman.

Source: Statistical Abstracts

Since Kuwait had achieved the most favourable ratios in 1990, and it is assumed that the life expectancy levels of Kuwaitis will be achieved in other Gulf States, it follows that similar ratios of facilities and personnel to population would have to be maintained. However, the cost per head was assumed to remain constant, as the cost may reflect other economic considerations that may be specific to each State.

Public Education

Enrolment-Finance Model The enrolment-finance model used by the International Labor Organization   illustrates the effects of population growth on education services.[16] The demand for education services in this model is based on the school enrollment rate (SER) where

$$SER_{(t)} = NS_{(t)}/SPOP_{(t)} \qquad \text{where}$$

$NS_{(t)}$ is the number of students in the relevant age group
$SPOP_{(t)}$ is the school age population

Change in the size and composition of the student population is assumed to imply a change in the level of resources required for education. These are then introduced by defining student/teacher ratios (STRs) and relative educational costs (RECs) by student age group.

$$STR_{(t)} = NT_{(t)}/NS_{(t)} \qquad \text{where}$$

$NT_{(t)}$ is the total number of teachers in the education system
$STR_{(t)}$ is the student/teacher ratio at time t

---

[16] Green, G. (1986). Planning for Population, Labour Force and Service Demand: A Microcomputer based Training Module. In ILO, *Background Papers For Training In Population, Human Resources and Development Planning.* Geneva: ILO

Given the size and distribution of the student population and student/teacher ratios for each educational level, the required number of teachers are then calculated by:

$$NT_{(t)} = \Sigma\{NS_{(t)}/STR_{(t)}\}$$

Similarly $REC_{(t)}$, is considered as the relative cost of educating a student in educational group i, and $EC_{(t)}$ as the total cost, therefore,

$$EC_{(t)} = \Sigma_i REC_{(i,t)} * NS_{(i,t)}$$

Taking the cost of educating a person in the youngest educational group as the base cost, $EC_{(t)}$ becomes the total cost of educating the student age population in terms of this base cost. Multiplying $EC_{(t)}$ by the actual monetary cost of educating a student in this educational group then gives the total financial cost of the educational system. The variation in the projected enrollments is then translated into needs for classrooms, teachers and budget, assuming constant per pupil inputs. This illustrates the additional demands for facilities staff and budget that is associated with larger numbers of school aged children.

For each of the Gulf States, the latest available Census results provided the Primary, Intermediate and Secondary enrollment ratios by sex and age. The student/teacher ratios and (total and capital) educational costs were obtained from the UNESCO database for each educational level for the latest available year (see Table 7.7).

Table 7.7 Estimates for Base Year Education Service

Education Level	Students	GER	pupil/ teacher ratio	Total Cost $
Bahrain				
Primary	48486	96	22	47827
Intermediate	17592	76	17	5488
Secondary	11755	59	11	23393
Kuwait				
Primary	89345	70	19	732633
Intermediate	47348	85	13	45407
Secondary	34642	80	13	19504
Oman				
Primary	199700	79	27	473900
Intermediate	63140	58	16	242560
Secondary	41780	45	16	114800

Source: UNESCO Statistical Yearbooks, Annual Statistical Abstracts.

The assumptions for the Alternative Projections were based on achieving 100 percent school enrollment for males and females at all educational levels by 2025, a quite realistic assumption, given the high school rates already achieved. In addition, it was assumed that the educational costs per student, and the current student/teacher ratios of Kuwait (which were the best in the Gulf in 1990) would be achieved by Bahrain and Oman, whilst Kuwait would maintain them to the year 2025. They further assume that the costs of different education levels per student will remain constant thereby ensuring that the currently relatively high standards are maintained. In addition, the costs of the different education levels retain the same relationship to each other, thereby the proportion of the primary education will remain constant. The objective in these projections is to assess enrollment, classroom and teachers requirements and budget associated with different rates of population growth.

The Gulf Labour Force Projections

Population parameters figure prominently in labour market dynamics, especially on the supply side. Increments in the working age population and labour force size depend primarily on demographic changes. In addition, continued rapid population growth makes the labour force younger even with no change in participation rates.

Since the labour force is always a fraction of the population, the total labour force participation rate (LFPR) can be defined as:

$$LFPR_t = LF_t/POP_t$$

Where $LFPR_t$ = total LFPR in period t

               LF_t = size of the labour force at time t

Therefore, the age and sex specific labour force participation rates would be:

$$LFPR_{ijt} = LF_{tij}/POP_{tij}$$

Where   LFPR = persons of sex j in age group i

Since the total labour force is the sum of the labour force of each sex in the 12 age groups (10-14 to 65+), then:

$$LF_t = \Sigma_{t,j} Lf_{tij}$$

Therefore, the total labour force in terms of the population distribution is:

$$LF_t = \Sigma_{.ij} LFPR_{tij} \times POP_{tij}$$

Table 7.8 outlines the base year labour force age and sex distribution used in the Alternative Scenarios, as obtained from the Census and Statistical Abstracts:

Table 7.8   Base Year Age and Sex Specific Labour Force Distribution

	Bahrain			Oman			Kuwait		
	Male	Female	Total	Male	Female	Total	Male	Fem.	Total
10-14	818	145	963	4920	2550	7460	0	0	0
15-19	3973	1130	5103	11190	680	11870	2026	168	2194
20-24	14609	4339	18948	42510	6280	48800	14338	3014	17352
25-29	12880	4489	17369	36920	4430	41340	17769	5362	23131
30-34	10189	3404	13593	29290	2350	31640	13508	4769	18277
35-39	8970	2078	11048	25560	1600	27160	8547	2264	10810
40-44	5457	1087	6544	20560	1070	21620	5559	994	6553
45-49	4930	459	5389	17970	840	18810	3109	341	3450
50-54	4566	195	4760	15840	610	16440	1883	98	1981
55-59	4029	115	4144	9180	260	9440	1301	35	1336
60-64	2330	21	2351	1870	110	1980	308	3	311
65+	2038	12	2050	2800	200	3000	5	1	6
Total	74789	17474	92263	218600	20970	239570	68353	17049	85402

Omani data in multiples of 10

Source: ILO estimates, Bahrain Census and Omani Census results

ILO's standardized labour force participation rates (SLFPR) projected to 2025 were assumed to apply. These SLFPRs have been constructed using the initial period population distribution together with the current participation rates to calculate an analogue of the total labour force participation rate:

$$\text{SLFPR}_t = (\Sigma_{i,j} \text{LFPR}_{tij} \times \text{POP}_{ij0}) / \text{POP}_0$$

Therefore, the changes that may feature in the SLFPR over time will only reflect changes in activity rates.

The maximum labour force participation rates that could be attained (given the demographic structure of the population) for males was also assumed. This fell within the ILO's forecasts for the 2025 labour force participation rates for the Gulf States (Table 7.9).

Table 7.9 Labour Force Participation Rates for 2025

	Bahrain			Kuwait			Oman		
	Males	Females	Total	Males	Females	Total	Males	Females	Total
10-14	0.3	0.0	0.1	0.3	0.0	0.1	0.4	1.3	0.8
15-19	30.4	10.6	20.7	30.1	5.6	18.1	36.3	6.5	21.6
20-24	89.8	43.0	66.8	88.7	22.6	56.3	83.7	25.7	55.2
25-29	98.9	42.2	71.0	97.7	22.2	60.7	95.6	31.3	63.9
30-34	100.0	33.2	67.1	98.8	17.5	58.9	97.9	28.3	63.6
35-39	100.0	23.5	62.5	98.8	12.4	56.5	97.9	17.6	58.2
40-44	99.6	17.6	58.9	98.4	9.3	54.5	96.6	15.8	56.5
45-49	98.7	13.2	55.9	97.5	7.0	52.6	96.2	12.1	54.6
50-54	94.6	8.4	51.9	93.5	4.4	49.3	88.8	14.3	52.2
55-59	88.2	4.7	47.1	87.1	2.5	44.4	79.2	8.8	45.0
60-64	68.4	2.2	33.1	67.6	1.2	32.5	55.7	6.4	30.3
65+	37.4	0.3	17.0	36.9	0.1	16.1	18.1	2.5	9.4
Total	73.8	18.2	46.0	71.5	10.3	41.1	59.5	14.3	37.1

Given the analysis in Chapter 6 a doubling of the female labour force participation rates by 2025 is assumed. Further improvements would not be realistic, because of the various cultural, social and political constraints to the full utilization of the female labour force.

Compulsory education has not been introduced[17] and this is reflected in the relatively higher rates of female illiteracy and their lower educational attainment levels. Social and cultural pressures discourage women from even considering a career as an option to motherhood and marriage and is reflected in the low proportion of women, of working age, who are employed in comparison to those who are classified as 'home makers'. For those who pursue education, certain educational paths are encouraged most of which are geared towards particular 'appropriate' occupations: the sciences for careers in medicine and nursing and the humanities and secretarial for employment as teachers and secretaries.[18] However, upon completion of their studies, it is economic necessity, rather than the urge to pursue a career that is the major reason for a job search. Further, the inefficiency of childcare services is another limiting factor: day care centers and nurseries are few, inadequate, inefficient and expensive. In addition, as identified in the author's survey, when given a choice between practicing family planning (to pursue a career) and childbearing, even Bahraini women (who enjoy one of the highest

[17] This was because the existing educational system could not accommodate all potential Bahraini students, see Nakhleh, E. (1976). *Bahrain: Political Development in a Modernizing Society.* Mass.: Lexington Books.
[18] Sanabary, N. (1994). Female Education in Saudi Arabia and the Reproduction of Gender Division. *Gender and Education,* 6(2), 141-150.

levels of literacy and employment amongst Gulf women) tend to opt for reproduction.

Finally, rapid population growth and the intensified pressure of excess labour supply may work towards keeping women from working (through increased discrimination at work), or discouraging any further participation of women in the workforce. Therefore, the onus is on men to provide for the family needs, which means that men would have to continue supporting large families.

Another aspect of the labour force is the non-national segment. Non-national workers account for an average of 62 percent of the total workforce. Thus far, this sub-population has been predominantly male, given the nature of the work required (construction), and the socio-cultural background of the States. However, the shift in the structure of the economy towards services has necessitated an increase in the proportion of female non-national workers (increases of 2.6 percent per annum (1980-1993) in Kuwait, and a steady increase of 1.2 percent per annum between 1971 and 1993 in Bahrain). However, while Gulf governments have attempted to reduce the number of foreign workers, through stricter procedures for issuing work permits, contract labour, tightening regulations on accompanying dependents, deporting illegal migrants and setting quotas for a minimum proportion of national workers in each economic sector, no quantitative targets have been set, nor have any strategies been implemented to reduce their numbers, nor have the current regulatory policies been made more effective and concrete.

Therefore, the Scenario for the non-national worker populations assume that the current labour force distribution found in Bahrain (the lowest in the Gulf) prevails across the three Gulf States.[19] Hence, by 2025, the proportion of working non-national females will increase, whilst that of the males will remain constant (Table 7.10).

[19]The Bahraini Census has published the most detailed information on migrant workers.

Table 7.10 Non-National Labour Force Participation Rates for 2025

Age	Male	Female	1995	Male	Female	2025
15-19	33.3	18.7	27.6	33.3	25.6	29.5
20-24	97.2	63.1	82.2	97.2	86.4	91.9
25-29	99.6	59.4	83.9	99.6	81.3	90.6
30-34	100.0	58.4	88.0	100.0	79.9	90.1
35-39	100.0	57.2	89.3	100.0	78.3	91.3
40-44	100.0	57.1	89.8	100.0	78.2	91.1
45-49	100.0	48.5	88.4	100.0	66.4	86.3
50-54	99.2	35.4	85.9	99.2	48.5	79.1
55-59	98.0	30.0	85.0	98.0	41.1	72.3
60-64	90.0	15.3	76.2	90.0	20.9	61.9
65+	62.0	8.6	47.6	62.0	11.8	47.4
Total	84.1	41.5	71.4	78.3	48.7	66.2

Chapter 8

Towards 2025: Public Services Provision

Population growth and educational and health care development affect and are affected by each other: rapid population growth constrains a country's ability to improve its human resource base, while poor coverage, low quality and minimal use of public services is itself a major cause of sustained population growth. This Chapter will consider the effects that population growth would have on educational and healthcare provision. The Alternative Scenario approach will illustrate that a reduction in the birth rates currently experienced by the Gulf States, would reduce the burden that the governments would have to bear with respect to student and patient numbers, demand for facilities and hence reduce the overall cost of providing educational and health care services.

Generally, development planners tend to formulate long-term goals based on only one population projection. Schemes for accommodating the rapidly growing numbers are then discussed. This ensures that the focus of individual ministries continues to be on the short term problems of coping with additional population going through the system, thereby obscuring the vital effects of long term trends in variables like population growth. This relegates population policy matters to the attention of public health officials and economists. Yet, an integration of population into development planning is vital, as the results of the Alternative Scenario projections highlight below.

The Demand for Education Services

All three Gulf States would stand to gain if their fertility levels were to decline immediately. The more rapid declines in the fertility rates, experienced under Scenario 1 conditions, result in the lowest growth rate and the smallest absolute increase in population numbers, than under the slowest fertility decline conditions of Scenario 3. As Figure 8.1 shows, the differences between the alternative fertility levels become evident after 2005, when the absolute number of students in the Gulf States increases at different levels: by 2025, Bahraini students would have increased 1.4 times under Scenario 3 conditions versus Scenario 1, whilst Kuwaitis and Omanis would have increased 1.2 times.

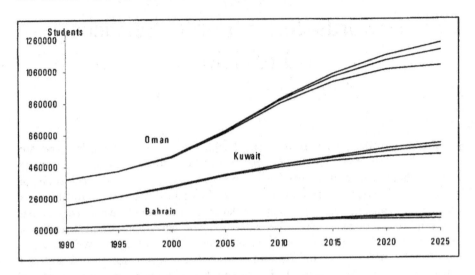

Figure 8.1 Increase in Student Populations Aged 6-17

Figure 8.2 traces the per annum changes in growth rates for the student population. Under Scenario 1 conditions, the average annual growth rate in Bahraini students would decline by 3 percent, while the decline would be slower, at 2 percent per annum under Scenario 3 conditions.

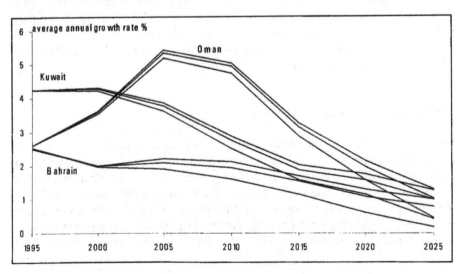

Figure 8.2 Change in Per Annum Growth Rates in Student Population

Oman, which begins experiencing declines in the student growth rate in 2010, would also gain if fertility declines were faster: Scenario 3 results in per annum growth rate declines of 4 percent per annum, in comparison to declines of 5 percent under Scenario 1. Similarly, Kuwaiti growth rates begin declining by the year 2000 with Scenario 1 declining by 3.6 percent per annum, and Scenario 3 declining by 2.8 percent per annum.

Similarly, the absolute number of teachers that would need to be employed by the public education system would increase more rapidly under Scenario 3 than under Scenario 1. The difference between Scenarios becomes apparent after 2005 in Oman, and only after 2010 in Kuwait and Bahrain (see Figure 8.3).

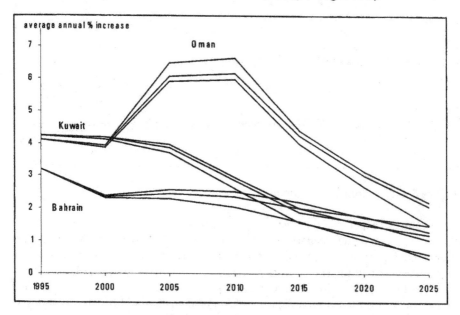

Figure 8.3 Increase in the Need for Teachers

The number of additional teachers required per annum would be lower under the high fertility decline scenario, in comparison to the slow fertility decline Scenario (Figure 8.4). The Bahraini education service would require an average of 114 additional teachers per annum under Scenario 1 conditions, verses 151 additional teachers per annum under Scenario 3 conditions. Kuwait would require an average of 582 additional teachers per annum under Scenario 1, verses 714 teachers per annum under Scenario 3. Oman would require an average of 1530 additional teachers per annum versus 1780 teachers per annum under Scenario 3.

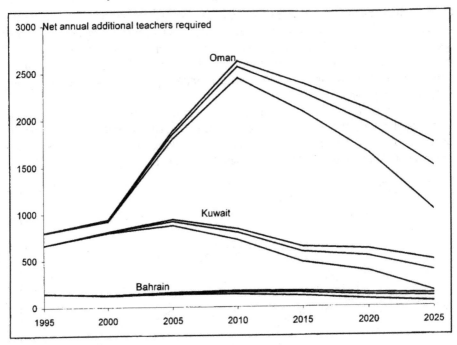

Figure 8.4 Net Annual Additional Teachers Required

As would be expected, the average educational costs would be higher under Scenario 3, than under Scenario 1 in all three States: 4.5 percent higher in Oman, six percent higher in Kuwait and 15 percent higher in Bahrain. This translates into higher average net additional costs per annum under Scenario 3 conditions (than Scenario 1): 14 percent higher in Oman, 27 percent higher in Kuwait and Bahrain. The average annual growth rate in total educational costs would be correspondingly higher under Scenario 3 conditions than Scenario 1: 7 percent higher in Oman, 18 percent higher in Bahrain and 17 percent higher in Kuwait.

The Demand for Healthcare Services

Just as in the demand for education, the demand for health care increases with increasing population numbers. High population growth with a target health coverage ratio of 100 percent by 2025, translates into more people that need to be covered by the public health sector (Table 8.1). The health systems of Bahrain, Kuwait and Oman would have to treat 1.2 times more patients in general, and one times more maternal health patients under Scenario 3 conditions than Scenario 1. Further, Bahrain would have to deal with 4 times more infants and 3 times more children per annum if fertility declines were slower. Kuwait's public health system would have to handle on average 2.6 times more infant and 2.1 times more children per annum if the high population growth scenario were followed rather than the low population growth scenario. Oman, would have to treat an average of 1.1 times more infant, and 1.8 times more children per annum, if the high population growth scenario were followed rather than the low population growth scenario.

Table 8.1 Average Annual Additional Population to be Covered by Health Services (1995-2025)

	Bahrain			Kuwait			Oman		
Scenario	1	2	3	1	2	3	1	2	3
General	834	923	970	3786	4111	4275	804	865	896
Infant	6	3	0	7	3	1	3	7	8
Child	31	169	127	226	469	594	662	723	754
Maternal	253	555	704	1537	2632	3190	4	6	6
	252	263	269	1196	1235	1254	423	638	747
	3	3	8	6	2	4	273	280	284
							9	7	1

*Omani data in multiples of 10

The gains to be made from rapid fertility decline are particularly evident in the infant health sector: immediate fertility declines would result in a growth rate that would be 2.2 times lower in Kuwait, 3.4 times lower in Bahrain, and 1.5 times lower in Oman (Table 8.2).

Table 8.2 Average Annual Growth Rate in Health Coverage Requirements

	Infant Health			Child Health			Maternal Health		
Scenario	1	2	3	1	2	3	1	2	3
Kuwait	0.8	1.4	1.7	1.8	1.8	1.9	3.2	3.3	3.3
Bahrain	0.4	1.0	1.2	0.6	1.2	1.5	2.2	2.3	2.4
Oman	1.8	2.4	2.8	1.6	2.1	2.3	4.7	4.7	4.8

With more potential patients, the public health sector would need to equip itself with more facilities and more personnel (Figures 8.5 and 8.6). Specifically, an average of 1.1 times more medical personnel would be required in Bahrain, Kuwait and Oman, if the high population scenario were followed rather than Scenario 1. A similar pattern is found for requirements for hospital beds (Figure 8.5).

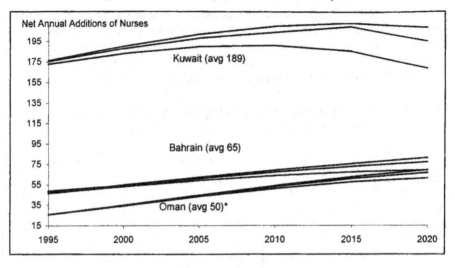

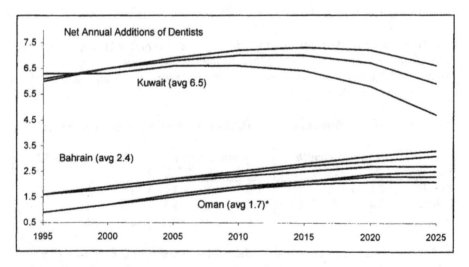

Oman's estimates in multiples of 10

Figure 8.5 Net Additional New Medical Personnel Requirements

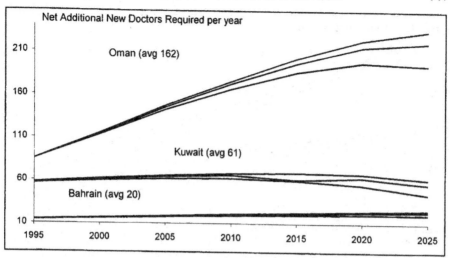

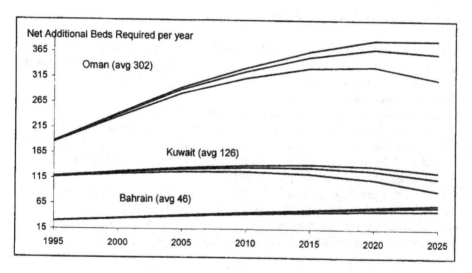

Figure 8.6 Net Additional Doctors and Hospital Beds Required

With fixed unit costs, these increases in public health facilities and personnel, would imply more public health expenditures. Very crude estimates of total costs were calculated, assuming constant per capita expenditure for Kuwait and Bahrain and no inflation. By 2025, Bahrain and Kuwait would have to spend eight percent more on public health expenditures if Scenario 3 were followed rather than Scenario 1 (Figure 8.7). Between 1990 and 2025, Bahrain could save about $300000; and Kuwait could save about $1.5 million per annum if the birth rate were to decline immediately.

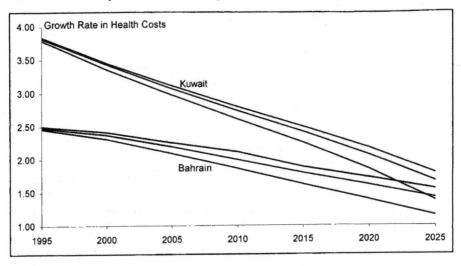

Figure 8.7 Growth Rate in Public Health Costs

The relatively more modest assumptions (basic health (of a quality existing today) for all by the year 2025), show dramatic increases in the annual requirements under the various population growth scenarios.   The qualitative in-depth Bahraini interviews threw doubts on whether the health service could cope under today's population growth rates, given the current levels of investment. The learnings from the Bahraini case can shed light on the possible future course of development of the other Gulf States, which are not yet undergoing the financial constraints experienced by Bahrain.   It also raised questions about the feasibility of the ambitious targets of the Development Plans.

There are definite benefits to achieving replacement level fertility. While the oil rich Gulf States may have achieved considerable improvements in their health indicators over the past two decades, rapid population growth rates in an uncertain economic environment may make further improvements more difficult to attain, and may even lead to a regression back to poor service, with all its implications for human capital development.

Chapter 9

Towards 2025: Human Resources in the Gulf States

By 2025, Scenario 3 would lead to a population which is two times larger in Bahrain and Kuwait and 2.5 times greater in Oman. The implied per annum growth rates (between 1990 and 2025) for the total population are relatively high for all three States, even under Scenario 1: averaging five in Oman, four in Kuwait and in Bahrain under the three alternatives (Table 9.1).

Table 9.1 Per Annum Growth Rates for Nationals in Various Age Groups

	Bahrain			Kuwait			Oman		
Scenario	1	2	3	1	2	3	1	2	3
0-14	0.5	1.0	1.3	0.9	1.4	1.6	1.6	2.2	2.5
15-64	3.9	4.1	4.2	7.7	7.9	8.0	9.3	9.5	9.7
65+	8.6	8.6	8.6	11.8	11.8	11.8	6.0	6.0	6.0
15-49	2.5	3.6	3.7	4.8	7.1	7.2	6.1	10.1	10.3
Total	2.7	3.0	3.2	4.2	4.5	4.7	4.9	5.3	5.5

However, the trend in the growth rates differ (Figure 9.1). Bahraini population increases by an average of 2.6 percent per annum until 2005-10 after which it declines to 1.6 percent per annum until 2025. Similarly Kuwaiti population increases by an average of 3.4 percent per annum until 2010 after which it declines to 2.2 percent per annum until 2025. Finally, Omani population fluctuates at an average of 3.8 percent per annum until 2005, and then declines to 2.8 percent per annum until 2025.

These relatively high population growth rates produce population pyramids that are broad at the base (large proportion of those aged less than 14) and narrow at the top (very few aged over 60). On average 34 percent of Bahrainis, 43 percent of Kuwaitis and Omanis will be aged below 15, and 4.8 percent of Bahrainis, 2.7 percent of Kuwaitis and 3.4 percent of Omanis will be aged over 64 between 1990-2025.

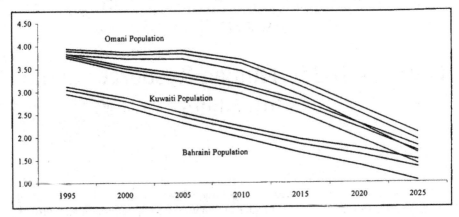

Figure 9.1 Per Annum Population Growth Rates

The rate of increase is uneven across time (Figure 9.2): Bahraini 0-14 year old population growth rate averages 2.1 percent per annum until 2005, after which it declines, averaging -0.1 percent per annum until 2025. That in Kuwait fluctuates at an average of 1.8 percent until 2010 after which it declines, averaging 0.3 percent per annum by 2025. Omani 0-14 year olds growth rate averages 2.4 percent per annum until 2010, and then declines, averaging 0.6 percent per annum until 2025.

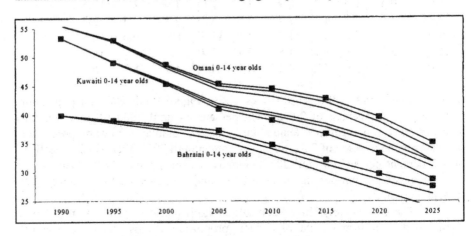

Figure 9.2 Proportion of Gulf Population Aged 0-14

Similarly, as tracked in Figure 9.3, the growth rates for those aged 15-64 in Bahrain and Kuwait's will average three percent and five percent, respectively by 2005, after which they average two and three percent respectively. Omani growth rates fluctuate around five percent until 2010 after which they decline, averaging four percent per annum until 2025.

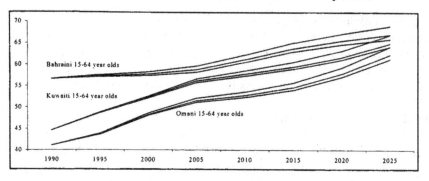

Figure 9.3 Proportion of Gulf Population Aged 15-64

This age structure has important implications for the ratio of productive to non-productive population (dependency ratio) and for health and education services. In later years, as these young people start looking for employment, the ratio of young, relatively inexperienced workers to older, experienced workers affects the labour market.

In these outer years, the shape of the pyramid affects future population growth because today's young girls are tomorrow's mothers. In Bahrain, there will be 120,887 women of childbearing age in 2005 compared to an average of 175,947 in 2025. In Kuwait, they will average 270,047 in 2005 in comparison to 462,403 in 2025. Finally, in Oman, there will be 572,475 women aged 15-49, in comparison to 1,167,844 in 2025. A more active population policy and a vigorous family planning program could moderate these Gulf State's rate of population growth. This would reduce the size of the overall population, narrow the base of the population pyramid and reduce the momentum of future population growth.

The variation between the high and low rates of population growth (Scenarios 3 and 1), are quite apparent, especially in the later years. But, between 2005 and 2025, the differences in population size and structure would become important for each State and its people: the proportion of those aged 0-15 would be 15 percent less in Bahrain, ten percent less in Kuwait and 11 percent less in Oman, whilst those aged 15-64 would be 2 percent less in Bahrain and Oman, and 1 percent less in Kuwait.

The National Labour Force

The age structure has a bearing on the size and composition of the work force since it determines the dependency ratios[1] and the productivity of the population.

---

[1] Dependency ratios are the number of dependent children aged less than 15 per 100 persons in the economically active population, whether or not they are actually in the labour force. Petersen, W. (1970). *Population*. USA: Macmillan.

The Gulf States are characterized by a young age structure: the proportion of the population under the age of 15 is large (averaging 40-50 percent of the total population) relative to the population of the older age groups. Further, the population aged 65 years and older is increasing. This translates into a dependency ratio averaging almost one dependent per working adult in all three States (Table 9.2).

Table 9.2 Total Dependency Ratios

	Bahrain			Kuwait			Oman		
Scenario	1	2	3	1	2	3	1	2	3
1990	76.5	76.5	76.5	97.3	97.3	97.3	120.2	120.2	120.2
1995	71.5	71.7	71.8	94.3	94.7	94.8	105.1	105.5	105.6
2000	68.0	68.6	69.1	89.0	90.0	90.5	96.4	97.3	97.8
2005	63.3	64.7	65.7	82.1	83.9	84.8	98.1	100.0	101.0
2010	58.4	60.7	62.0	72.3	74.8	76.0	88.8	91.5	92.8
2015	53.1	56.1	57.7	63.9	67.0	68.6	75.8	79.2	80.9
2020	49.2	53.0	54.9	56.4	60.3	62.3	62.8	66.9	69.0
2025	46.2	50.7	53.0	49.0	53.7	56.1	50.3	55.3	57.8
Average	60.8	62.8	63.9	75.5	77.7	78.8	87.2	89.5	90.6

In all three States, the highest ratios are found under the conditions of slowest fertility decline (Scenario 3), and lowest ratios are found under the most rapid fertility decline conditions (Scenario 1). While the difference is not that dramatic in the initial years, by 2010, the situation changes. The average annual change in the ratios paint a similar picture: the most rapid declines in the dependency ratios occur under Scenario 1 conditions, and the slowest under Scenario 3: the average annual rate of decline in the dependency ratios is one, 1.5 and 1.9 percent under Scenario 3 in Bahrain, Kuwait and Oman, respectively, as against 1.4, 1.9 and 2.3 percent per annum under Scenario 1 conditions in Bahrain, Kuwait and Oman, respectively.

An important element of Gulf dependency ratios that needs to be highlighted is the status of Gulf women as 'dependents'. Few working aged women are involved in income earning employment outside the home, and most are supported by the men in the household: husbands, fathers or brothers. Table 9.3 outlines female and total non-working population as a proportion of total labour force. This clearly shows the high dependency ratios that would be expected in the Gulf States, even if the proportion of working female population in the Gulf were to double by the year 2025.

Table 9.3 Female and Non-Worker Dependency Ratios

	Scenario 1		Scenario 2		Scenario 3	
	females	non-workers	females	non-workers	females	non-workers
			Oman			
2005	109.4	144.4	109.4	144.4	109.4	144.3
2015	102.3	131.2	102.5	131.6	102.6	131.8
2025	92.0	112.3	92.3	112.9	92.4	113.2
			Bahrain			
2005	81.2	101.7	81.2	101.7	81.2	101.7
2015	78.8	96.8	78.9	97.1	79.0	97.3
2025	77.7	94.7	77.7	95.1	77.7	95.3
			Kuwait			
2005	153.0	234.6	153.0	234.6	153.0	234.6
2015	117.2	161.8	117.5	162.3	117.6	162.6
2025	94.1	113.7	94.3	114.3	94.4	114.6

Generally, a young population would have a lower production per capita than a population with a smaller proportion of such persons (this is also true for ageing populations). This relationship is not strictly relevant in any of the three Gulf States in the 1970s, because oil revenues and the resultant rentier mutation have divorced production from labour activity.

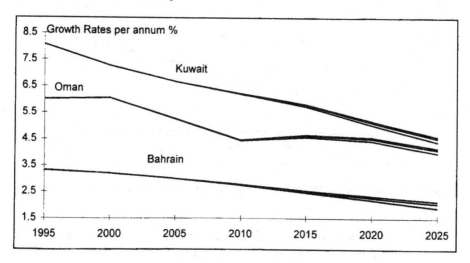

Figure 9.4 Average Annual Growth Rates in the Labour Force

However, under the currently globally depressed economic situation, dependency ratios are gaining in importance. This is because, a population of dependents is a population of consumers: higher public sector expenditures are necessary to ensure provision of adequate schooling and health care services. In all three States, the population growth changes manifest themselves by 2015, when there is a perceptible difference in the annual growth rate in labour force numbers, with Scenario 3 showing the highest growth (averaging 2.8 percent for Bahrain, 6.3 percent for Kuwait and 5.1 percent for Oman) and the Scenario 1 showing the least growth (averaging 2.7 percent for Bahrain, 6.2 percent for Kuwait and 4.9 percent for Oman). Such a projected labour force growth will effect future economic prospects through its impact on the growth of potential labour surpluses and labour force quality.

Projections of labour surpluses or unemployment depend on prospects of the demand for labour, which in turn depend on expectations about how the economy and the population will grow. By 2025, employment would need to be found for 14.3 percent more Bahrainis, and an average of 6.3 percent more Kuwaitis and Omanis, if the low fertility decline scenario were followed, than if fertility were to decline immediately (assuming the absolute number of openly unemployed is held constant, or if unemployment stays at current levels and no changes in the labour policies occur). Between 1995 and 2025, every Gulf government would need to find employment for on average of 1.1 times more national workers per annum.

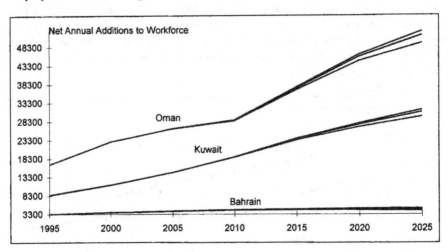

Figure 9.5 Net Additional Workers Requiring Employment Per Year

This would also mean that the average annual growth rate in the inactive population segment would be higher under Scenario 3 conditions: by 2025, this would be 4.5 percent in Bahrain, three percent in Kuwait and 6.6 percent in Oman, as against four percent, 2.6 percent and 6.1 percent, respectively, per annum under Scenario 1 conditions.

Therefore, by 2025, Bahrain could expect about 5.7 percent more economically inactive males and 2.4 percent more economically inactive females under the rapid population growth scenario in comparison with the slow population growth scenario. Kuwait will experience 5.2 percent more inactive males, and 2.5 percent more inactive females under the high population growth scenarios in comparison with the low population growth scenario. Oman could expect 4.8 percent more inactive males, and 2.5 percent more inactive females under the high population growth scenarios in comparison with the low population growth scenario.

The alternative scenario projections assume that economic growth will be independent of population growth. In addition, the macro economic framework for projecting labour demand assumes an environment of sustained growth supported by adjustment policies that seek to minimize distortions and promote efficient use of human resources. However, should population growth affect economic growth adversely, the level and rate of unemployment increases will be higher than those expected and reported above.

The second means through which the projected labour force growth will effect future economic prospects is through its impact on the quality of the labour force. Demographic shifts are an important determinant of the extent of this impact. The age composition of the labour force will change as past population increases raise the proportion of labour force in the younger age groups (aged 15-24). This is particularly true for Oman, where fertility levels are still relatively high: average TFRs in 1990 were 6.8 per woman. Oman's median age of labour force, which stood at 35 years in 1990, would be reduced to 33 by 2025 under Scenario 1 and to 32 years under Scenarios 2 and 3. This would be mainly due to a reduction in the male median age from 36 years in 1990, to 33 years by 2025 under all three Scenario conditions. On the other hand, Bahrain and Kuwait, with their relatively older population (given their starting fertility levels were relatively lower), would experience an ageing of the labour force: the 1990 median age of the Bahraini labour force of 33 years, would increase to 35 by 2025. While the male Bahraini labour force age would increase (from 33 to about 36 years), that of the female labour force would decline (from 30 to 29 years). Similarly, the median age of the Kuwaiti labour force would increase from 31 years in 1990, to 33.5 by 2025.

Despite these increases, such average ages are relatively young, in comparison to international estimates.[2] Such a youthful labour force implies a less experienced labour force with a greater need for job training. Even if rising school enrollments increase the educational attainment of the labour force, its effect will not be dramatic, as the change will be gradual and 'on-the-job', practical skills will still need to be developed if quality of work is not to be compromised.

The gender distribution of the workforce affects productivity and incomes. Given our assumptions were based on increasing the participation of women, it is expected that the numbers of females at work will increase by 2025. However, the

---

[2] Average age of the labour force in the US is 40 years (1996-2000). Fullerton, H.N. (1997). Labor Force 2006: Slowing Down and Changing Composition. *Monthly Labour Review Online*, 120(11). http://www.bls.gov/opub.

growth rate in the net number of females that would be added to the workforce would be faster under Scenario 3 conditions (Figure 9.6): 8.5 percent, five percent and 0.5 percent per annum for Oman, Kuwait and Bahrain, respectively, under Scenario 1 as against 9.3 percent, 5.9 percent and 1.3 percent growth per annum under Scenario 3 conditions.

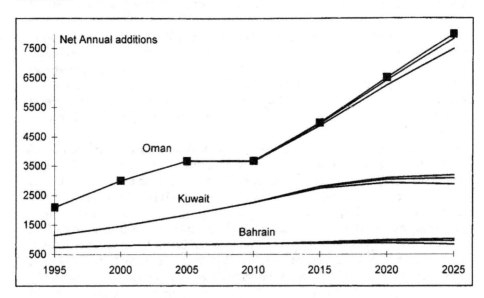

Figure 9.6 Net Annual Additions of Females to the Workforce

The Non-National Population Projections

The national population size is affected by the presence of the non-national population, even though the sub-population is separate from the national segment demographically, economically and socially.

By 2025, non-nationals will account for (on average) 26 percent of the total population in Bahrain, 52 percent in Kuwait and 34 percent in Oman by 2025. This will increase the total population in each State by an average of 36 percent in Bahrain, 55 percent in Oman and 116 percent in Kuwait (Table 9.4).

Table 9.4 Non-National Population Size Under Alternative Scenarios

	Non-Nationals	Scenario 1 *Nationals*	Scenario 2	Scenario 3
Bahrain	236,685	613,318	644,064	663,119
Oman	2,196,313	3,867,255	4,043,536	4,146,390
Kuwait	1,829,870	1,525,263	1,588,405	1,619,715

As Figure 6.7 demonstrates, an average of 76 percent of the non-nationals in the Gulf will remain in the working age group.

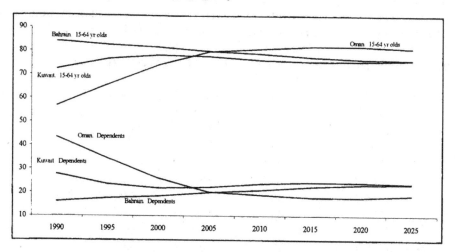

Figure 9.7 Age Structure of Non-National Population

The absolute numbers of non-national workers will continue to increase in Kuwait and Oman, though they will decline in Bahrain (Table 9.5). Oman shows the most significant increase. In addition, with the exception of Oman, the increase will be due to an increase in the proportion of working females rather than males.

Table 9.5 Non-National Labour Forces

Total	Total Expatriate Labour Force				Annual	
	1995	2005	2015	2025	% Growth	Net Change
Kuwait	583933	785783	985444	1201104	3.5	20572
Oman	346183	729903	1247978	1782642	13.8	47882
Bahrain	151171	157058	133354	156392	0.1	174
Female						
Kuwait	119737	210174	321924	449722	9.2	10999
Oman	72816	135444	199208	268861	9.0	6535
Bahrain	28999	42712	51733	71630	4.9	1421
Male						
Kuwait	464195	575609	663520	751383	2.1	9573
Oman	273367	594459	1048770	1513780	15.1	41347
Bahrain	122172	114346	81621	84762	-1.0	-1247

This will translate into a significant, though declining proportion of non-national workers in the total labour force in the Gulf. Bahrain, would continue having the lowest proportion, whilst Kuwait would continue having the highest proportion. After peaking in 2000, the non-national proportion would decline (Table 9.6).

Table 9.6 Proportion of Non-Nationals in the Total Workforce

YEAR	Kuwait	Oman	Bahrain
1990	85.3	90.6	59.6
1995	80.7	89.2	56.0
2000	75.7	87.9	52.6
2005	70.0	86.6	49.4
2010	63.3	85.1	46.2
2015	55.8	82.6	42.9
2020	48.7	80.0	38.9
2025	42.5	77.5	34.8
Actual avg (1957-90)	79.0	n/a	49.0

Since the projections built in the assumption that most of the males and an increasing proportion of the females will be working, the resultant dependency ratios are relatively low (Table 9.7).

Table 9.7 Dependency Ratios for Non-Nationals

	Bahrain	Kuwait	Oman
1990	18.5	36.6	72.7
1995	13.9	39.7	75.2
2000	20.1	37.1	70.1
2005	51.0	37.5	77.3
2010	35.3	16.0	20.3
2015	25.2	12.9	11.8
2020	22.4	15.4	10.3
2025	14.7	14.6	8.0

Yet this non-national scenario could be easily and quickly altered were Gulf governments to decide to change the legal context of the non-national workers. More important than these quantitative changes are the indirect means by which the presence of these workers disadvantage the national labour force. The non-national workers tend to be educated in institutions in their home countries, tend to be fluent in at least two languages and are overall more experienced. Therefore, they are in a better position to compete for employment in the Gulf, particularly in the higher paying private sector, which includes foreign companies that demand specific communication and working skills that the nationals may not have yet refined. Their continued presence also ensures that nationals continue to segregate economic activities along ethnic lines: with expatriates doing manual labour, and nationals performing white collar jobs. This works against the development of a healthy work ethic in the long run, and reinforces the dependence on non-nationals into the future: as nationals will either not be sufficiently trained or wish to handle the maintenance of the infrastructure set up by the expatriates.

Concluding Remarks

The alternative scenario projections have shown that the impact of population growth would be to increase the labour supply through the next decade so that it would not be unrealistic to assume an increase in unemployment even with healthy economic growth (as has already occurred in Bahrain). The growing numbers of young people will swell the labour force and even a rapidly growing economy will be strained in its ability to create sufficient new jobs. Macro policies which do not take into account the social culture and political framework of the State, will not be able to contain the growing labour surpluses, as they necessarily rest on some basic assumptions that may prove unrealistic:

> nationals will accept any employment offered,
> the private sector will be enticed to set up large industries in the Gulf,
> the private sector will also agree to trade off cheaper, better skilled and more experienced non-nationals with unskilled fresh graduate nationals.

There is a need for policies that simultaneously stimulate growth and labour intensity in production (to promote long-term employment), and for training youth so as to overcome their lack of skills. The labour force is relatively young, and in the case of Oman continuing to get younger, and Gulf governments should pay attention to providing productive employment opportunities for younger workers. However, in the long run, demographic factors will determine the size and structure of labour surpluses. And the only certain way to stem or arrest the surplus (in a decade or so) is to formulate appropriate population policies through appropriate child spacing complemented by improved health and education services since in the longer term only population policies will be able to ease the stress on future labour markets.

Chapter 10

The Need for Population Management

Chapter 1 to Chapter 4 considered the components of population growth in the Gulf States. While the Demographic Transition in the Gulf States has been underway at least since the mid 1980s, the population growth rate (averaging 2.8 percent per annum for the total population) remains one of the highest in the world.

The Gulf States have a unique migratory situation. Before the 1970s, Iranians, Omanis, Saudis and Bahrainis migrated across the porous borders within the region seeking employment in the shipping and pearling industries. The oil boom of the 1970s stimulated a change in this pattern: Gulf nationals remained in their countries of origin while Arabs from North Africa and the Levant flocked to the Gulf States. The 1980s saw Asians flooding into the Gulf region, a trend which has yet to abate. While these non-national workers have contributed significantly to the rapid economic progress witnessed by these States, they have remained a distinct sub-population, outside the main social, political and demographic framework, stripped of political or economic rights.

Today's low mortality levels and high average life expectancies (averaging 72 years), have been achieved through investing the oil revenues in an extensive network of Hospitals and Clinics, and a modern urban infrastructure that has rapidly improved living standards. In addition, imports of a diverse range of foodstuff, sold at reasonable prices, have ensured a well-nourished population. However, while mortality rates of Gulf nationals have declined to levels comparable to those found in the West, there is room for improvement, particularly in the area of infant and maternal mortality.

Therefore, underlying the rapid population growth rates of the Gulf States is the high fertility levels, with TFRs averaging five children per woman. Bongaart's Proximate Determinant approach identified the low prevalence of contraceptive use, high marriage rates and low effectiveness of the types of contraceptives used, as the main factors accounting for the fertility rate. In addition, the patriarchal norms on which the social and legal infrastructure in the Gulf is built support a 'high-fertility' regimen, and contribute towards slowing down the pace of fertility decline. Finally, the young age structure of Gulf populations translates into an inbuilt population momentum – the fact that even more females would be entering the reproductive age bracket – and further ensures that fertility declines are slow.

The development of the human capital assets of the Gulf States was the focus of the analyses in Chapters 5 to 6. Non-national workers have dominated the labour market in the Gulf States. The low prevalence of nationals in the workforce was attributed to the low female participation rates, the young age structure of the national population, the lack of relevant skills and training, and a rentier ethic, which regards only white collar employment as acceptable. This was compounded by the availability of generous allowances, grants and subsidies which reduce the need to seek employment. However, the decline in oil revenues has coincided with the time when the 1970s baby boom has reached working age. The increased pressure on the governments to create employment has led to the proliferation of various training centers (for example, the '10,000 Project' in Bahrain and other localisation schemes in which minimum quotas of national employees in each industry are specified) and the wave of privatisation across the Gulf.

In quantitative terms, the national human capital resources are relatively good, given the heavy oil-fuelled investments in the public health and education infrastructures. High enrolment ratios and literacy rates, low population per physician and an extensive network of Clinics and Hospitals have been achieved within a short time frame. However, in both cases there are indicators of a decline in the quality of these services: a morning and an afternoon shift for primary school students, ratios of pupils per teacher increasing in Bahrain, and the replacement of drugs by cheaper less effective versions.

Chapters 7 to 9 focussed on the Alternative Scenarios. Based on the expectations raised by the analysis of the components of population growth and declared policy direction of the Gulf States, the main assumptions underlying the Alternative Scenario Projections were outlined. Three alternative scenario projections for the national populations, and one for the non-national population were then generated. These traced the different paths along which the Gulf Demographic Transition could proceed toward a low-mortality-low-fertility equilibrium by 2025, and illustrated the implications for population growth of three potential fertility trends. Through the projections, the Scenarios outlined the socio-economic implications of alternative fertility pathways, and hence the modifications that could be made through the implementation of a public policy strategy that would integrate population and development matters. They were not generated to obtain one most probable variant based on a complex set of assumptions.

In all three States, Scenario 3 with the slowest trend in fertility decline resulted in the highest growth rates, and highest population numbers, whilst Scenario 1, with the most rapid fertility decline was the opposite. On average, Scenario 3 experienced an average per annum growth rate that was 8 percent, 12 percent and 7 percent higher than the growth rate under the conditions of Scenario 1 in Kuwait, Bahrain and Oman, respectively. Similarly, the dependency ratios were, on average, 4 percent greater under Scenario 3, than Scenario 1. By 2025, the composition of the populations would be as follows: 662,789 Bahrainis and 236,685 non-nationals in Bahrain, 4,473,356 Omanis and 2,196,313 non-nationals in Oman, and 2392336 Kuwaitis and 1829870 non-nationals in Kuwait.

This rapid population growth would have a significant impact on the provision of public services and the creation of employment, especially given the strain that these Gulf States are already facing. This would be occurring at a time when their revenues are not expected to be similarly increasing. Even under the relatively conservative assumptions, of the female labour force participation rate doubling from a low base, and the current labour force participation rates remaining constant, the absolute numbers of working age nationals seeking employment will increase by 160 percent in Bahrain, 790 percent in Kuwait and 480 percent in Oman between 1990 and 2025. The lack of detailed and rigorous development planning, which tends not to take into account population growth, would only compound these strains.

Towards Effective Population Policies: Influencing the Regulators of Fertility

The effective management of the population and its growth is vital if Gulf States are to avoid the costs identified, especially if the current socio-political system were to remain constant. However, achieving the ambitious declines envisioned in Scenario 1 (from which Gulf States stand to benefit the most) will require a strong and sustained effort by the government and the private sector, to give the necessary momentum to start the fertility decline now. Present government policies, neither recognise these factors, nor the need for a multi-sectoral approach. A comprehensive population policy that informs about and supplies family planning services would lower the population growth rate and give a less youthful population structure through fertility moderation.

Yet, an all-encompassing population policy involving family planning, distribution of education and health services aimed at reducing fertility would require time before its effect becomes visible, the duration depending upon the extent to which the change requires a shift in attitudes, traditions and behaviour (Table 10.1).

Family Planning programmes tend to initially affect those families that already want to limit their fertility, and then spread gradually through to other families, in which the concept of birth limitation is alien. While the effects of devising programmes that reduce mortality, educate women and encourage female employment may only be visible in five to ten years, this should not justify delaying action, as past inaction has already ensured that the population will double within a generation. It is the very long gestation period that makes action as early as possible necessary.

Attempting to increase the age at marriage will be effective (as it would reduce the number of years that a woman is exposed to conception) in rural areas of Oman and Saudi, where the mean age at marriage is still relatively young. It is generally accepted that the average age at marriage for women must exceed 20 to have a positive demographic impact. Development, education, increased job opportunities and media campaigns would all help to increase the age at marriage over time, while imposing and/or raising the legal minimum age at marriage would help speed this process.

Table 10.1 Population Policies and Lag Times for their Effects

Time Lag between Action & Fertility Impact	Short Time Lag: 0-5 yrs	Medium Time Lag: 6-10 yrs	Long Time Lag: 10+ yrs
Direct Fertility Control Birth Spacing/Timing (contraception, lactation) Age at Marriage Information, Education, Media	X X	X	
Reducing Desired Family Size Access to MCH services Nutrition programmes Maternal Education (nutrition, childbirth, child care) Water and Sanitation Programmes Access to Formal Education (boys and girls) Adult Literacy Programmes Improved Female Work Conditions Social Security, Pensions Fiscal Policies: subsidies/tax relief for small families	X	X X X X X	X X X
General Development Policies Higher incomes/living standards (quality vs quantity) Shift to industrial society Improved job opportunities Change social views of women's role and status		X	X X X

Source: World Bank

While breast-feeding is an important fertility regulator, it is difficult to prevent a decline in breastfeeding within the context of modern health care systems (pre and post natal care, delivery in hospitals, nutrition supplements), increased education, female employment and urbanisation.[1] However, its small contraceptive effects are generally limited to six months. Oman and Bahrain are already advocating this in their Birth Spacing Programmes, and given it is a culturally accepted form of contraception and an important source of infant nutrition, such programs should be continued and strengthened to ensure the long, frequent and exclusive nursing that best inhibits fertility.

However, for the population growth rate of the Gulf States to be managed, the option of effective contraceptive use must be accessible. Not only is it the only effective means of fertility reduction,[2] but it is a basic human right. Most current users of contraceptives in the Gulf obtain their supplies from the local health clinics or pharmacists. The range offered is limited and women are not always aware of the alternatives available to them. The integration of family planning services and education with the Maternal-Child Health services would increase their cost and general effectiveness, as this would fully utilise the interaction between fertility and infant mortality. Health personnel would therefore need to be fully trained in this field, given full responsibility to deliver the service and supported by enhanced supervision and logistics. The availability and quality of MCH services should also be enhanced to encourage their use particularly by those most in need – the rural poor and least educated.

The media has an important role to play in seeking out women at home and workplaces, and motivating them to delay marriage and childbirth to benefit from smaller family sizes and informing them on where to obtain family planning/MCH services. While there is a need for care and sensitivity, so as not to arouse opposition, suitable contraceptive methods – those that delay first births, and that prolong the spacing between births need to be further promoted. While Bahrain and Oman are promoting a birth spacing programme, the Gulf States need to switch to a higher profile media policy to ensure that this approach is operational. Males, who have been hitherto ignored, should be educated about their role in the reproductive process, the benefits of birth control and its usage. This should also be fully integrated with messages stressing the importance of child spacing for infant, child and maternal health. In parallel with such a campaign, health and population education should be introduced in primary schools and strengthened at other levels. Such a wide ranging initiative will require good co-ordination and co-operation between the agencies concerned and a sustained commitment at the highest level to the campaign's objectives.

---

[1] World Bank. (1988). *Development Report 1988*.

[2] 70 percent of fertility reductions (of the order five births) that occurred amongst 31 countries was through the use of more contraceptives, 30 percent was through increasing the age at marriage and abortion while reduced breast-feeding actually increased fertility. World Bank. (1984). *Development Report 1984*.

Other measures include increasing female education and ensuring equal opportunities at work. Gulf governments should emphasise less on constructing new buildings and more on the availability of good quality education. Expanding employment opportunities for women are complementary to education. As education extends, women's participation in the labour force is likely to increase, and this will have a depressing effect on fertility in the long term.

Concluding Remarks

The Arab Gulf States would gain if the pace of decline in the fertility rates were speeded up (that is, following a Scenario 1 pathway, rather than Scenario 3). If the national fertility rates were left to continue declining as gradually as they currently have been, the demand for public health and education services and the need to provide employment would increase at a rate for which Gulf governments may not be adequately prepared for. This would be particularly significant, if it occurs within a context of depressed economic performance and/or reduced oil revenues. Specifically, the lower levels of human capital formation, resultant upon the strain on public service provision, could not only result in lower labour productivity and a slow adoption of new technologies, but would affect the possibilities of achieving sustainable development in the long run.

The population growth rate is not the only culprit for lower levels of development, and the optimum population for any particular society depends on which objective function the society 'chooses' to maximize. However, the number and quality of the population that can exist in any Gulf State is constrained by natural and economic limitations. Thus far, the population growth of the Gulf States did not impact the rate of growth of average per capita income, mainly because in such rentier economies, growth tends to be independent of the productive activities of the population. Therefore, the governments could afford to take a neutral stand on population matters, based on perceived political benefits.

However, the current economic climate – the reduction in oil revenues, whether from reduced demand, or reduced oil prices, the world recession and so on – are making the previous levels of growth extremely difficult to achieve.[3] More importantly, maintaining (let alone increasing) the living conditions of the growing population, which was relatively easy to do in the oil boom era, are proving challenging.

The arguments in this book have focussed on the 'accounting' issues of rapid population growth. However, the problem is potentially greater: such a rapid population growth will have political repercussions. Kuwait continues to face an external enemy – Iraq. In the post-liberation era, many of the previous subsidies offered to Kuwaitis have had to be reduced or removed. In fact, such has been the

---

[3] Bahrain's GDP growth rate declined from 6.7 percent in 1988 to 2.9 percent in 1990. *Middle East Monito*, May 1992, 199.

deficit that there were discussions of devaluation of the Kuwaiti Dinar.[4] How will Kuwait employee the increasing numbers of young nationals? Will the increasingly eloquent Parliament use their powers to enforce change?

Bahrain has had a history of political unrest and the ruling family does not boast many staunch supporters. In 2025, of the 662,789 Bahrainis, approximately 198,837 (32 percent) will be Sunnis and 463,952 (68 percent) will be Shi'as[5] (this is assuming the rate of growth of Sunnis and/or Shi'as remain constant, and no further naturalisations occur).[6] Will the Shi'a continue accepting the inherent inequalities of the system if the economic situation deteriorates further? The 1996 riots were instigated by unemployment, but have since evolved into a call for parliamentary democracy, and the re-establishment of the Parliament. Can political stability, under such circumstances, be guaranteed, if the unemployment rate increases beyond its present 15 percent? Bahraini physical oil resources have already been nearly exhausted and it was only with the Saudi donation of the Abu S'afa oil fields to the royal family that Bahrain has an income. This begs the questions: why should Saudi Arabia, itself under severe economic and financial strain, be so generous towards its largely Shi'i, little neighbour? If this is part of Saudi Arabia's expansionist policy, how will the largely Shi'i population of Bahrain react to Wahhabi control?

Oman's Sultan needs to retain a fine balance between the interior nobles and the coastal tribes. Were the economic subsidies reduced or rate at which infrastructure developed is slowed, will the Sultan continue enjoying the support of the interior nobles, or will it face internal strife?

High fertility and rapid population growth do not preclude social and economic development, but in the main, were fertility to decline more rapidly, the development of the Gulf States would be greater. The tempo of economic development depends on the diversion of resources from consumption to uses that promote future output. A population with a high ratio of dependants to producers (resultant from high fertility) consumes more of a given output and devotes less to investment. During an interim of two to three decades, reduced fertility would result in approximately the same number of available workers. However, with fewer dependants, the population could invest more and hence develop faster. With progressively fewer consumers sharing the same total product, reduced fertility would result in a distinctly higher living standard. In fact, reducing dependency ratios would increase the investment possible per child for education and the procurement of skills (that is, investment in human resources) which is essential for improving population quality (a process termed 'capital deepening').

Thus far, the governments of the Gulf States, have not (at least publicly) managed their population growth, nor monitored it as part of their development

[4] *Gulf News*, 11 Sept. 1998.
[5] The ratio of 32:68 was derived from the results of the random Survey conducted by the Author. International estimates place it at 30:70.
[6] During riots of 1995-8, many Sunni Jordanian and Baluchis were recruited into the Bahraini Defence Force and were given Bahraini passports.

planning.   Whether purposefully or by accident, they have tended towards a pronatalist, or at best a laissez faire approach.   Their most active attempts at regulating their population began in the 1990s when Oman and Bahrain (to varying extents) initiated birth spacing programmes.   Yet even this has not been wholeheartedly followed, and has been implemented within a framework of 'improving maternal health'.   There have been few indications of a change in the official approach, with the argument being that a high fertility rate is necessary to increase the size of the indigenous labour force and the absorptive capacity of the economy.   However, given that the main industry, oil, is capital intensive and employs limited numbers of skilled labour, and that the infrastructural investments have been largely completed (hence reducing the demand for manual labourers), it is short-sighted to pursue a high fertility regime, to provide 15 to 20 years later, manpower for industries that would no longer require a large labour force.

Demographic Transition theory expects that with economic growth and modernization, comes the gradual weakening of the factors underlying high population growth and the moderation of fertility and mortality rates.   However, Bahrain, Kuwait and Oman (and the rest of the Gulf States) cannot afford to (and should not) wait for that time to come under its own steam. The Gulf States need to re-evaluate their strategic direction, and formulate comprehensive population policies that would be sensitive to Gulf cultural norms, but would take the economic and political realities into account. This would necessarily encompass amongst its aims, increasing female labour participation, improving education especially with respect to birth control, increasing access to effective contraception, and promoting its proper use.

The economic (and political) advantages of reduced fertility begin immediately and accumulate for an indefinite period into the future. Developing appropriate population policies that aim to reduce the annual natural increase rate of 2.4 percent,[7] and hence the current dependency ratios would reap economic advantages. To postpone population management is to risk the erosion of the gains secured in living standards and hence slow down the process of the Gulf's socio-economic development for the near future.

---

[7] United States Bureau of the Census. Report WP/91. (1991). *World Population Profile: 1991* (p. A-10). US Government Printing Office D.C.

Bibliography

Abdulla, K. (1991), 'The Evolution Of and Prospects for the Rentier Economy in a Small Open and Oil based Society: The Case Of Bahrain,' Ph.D. Dissertation, University Of Exeter.

Allman, J. (1978), *Women's Status and Fertility in the Muslim World*, New York, Praeger.

Al Kuwari, A.K. (1978), *Oil Revenues in the Gulf Emirates*, Bowker Publishing Company Ltd., Essex.

El Azhari, M.S. (1981), *The Impact of Oil Revenues on Arab Gulf Development*, Croom Helm, London and Sydney.

Azzam, H. (1988), *The Gulf Economies in Transition*, George Allen and Unwin Ltd., London.

Beblawi, H. (1987), *The Arab Gulf Economy in a Turbulent Age*, Croom Helm, London.

Beblawi, H. and Luciani, G. (1987), *The Rentier State*, Croom Helm Ltd, London.

Bina, C. (1985), *The Economics of the Oil Crisis*, Merlin Press Ltd, London.

Al Baharna, H. (1968), *The Legal Status of the Arabian Gulf States*, Manchester University Press, Manchester.

Birks J.S. and Sinclair, Clive A. (1980), *International Migration and Development in the Arab Region*, International Labour Office, Geneva.

Birks, J.S. (1988), *International Labour and Associated Population Movements in the Arab Region*, University of Durham, Durham.

Bongaarts, J.C. and Potter, R.G. (1983), *Fertility, Biology, and Behaviour: An Analysis of the Proximate Determinants*, Academic Press Inc., New York.

Brunborg, H. (1983), 'An Economic Model of Fertility, Sex and Contraception', Unpublished Ph.D. thesis in Economics, University of Michigan.

Caldwell, John C. (1982), *Theory of Fertility Decline*, Academic Press, New York.

Castles, S. and Miller, M.J. (1993), *The Age of Migration: International Population Movements in the Modern World*, Macmillan Press Ltd., London.

Cleland, J. and Scott, J.C. (1986), *World Fertility Survey: An Assessment of its Contribution*, Oxford University Press, London.

Cleland, J. and Hobcroft, J. (1985), *Reproductive Change in Developing Countries: Insight form the World Fertility Survey*, Oxford University Press, Oxford.

Coale, A.J. (1967), 'Factors Associated with the Development of Low Fertility: An Historic Summary.' *Proceedings of the World Population Conference*, United Nations, New York.

Coale, A.J. (1976), *Economic Factors in Population Growth*, Halstead Press, New York.

Coale, A.J. (1960), *Demographic and Economic Change in Developed Countries*, Princeton University Press, Princeton.

Coale, A.J. and Hoover, E.M. (1958), *Population Growth and Economic Development in Low Income Countries: A Case Study of India's Prospects*, Princeton University Press, Princeton.

Cottrell, A.J. (1980), *The Persian Gulf States*, John Hopkins University Press, Baltimore.

Directorate of Statistics (various years), *Statistical Abstract: State of Bahrain*, Arabian Printing and Publishing House W.L.L., Bahrain.

Directorate of Statistics (1989), *Fourth Population Census*, Arabian Printing and Publishing House, Bahrain.

Directorate of Statistics (1989), *Fifth Population Census*, Arabian Printing and Publishing House, Bahrain.

Directorate of Evaluation and Economic Research (1991), *30 Years of Economic and Social Development in the State of Bahrain*, Ministry of Finance and National Economy, Bahrain.

Donaldson, W.J. (1981), *Change and Development in the Middle East*, Methuen, London.

Easterlin, R.A. (1982), *Population and Economic Change in Developing Countries*, University of Chicago Press, Chicago.

Eberstadt, N. (1963), *Measurement in Economics: Studies in Mathematical Economics and Econometrics in Memory of Yehuda Grunfeld*, Stanford University Press, Stanford.

Fakhro, H.A. (1984), 'The Bahrain Oil Industry Past and Present', Ph.D. Dissertation, University of Exeter.

Fakhro, M.A. (1990), *Women at Work in the Gulf: A Case Study of Bahrain*, Kegan Paul International Ltd., London.

Farid, S. and Rashood, R. (1991), *Kuwait Child Health Survey*, Ministry of Health, Kuwait.

Farid, S., Yacoub, I., Khalfan, N.T., Hafadh, N., Mattar, I., Naser, Y. and Radhi, L. (1992) *Bahrain Child Health Survey*, Ministry of Health, Bahrain.

Farid, S., Suleiman, M.J. and Ghassany, A. (1992), *Oman Child Health Survey*, Ministry of Health, Oman.

Farid, S., Muhaideb, A. and Abdul-Ghafour, A. (1991), *United Arab Emirates Child Health Survey*, Ministry of Health, Abu Dhabi.

Farooq, G.M. and DeGraff, D.S. (1988), *Fertility and Development: An Introduction to Theory, Empirical Research and Policy Issues, Paper No 7*, International Labour Office, Geneva.

Field, M. (1984), *The Merchants: The Big Business Families of Arabia*, John Murray Publishers Ltd, London.

Finne, D.H. (1958), *Desert Enterprise: the Middle East Oil Industry in its Local Environment*, Harvard University Press, Cambridge.

Galtung, J., O'Brien, P., and Preiswerk, P. (1980), *Self Reliance: A Strategy for Development*, Boghe-L'Ouverture Publications, London.

Gillis, M., Perkins, D., Roemer, M. and Snodgrass, D. (1992), *Economics of Development*, 3rd Edition, Norton and Co., New York.

Goldziher, I. (1981), *Introduction to Islamic Theology and Law*, Princeton University Press, Princeton.

Gunatilleke, G. (1991), *Migration to the Arab World Experience of Returning Migrants*, United Nations University Press, Japan.

Guzman, J.M. (1984), 'Trends in Socioeconomic differentials in infant mortality in selected Latin American Countries', Paper presented at the *Seminar on Social and Biological Correlates of Mortality*, International Union for the Scientific Study of Populations, Washington.

Hallak, J. (1990), *UNDP: Investing in the Future: Setting Educational Properties in the Developing World*, Pergamon Press, UNESCO.

Hauser, P.M. (1979), *World Population and Development: Challenges and Prospects*, UNFPA, New York.

Hopwood, D. (1972), *The Arabian Peninsula: Society and Politics*, George Allen and Unwin Ltd., London.

Hourani, A. (1991), *A History of the Arab Peoples*, Faber and Faber, London.

170   *Population and Development of the Arab Gulf States*

Ibrahim, S.E. (1982), *The New Arab Social Order: A study of Social Impact of Oil Wealth*, Croom Helm, London.
International Planned Parenthood Federation Arab World Region (1993), *Unsafe Abortion and Sexual Health in the Arab World*, KPC, England.
Issawi, C. (1977), *The Economics of Middle Eastern Oil*, Greenwood Press, Connecticut, USA.
Khuri, F.I. (1980), *Tribe and State in Bahrain: The Transformation of Social and Political Authority in an Arab State*, University of Chicago Press, Chicago.
Lawson, F.H. (1989), *Bahrain: the Modernisation of Autocracy*, Westview Press, Boulder, Colorado.
Littlefield, R.E. (1958), *Bahrain as a Persian Gulf State*, M.A. Thesis, American University of Beirut, Beirut.
Lutz, W. (1994), *The Future Population of the World: What Can We Assume Today?* Earthscan Publications, London.
Lutz, W. (1991), *Future Demographic Trends in Europe and North America: What Can We Assume Today?* Academic Press Ltd., London.
Hobcraft, J.C, Ruzicka L.T., and Caldwell, J.C. (1981), 'Interrelations between Nuptiality and Fertility: Evidence form the World Fertility Survey', *World Fertility Conference 1980: Record of Proceedings*.
McLachlan, M. and Ghorban, N. (1978), *Economic Development of the Middle East Oil Exporting States*, Economic Intelligence Unit, London.
Ministry of Planning (various years), *State of Kuwait Statistical Abstract*, Central Statistics Organisation, Kuwait.
Ministry of Development (1996), *Sultanate of Oman, Statistical Yearbook 24th Issue*, Information and Documentation Center, Oman.
Mahadevan, E. (1989), *Fertility Policies of Asian Countries*, Sage Publications, London.
More, P. and Turner. T. (1980), *Oil and Class Struggle*, Zed Press, London.
Moomen, M. (1985), *An Introduction to Shi'i Islam*, George Ronald, Oxford.
Nakhleh, E. (1976), *Bahrain: Political Development in a Modernizing Society*, Lexington Books, Massachusetts.
Niblock, T. (1980), 'Dilemmas of Non Oil Economic Development in the Arab Gulf,' *Arab Papers* No 1, Arab Research Centre's Publications.
Niblock, T. (1980), *Social and Economic Development in the Arab Gulf*, Croom Helm, London.
Nugent, J. and Thomas, T.H. (1985), *Bahrain and the Gulf*, Croom Helm, Kent.
Omran, A.R. (1971), 'The Epidemiological Transition: A Theory of Population Change', *Milbank Memorial Fund Quarterly*, 49(4).
Omran, A.R. (1983), 'The Epidemiological Transition Theory: A Preliminary Update', *Journal of Tropical Paediatrics*, 29.
Omran, A.R. (1992), *Family Planning in the Legacy of Islam*, Routeledge, London.
Omran, A.R. and Roudi, F. (1993), 'The Middle East Population Puzzle', *Population Bulletin* 48(1), July.
Petersen, W. (1970), *Population*, Macmillan, USA.
Pollard, A.H., Yusuf, F., and Pollard, G.H. (1974), *Demographic Techniques*, Pergamon Press Pty Ltd, Australia.
Preston, S. (1978), 'Mortality Morbidity and Development', *Population Bulletin of the United Nations Economic Commission for Western Asia*, 15, Decmber.
Preston, S., and Farah, A. (1993), 'Child Mortality Differentials in Sudan', *Population and*

Development Review, 8(2), June.

Roberts, G. (1990), *Population Policies: Contemporary Issues*, Praeger, New York.

Robins, P. (1989), *The Future of the Gulf, Politics and Oil in the 1990s*, Dartmouth Publishing Co, Dartmouth.

Rumaihi, M.G. (1986), *Beyond Oil: Unity and Development in the Gulf*, Al-Saqi Books, London.

Rumaihi, M.G. (1976), *Bahrain: Social and Political Change since the First World War*, Bowker, London and New York.

Rumaihi, M.G. (1973), *'Social And Political Change in Bahrain Since the First World War'*, D.Phil. Dissertation, University of Durham.

Sayigh, Y. (1978), *The Determinants of Arab Economic Development*, Croom Helm, London.

Sayigh, Y. (1991), *Elusive Development: From Dependence to Self Reliance in the Arab Region*, Routledge, Chapman and Hall, Inc., London, USA and Canada.

Serageldin, I., James, A., and Sinclair, C. A. (1983), *Manpower and International Labour Migration in the Middle East and North Africa*, Oxford University Press, New York.

Simmons, G.B., and Farooq, G.M. (1985), *Fertility in Developing Countries: An Economic Perspective on Research and Policy Issues*, Macmillan Press, London.

Stauffer, T. (1981), 'The Dynamics of Petroleum Dependency Growth in Oil Rentier States', *Finance and Industry* 2.

Thornburg, M.W. (1964), *People and Policy in the Middle East*, W.W. Norton and Co, New York.

Tilak, J.P.G. (1988), *Education, Economic Growth, Poverty and Income Distribution: A Survey of Evidence and Further Research*, World Bank, Washington, D.C.

Toubia, N. (1994), *Arab Women: A Profile of Diversity and Change*, Population Council, New York.

Todaro, M.P. (1989), *Economic Development in the Third World*, Longman Group Ltd., Essex.

United Nations Department of Economic and Social Affairs (1970), *Variables and Questionnaire For Comparative Fertility Surveys, Population Studies*, No 45, ST/SOA/Series A/45, New York.

United Nations Department for Economic and Social Information and Policy Analysis (1994), *Population Bulletin of the United Nations*, No 37/38-1994, New York.

United Nations Population Division (1985), *Concise Report on the World Population Situation in 1983: Conditions, Trends, Prospects and Policies*, Population Studies, No. 85, (ST/ESA/SER.A/85), New York.

United Nations Population Division (1985), *Socio-economic Differentials in Child Mortality in Developing Countries*, Sales No E85,XIII.6, New York.

United Nations Population Division (1984), *International Conference on Population: 1984 Mortality and Health Policy: Proceedings of the Expert Group on Mortality and Health Policy*, Rome, 30 May to 3 June 1983, ST/ESA/SER.A/91, New York.

United Nations Population Division (1985), *World Population Trends and Population Policies, 1983 Monitoring Report, Volume II*, ST/ESA/SER.A/93/Add.1, Population Studies No 93, New York.

United Nations Population Division (1987), *Fertility Behaviour in the Context of Development: Evidence from the World Fertility Survey*, ST/ESA/SER.A/86, New York.

United Nations Population Division (1992), *Long Range World Population Projections: Two Centuries of Population Growth 1950-2150*, ST/ESA/SER.A/125, New York.

United Nations Population Division (1991), *World Population Prospects, 1990*, Population

Studies No 120, Department of International Economic and Social Affairs, ST/ESA/SER.A/120, New York.

United Nations Population Division (1993), *World Population Prospects, 1992*, Department of International Economic and Social Affairs, ST/ESA/SER.A/135, New York.

United Nations Population Division (1992), *Long Range World Population Projections: Two Centuries of Population Growth 1950-2150*, ST/ESA/SER.A/125, New York.

United Nations Population Division (1989), *Trends in Population Policy: Population Studies No 114*, ST/ESA/SER.A/114, New York.

United Nations Population Division (1990), *World Population Trends and Population Policies, 1989 Monitoring Report Vol. II*, ST/ESA/SER.A/Add.1, New York.

UNDP (1996), *Human Development Report 1995*, Oxford University Press, Oxford.

United States Bureau of the Census (1991), *World Population Profile: 1991*, US Government Printing Office, Washington.

World Bank (1994), *World Bank Development in Practice: Population and Development: Implications for the World Bank*, Washington, DC.

Yergin, D. (1993), *The Prize*, Princeton Press, Washington, D.C.

El Zaim, I. (1980), *Bahrain: Recent Industrial and Economic Development - New Trends and Regional Prospects*, United Nations Industrial Development Organisation (UNIDO), Geneva.

Ziwar-Daftari, M. (1980), *Issues in Development: The Arab Gulf States*, MD Research and Services, London.

Index